Religion
The Basics

Is religion the same as culture? How does it fit with life in the modern world? Do you have to 'believe' to be part of one?

From televangelism in the American South to the wearing of hijab in Britain and Egypt; from the rise of paganism to the aftermath of 9/11, this accessible guide looks at the ways in which religion interacts with the everyday world in which we live. A comprehensive introduction to the world of religion, it covers aspects including:

- religion and culture;
- how power operates in religion;
- gender issues;
- the role of belief, rituals and religious texts;
- religion in the contemporary world.

Religion: The Basics offers an invaluable and up-to-date overview for anyone wanting to find out more about this fascinating subject.

Malory Nye is Professor of Multiculturalism at the Al-Maktoum Institute, Dundee, Scotland.

D0916462

Also available from Routledge in this series:

Archaeology: The Basics
Clive Gamble

The Internet: The Basics
Jason Whittaker

Language: The Basics (Second edition)
R. L. Trask

Literary Theory: The Basics
Hans Bertens

Philosophy: The Basics (Third edition)
Nigel Warburton

Politics: The Basics (Second edition)
Stephen Tansey

Religion: The Basics
Malory Nye

Semiotics: The Basics
Daniel Chandler

Shakespeare: The Basics
Sean McEvoy

Sociology: The Basics
Martin Albrow

Routledge
Taylor & Francis Group

LONDON AND NEW YORK

Religion

The Basics

■ Malory Nye

ROUTLEDGE

First published 2003
by Routledge
11 New Fetter Lane, London EC4P 4EE

Simultaneously published in the USA
and Canada
by Routledge
29 West 35th Street, New York, NY 10001

*Routledge is an imprint of the Taylor &
Francis Group*

© 2003 Malory Nye

Typeset in Times by Taylor & Francis
Books Ltd.
Printed and bound in Great Britain by
MPG Books Ltd, Bodmin

*British Library Cataloguing in Publication
Data*
A catalogue record for this book is
available from the British Library

*Library of Congress Cataloging in
Publication Data*

ISBN 0–415–26378–6 (hbk)
ISBN 0–415–26379–4 (pbk)

Contents

Preface   vi

1   **Religion: some basics**   1

2   **Culture**   21

3   **Power**   49

4   **Gender**   73

5   **Belief**   101

6   **Ritual**   125

7   **Texts**   149

8   **Contemporary religions,
    contemporary cultures**   177

Appendix: the study of religion and culture   207
Bibliography   211

Preface

This book is intended to give an accessible introduction to the contours of the contemporary study of religion. It was written out of a sense that there is a lot going on in recent debates that is shaping the discipline in new and exciting ways. For a long time the basic starting point for introductions to religious studies has been the distance of the subject from the traditional faith-based (and often church-funded) approaches of theology and divinity. This book is no exception, but I am intending the discussions that lead from this to go a bit further. It is not simply a matter of stating what religious studies is not, but rather what there is to say in a dynamic field of study relevant not only to the past, but also to the contemporary world. Hence in this book I have tried to avoid – as much as possible – the familiar term 'religious studies' and instead put forward a more nuanced alternative: the study of religion and culture. As I explain in the introduction, this approach is not only about asking questions on how to distinguish religion *from* culture (if indeed that is possible). Rather it is about exploring religion – religions, religious traditions and practices – from a cultural perspective, as a means by which culture (in the different meanings of the term) and cultures can be understood.

There are many people who I would like to thank for their help, comments, ideas, and support during the time I was writing this book. I am grateful to my colleagues in the Department of Religious Studies, University of Stirling, particularly for allowing me to take sabbatical research leave in spring 2002, which gave me time to concentrate and work on the book. In particular I would like to thank the head of department, Gavin Flood. The department has been a challenging and stimulating place to work over the years, and I hope I show my debts to colleagues in my use of their work through this book. One colleague, who has had a most profound inspirational role in the formation of the ideas in the book, as well as a number of other areas, is Steven Sutcliffe, who has made huge contributions over the years to the developing department. I would like to thank him for his ideas, and for his friendship. I would also like to thank my students, both undergraduate and postgraduate, over the past decades for their ideas, comments, and refreshing insight which have led me to the places where I am at present. Postgraduate research students in recent years who have been inspirational are Kerry Huntly, Aislinn Jones, Jude Macpherson, and Cat McEarchern.

There are many others too, beyond the confines of Stirling: Kim Knott, Russell McCutcheon, Mark Hulsether, Simon Coleman, Robert Segal, Rosalind Hackett, Abd al-Fattah El-Awaisi, Ali Wardak, Ian Reader, Peter Clarke, and John Hinnells, to name just a few. I would also like to thank His Highness, Sheikh Hamdan bin Rashid Al-Maktoum, Deputy Ruler of Dubai, and Minister of Finance and Industry in the UAE, along with His Excellency Mirza al-Sayegh, and Abd al-Fattah El-Awaisi, for offering me the new challenge of the post of Professor of Multiculturalism at the Al-Maktoum Institute for Arabic and Islamic Studies, Dundee in 2003.

At Routledge I would like to thank Roger Thorp for initially encouraging me to write this book, and Milon Nagi for her extremely helpful support throughout many stages of the writing and publishing process. I am also very grateful to Rosie Waters, Susannah Trefgarne, and the three anonymous reviewers of the manuscript for their comments and suggestions.

Above all, though, the people I have most to thank for their patience, support, and love are Alex Nye and our children

Micah and Martha. They had to endure months of me hanging around in the upstairs room, trying to write this book, deflecting their enthusiasm to tell of the latest news from school. I am sure they are glad that the writing project is now over, and they can 'have the computer now'. I hope they feel that it was all worth it. Thanks and love to you all.

Chapter 1

Religion

Some Basics

The first defining moment of the twenty-first century occurred at around 9 a.m. in New York on 11 September 2001. The shocking and unforgettable images brought to us the nightmares of the modern world. Jet airplanes and tall steel and glass skyscrapers are key images of the modernity in which we all live, as are the instant media technologies of mobile cameras and satellite-relay, which enabled us to watch these horrific events as they happened. But such modernity has its surprises, not only in the terrible scale of the mass-murder, but also because of the motivations and cultural factors leading to the event. As emerged in the days and months following 9/11, one justification for the hijackings and deaths was religion (that is, a particular interpretation of Islamic traditions).

The contemporary world is shaped by religions: Waco, wars in the Middle-East, the Jonestown mass suicides, conflict in India, former Yugoslavia, Northern Ireland, environmental summits, peace demonstrations – the list goes on. Osama bin Laden and Al-Qa'eda draw justification for their

1

view of a holy war from the policies of Jewish settlement on Palestinian lands, which are themselves supported by American aid motivated by Christian biblical rhetoric. To understand the contemporary world, as well as the past, we need a sophisticated understanding of religion.

This book is not specifically about Al-Qa'eda or the events following 9/11, nor is it about any specific religious tradition (such as Islam or Christianity). In this book I will seek to give some sense of how we can begin to understand the complexities of religious traditions, and how they shape cultures and events. I will do this by introducing an approach premised on a simple point: that what we call 'religion' is something that humans do, and so the study of religion is primarily concerned with people and cultures.

The basics

The approach I advocate here could be loosely labelled the study of *religion and culture*. That is, 'religion' is not something abstract and set aside (nor necessarily 'god-given'), but it is integral to other aspects of cultural activity. This approach looks at how people are different – how cultural and religious differences across the world can be understood and put into context. In this sense, the study of religion is comparative.

It is more accurate, however, to say that this study of religion is *cross-cultural*, looking at religions across a range of different cultures. We should expect to look at more than one religious tradition (the study of religion is not simply a study of Christianity, for example), and we must also build into our approach a viewpoint that takes in the diversity of cultural locations across the world. It may be obvious to expect to find cultural differences if one looks at Christianity (in Europe), Islam (in the Arab world), and Buddhism (in China or Tibet). But any study of a particular religion will *also* need to be cross-cultural. For example, there are different cultural forms of Christianity (in the USA, in Latin America, in Poland, etc.), just as Islam in Saudi Arabia is quite different to Islam in Pakistan, or Indonesia, or Scotland. Therefore, this study of religion and culture is about looking at cultural and religious diversity, in different parts of the world, as well as close to home in our own cultural location. It is about exploring how current and historical events are shaped by practices and influences that could be labelled 'religious', and how much of what we see and do is affected by such religiosity.

What the study of religion and culture is *not* about, however, is finding 'ultimate' truths or answers. Liberation, salvation, morality, belief, and many other such key concepts may be subject matter under examination when studying religion, but we can speculate *ad infinitum* as to which set of ideas is closer to the 'truth'. On a personal basis, we might prefer certain ideas and perspectives to others, but then we may all differ as to *which* viewpoint we think is actually 'true'. Many (not all) religions are practised in a way that presumes a reality beyond humans such as gods, deities, supernaturalism. But scholars have to adopt an element of agnosticism, and so claim competence only in the field of experience which they know: the human world. This is not to argue that there is no 'supernatural' or spiritual reality beyond this, but rather that there are plenty of *other* interesting things to learn and think about religion without presuming (or refuting) this alternative reality.

This is *not* a god-centred approach (theology), we are not looking for answers to questions about whether or not god (one or more) exists and what she or he is like. Instead it is a human-centred approach: the study of religion as a human practice, a type of activity that appears to be integral to humans. This is not to say that such human practices of religion are exclusively human *creations*: the cultural forms of religion that we can study may or may not be 'divinely inspired'. And indeed many people practise their religions because *they assume that* they are derived from such divine principles. However, the exploration of whether there is a reality to such assumptions is the preserve of theologians. In contrast to this, the much broader cultural study of religion is the focus of this book. The religious life is the cultural life, one's religion (whether one pursues it fervently, indifferently, or somewhere in between) not only emerges from one's culture – religion is culture.

Religion and culture

There are many approaches that could be included in this cultural study of religion. A central part of these relies on the idea that human beings differ from each other along broad lines, particularly in terms of differences of personality and culture. Generally it has been psychologists who have looked at personality, whilst it has been sociologists and anthropologists who have looked at culture. Even so, the way in which one lives one's personality is bound up with one's culture, and the way in which a person embodies and lives their culture depends, of course, on their individual or particular personality.

At the beginning of the twentieth century most scholars looked at personality as a reason for the existence of religion. Making some very broad assumptions that religion was purely a matter of believing in some spiritual entity, writers tried to explain religion as part of the process by which individuals either thought through ideas in a semi-rational way, or tried to come to terms with the emotional and psychic legacy of their childhoods.

The most famous of these thinkers was probably Sigmund Freud (1990a [1918]), who proposed that religion is a misguided and unhealthy outcome of the problems inherent in a young boy working through his relationship with his father. But Freud ignored his own particularly cultural assumptions in putting forward such a theory. That is, his ideas about how humans become religious depended on ideas of behaviour specific to his particular culture. They also relied very heavily on a view which assumed all religions were similar to Christianity and Judaism. The assumption that religion comes from making up a heavenly father figure called god to compensate for relations with one's own father simply does not apply to those non-Christian traditions that don't image god as a father figure, or don't even image god at all.

If personality has a place in understanding religion, that personality is itself culturally dependent in many ways. To extend the Freudian example a little further, the father–son relationship is something that we all take for granted. It is seemingly biologically defined, and although there are many different ways of being both a father and a son, we are surrounded by images of what an ideal father should be. But consider for a moment that in different cultural groups fatherhood can take different forms. Indeed the idea of fatherhood can change over time even in the 'same' culture. What is now expected of a father in Britain in the early twenty-first century is very different from what was expected in Freud's late-nineteenth-century Austria. Although, we assume, biological fatherhood is the same everywhere, there are great cultural variations on what fatherhood is taken to be about.

This digression into the area of parenthood is simply to suggest that culture, and cultural difference, is a crucially important factor if we want to try to understand religion. Our assumptions are produced by the cultural world in which we live. Thus our culture gives us a worldview, a means of seeing and understanding the world, by which we live, and which may be radically different from those held by people living in cultures different to our own. Although as individuals we may interpret, live with, and reconstruct that worldview in a way that suits our own personality and needs, we can never fully escape the parameters of our own particular culture.

What, then, do we mean when we talk of culture? And with respect to the subject of religion, where does culture end and religion begin? What is the difference between the two? Particular religions are shaped by particular cultures, and of course the same occurs the other way round – most cultures are largely shaped by their dominant religions. To take obvious examples of this, Christianity is a religious tradition which has been manifest in many different cultural contexts – from Southern Baptists in the USA, to medieval Europe, to Viking Norse settlements at the end of the first millennium, to native (Indian) Catholics in contemporary South America. No one would suggest that all these forms of Christianity are the same – the experiences of being a Christian in each of these contexts are extremely different, at the level of language, dress, lifestyle, and many other areas of daily practice.

Thus Southern Baptists in contemporary America practise a form of Christianity embedded within the wider context of

English-speaking American cultural life. These churches' use of television as a central medium for the distribution of information and church life is closely related to the way television has become an essential and very powerful component of broader American cultural life. At the same time, the 'Bible Belt' areas where the Southern Baptists dominate are culturally influenced by the Christian values of the church: from the strict ethical code on heterosexual monogamy, to the emphasis on personal achievement and success as means of demonstrating one's moral fibre. Thus the religion strongly influences the culture, and the culture is itself the medium through which the religion is experienced and practised.

In contrast to this, there is the very different cultural setting of my own native experience – of Anglican Christianity in England (that is, the Church of England). Unlike in the USA, the Anglican church is bound up with the formal fabric of the state – thus the British monarch, presently Queen Elizabeth, is also the head of the church. Doctrinally and organisationally there are significant differences between the Church of England and the Southern Baptists. Most importantly, the Church of England has to be understood as a particularly *English* form of Christianity. Although the BBC TV series *The Vicar of Dibley* cannot be held to be a truly representative portrayal of contemporary English Anglicanism, it does demonstrate how innovation and significant cultural change (such as women's ministry) fit in with a world of coffee mornings and garden fetes which has seemingly been left unchanged for centuries. In both cases, and in any other example, the point is that the 'religion' is not some free-floating thing that exists outside of the cultural setting.

Religion and religions

So far I have given a few pointers to where we can start looking for religion, and how and why people are 'religious' in their various ways. The question remains, however, what do we mean when we talk about 'religion'? To start with, we can break our concept of 'religion' down in several directions, according to whether we talk about 'it' as a noun, an adjective or adverb, or

Table 1

Religion			
Noun	Noun	Adverb or Adjective	Verb
Specific	General category		
Religion(s)	Religion	Religious	Religioning
Refers to particular groups and traditions (e.g. Christianity, Islam, Hinduism, etc.)	'Universal' aspect of human culture	Used in general sense to describe a type of thing or behaviour or experience	Not a 'thing' but an action, more of a process of doing

even as a verb. That is, religion (as a noun) as either religious traditions or as something which is universal and can be found in all humans (irrespective of the particular religion/tradition they follow). Or otherwise, as an adjective (or adverb), as a way of describing certain things, activities, and behaviour (for example, religious books, religious buildings, or religious actions). And we could even extend and re-invent the word as a verb (religioning?), to think of the concept as something which is done, rather than something which does things to people. The differences between these can be seen in Table 1.

Religions: particular traditions

For some people there is only one religion in the world, that is the 'true' religion, which is usually their own. Thus, as Morton Klass points out, the fictional Parson Thwackum (an Englishman) was of the opinion:

> When I mention religion I mean the Christian religion; and not only the Christian religion, but the Protestant religion; and not only the Protestant religion, but the Church of England.
>
> (From Henry Fielding's *The History of Tom Jones*, quoted in Klass 1995: 17)

From this perspective what everybody else has is not 'religion', or at least not his religion – whether that be 'false religion', idolatry, superstition, or worse.

In most cases, however, it is far more common to talk of a number of different religions in the world. So, for example, there are Islam, Buddhism, and Christianity, each of which is distinct. A very influential way of describing such differences is called the 'world religions' paradigm. This approach looks at discrete, bounded religions – each different from the others – as the basis for making sense of the vast range of religious practices in the world. Thus, scholars have learnt to talk about particular world religions – Christianity, Buddhism, etc. – which exist as bounded blocs of humanity.

I will explore below some of the problems with this world religions approach below. But first, what is this approach saying? In particular, what is it that makes particular religions different? Differences are primarily framed in terms of each distinct religion having certain characteristics, which can be clustered in particular areas:

- major texts (sacred books)
- foundational ideas, 'beliefs', and worldviews
- particular histories and leaders
- and very often a sense of having a distinct identity.

In this way, we classify Christianity and Islam as different religions: they have different texts (the Bible, the Qur'an), different foundational ideas (broadly God/Trinity and Allah), quite different histories, as well as identities which mark out the distinctions between Christian and Islamic religions. Under these markers of difference we also classify other religions as distinct major religions of the world. Table 2 gives some examples.

If we wished to expand this further we could include a number of other religions – for example, Jainism from India, Taoism from China, and Shintoism from Japan. We could also discuss much further what the ideas are, the particular characteristics of the founders, and the histories, and the texts, and so

Table 2

Label and Identity	Main texts	Major ideas	Founder	Country of origin
Christianity	Bible (Old and New Testaments)	Single god – trinity	Jesus Christ	Palestine/ Rome
Islam	Qur'an	Single god – Allah	Muhammad	Arabia
Judaism	Hebrew Bible ('Old Testament')	Single god – Jehovah	Abraham	Israel
Buddhism	Pali Canon	No god, Four Noble Truths, etc.	Gautama Buddha	Northern India
Sikhism	Adi Granth	Single god – Vaheguru	Guru Nanak	North West India
Hinduism	Vedas, Upanishads, Puranas	Main deities – Brahma, Vishnu, Shiva. Many other deities	None	India

on. Indeed, there are many excellent books which do exactly this, they take one particular religion and introduce the reader to each of these main characteristics.

However, in setting out this table I do not intend to make it appear definitive, nor indeed is it meant as a point of reference for study-revision on the differences between 'world religions'. For a start, it is reminiscent of a butterfly collector's pin-board, with the complexity of cultural and religious diversity stripped bare to very basic and simplistic premises. The point of this table is to show how different religious traditions are systematically classified by scholars in terms of these key issues of difference. However, the differences, and the means of classifying and describing difference, are much more complex than such a table suggests.

Such an approach may give us a starting point for mapping out differences between 'religions', as well as the particularities about a 'religion'. It is of course very important to know the basic elements of Islam, what Hindus believe in, and so on. And such knowledge is not only useful for its own sake: in the world at the beginning of the twenty-first century we can be certain that we will encounter people from these religions at some point in our lives – as friends, work colleagues, when travelling, or in business.

But there are problems with this straightforward approach, mainly because it tells us some things, but misses out a lot more. For one thing, it is very dry. Surely there is more to know about being a Muslim than simply texts and history! Where is the sense of the lived experience, such as the sights, and smells, and tastes of Islam? We could add these to our list of characteristics, so as well as knowing that Muslims believe in Allah, we learn that Muslims avoid pork and alcohol. We could also add some helpful pictures – of main religious centres and religious leaders to show that visual sense.

What is more problematic, however, is that this suggests all Muslims (or Hindus, or Christians, etc.) are the same. It may, perhaps, lead us to think that we know what it is like to be a Muslim: all we need to do is learn about the basics of Islam. But as we have encountered already, being a Muslim in one part of the world may be quite different to what it is in another part – say between Saudi Arabia and Indonesia, or between Sudan and the Southern USA. Furthermore, there are the major historical divisions within many traditions, such as between Orthodox, Catholic, and Protestant forms of Christianity, or between Sunni and Shi'a forms of Islam. Looking at Islam, or any other religion, as a 'religion' means looking at the *variations* within that religion, how in different cultures the forms of the religion will have varied, even though some of the basic characteristics have remained constant.

This 'world religions' approach also leaves considerable geographical gaps. That is, Christianity, Islam, Judaism, Hinduism, Sikhism, Buddhism, Jainism, Taoism, and Shintoism are not the only religious traditions in the world. There are others that we could call 'religions': for example, the traditional religions of Africa, made up of numerous cultural traditions that some argue are diverse expressions of a single tradition.

There are strong arguments that African traditional religion is a religion in the same sense of Islam or Christianity, with a basic set of ideas (in a single creator deity, along with more minor deities, and ancestor spirits). This may be the case, although against this there are many who argue that the differences between, for example, religion amongst Yoruba people in Nigeria and Zulu or Shona people in South Africa are just too great to compound together as a single 'religion'.

In other parts of the world, the situation is equally complex. In Australia, there are numerous small cultural groups of Native (or Aboriginal) Australians, each of whom have religious traditions which are unique to their area. The same is true in many other regions, such as North and South America, the many Pacific Islands, and South-east Asia. Although major religious traditions such as Christianity, Islam, and Buddhism have spread to most countries in the contemporary world, there are still (and are likely to remain) alongside these much smaller-scale and culturally local religions. To describe these, we usually have to name them according to their cultural group, so we talk of Navajo religion among that particular Native American group, Yoruba religion in West Africa, and Arrernte religion for a central native Australian group, and so on.

So how do such small-scale traditions fit in with the world religions typology? They are more geographically bound, and have less global impact, and so offer quite a challenge to the idea of classifying religious differences in this way. One scholarly attempt to solve this has been to lump together how we perceive and label many of the smaller religious cultures (such as Navajo, Arrernte, and many of the religions of Africa) into a wider category, such as 'indigenous religions'. (Or in older terminology, they have been labelled as 'primal' or 'traditional' religions.) What this does is provide a sense of scale for classification – all these 'indigenous religions' cover an area of the globe that puts them on a more equal footing with other 'world' religions. Even though there are highly significant differences between the many indigenous religions in this category, there is similar diversity among the other 'world' religions, such as Christians, Buddhists, Hindus, and Muslims.

The problem with this 'world religions' approach, however, is that it is mainly about *classification* of cultures and traditions. In fact, it has been argued that it is primarily a *political* activity (see, for example Smith 1998, Fitzgerald 1990). It may be convenient to think of religions as distinct and qualitatively different from each other, but the differences are very often framed from a particular western perspective. The religions that are concentrated on, and are so classified in terms of 'world' or 'global' categories, are those that have figured most prominently in recent western history.

In sum, to talk in this way of world religions is merely a starting point – it points out to us the obvious differences between groups on a world-wide scale. And it encourages us to look further at the cultural issues which underlie these differences, as well as the political conditions in which they are found. But there is also much to be gained from looking at the issues from the other way around – that is, working from the particular to the global. Instead of assuming such large-scale entities as 'world religions', we should begin with reference to particular geographical contexts.

This would, for example, locate a study of Hinduism within the complexity and diversity of Indian culture and society. From this, there are many different Hinduisms, each emerging out of the many different geographical and cultural locations in India itself. Such a study of Hinduism from this level needs to encompass an understanding of the many different aspects of Hindu cultural and religious life in these locations – including texts and practices, as well as ideas and beliefs. Such a study of Hinduism could also start from another location, for example from a western context (in Britain, or America, or elsewhere), looking at the many aspects of Hindu religious life and culture in such places.

Similarly, this means we need to reconsider the perspective that there is a *single* Christianity, that encompasses *all* Christian traditions, across history and across the world. A study of Christianity entails a study of Christians in a *particular* time and place, for example in twenty-first century America, or medieval Europe. The assumption we often make that the Christian traditions found in such different contexts amount to the 'same thing' (the same 'religion') needs to be reassessed. Instead we should start with the assumption that these different *Christianities* can only be understood in their own particular terms

Such an approach, therefore, breaks down our basic assumptions of particular (world or otherwise) religions into a more pluralistic and diverse model. We should talk, then, of Hinduisms, or Christianities, or Islams, each specific to particular places and contexts. Likewise, small-scale religious cultures do not need to be lumped into a larger category (as 'indigenous' religions), but instead point to the specificity of *all* religious cultures in places and times. This might not be so tidy as the neat table I gave at the beginning of this section, but it does provide a basic starting point for talking about *religions* which more accurately represents the complexities of religious and cultural differences.

Religion as a universal

I am now going to talk about the other way in which we use the term 'religion' as a noun: that is, not as a label to divide and classify different traditions, but as a broad category for describing a universal aspect of human life. One immediate problem is that so many people in the contemporary western world do not seem to have any religion. So is it correct to assume that religion is universal?

So whereas in the past most people in the west were active practitioners of some form of Christianity, there are now many who do not go to any Christian church, and do not engage in any significant way with Christian teachings. Indeed, there are many who openly refute *any* religion, and who describe themselves as humanists, marxists, or just plain atheists. The presence of such people seems to indicate that religion is not something that is innate to humanity (after all there is no particular 'religion' gene), but is much more a matter of choice and socialisation.

Against this there are arguments that religion is universal, shared by all humans. That is, many argue that the need for an engagement with an alternative reality, a true meaning of existence, a ground of being, or an ultimate truth is a part of human nature. This experience is usually manifest through particular religions, such as Christianity, or Islam. But in a rapidly changing world, where old traditions and old certainties are being swept away, the manifestations of what we call religion are taking new shapes.

It can be argued that secular ideologies such as Marxism (or Communism) have developed to fulfil the roles and functions that were previously filled by religion, or otherwise that nationalism has provided a new set of 'gods' for many in the western and non-western world. Others have looked elsewhere, to the general national and state culture, or 'civil religion', which seeks to create a sense of religion that binds together those of many different religious backgrounds, as well as none. It is also suggested that new cultural manifestations have emerged to fill this gap, particularly sport – such as football, soccer, or baseball – or the power of film and cinema.

All of these appear to be substitutes for what more 'conventional religion' has been in the past, and they could be called quasi-religions for a post-traditional, postmodern, and secularised world. But to describe football as a religion does perhaps stretch too far the usual idea of what religion is. In some ways, the cult status of football heroes, the veneration of teams, the sacredness of football grounds, and the mysticism and magic that is associated with the game all suggest something that could be said to be *like* religion. But even so, is that the same as saying it actually *is* religion? It might seem to be trivialising the concept of religion to include things such as football or other sports. But if we are assuming that religion is something universal and basic to humans, then there must still be some kinds of religious manifestations in contemporary western cultures, other than Christianity.

To make this argument work, we need to show that religion can be found in *every* culture. Is religion everywhere, and does everyone have a religion, irrespective of their culture? One problem with answering this question is that 'religion' is an *English* word, and has a particular history within the English-speaking world. The world 'religion' does not easily translate into other languages, and terms found in different cultures might not translate all that happily into the English term religion.

For example, Hindus talk about *dharma*, and often use the term *sanatan dharma* as a name for their religion (a literal translation of this is 'eternal religion'). But *dharma* encompasses other concepts too within its range of meanings. Thus *dharma* also describes the order of the world, the way things are, in a sense that is religious, social, and 'natural' (or inherent). For example, each person has their own *dharma*, which derives from their place in life – the *dharma* of a student is to study (and remain celibate), the *dharma* of a married householder is to have and raise children. And each person will have their own *dharma* (depending on the family into which they are born), which determines their occupation (or vocation): to be a soldier, trader, blacksmith, carpenter, or whatever. So we might find a broad correspondence or affinity between what we call religion and what Hindus call *dharma*, but they are not the same. This raises the tricky question of what we are studying when we look at the 'religion' of Hindus: should we limit ourselves to what we think is 'religion', or look instead at those things described by the word *dharma*?

To complicate matters further, in many cultures there is *no* obvious word that can be translated as religion. As Gary Cooper points out, for Native American groups 'No tribe has a word for "religion" as a separate sphere of existence' (Cooper 1988: 873, see also Fitzgerald 1999: 81). So when we talk in English of Navajo 'religion', we are not *translating* any particular word or concept – what is happening is that the scholar is *imposing* the term religion. And in this case we must remember the raw sensitivities in such an encounter. European Americans have imposed a great deal onto Native Americans – most of which has been negative – through a history of conquest and appropriation of land.

Defining (or mapping out) the term 'religion'

If, then, we have to be careful with the words we use, does that mean we cannot talk about religion at all? Surely, even if the word 'religion' itself is not universally translatable, then perhaps the broad area of life it describes is? It seems fairly reasonable to assume that most, if not all, people have something about their lives that if we look closely and sensitively enough we can say is like religion, even if they do not call it that? If so, what is this 'religion' in the general sense? Can such a 'thing' be defined in a way that it includes activities in a range of different cultures that look like they are 'religious'?

As one might expect, the answer to this question is not straightforward. There are indeed many different ways to define religion. For example, Jonathan Z. Smith cites a list (by James H. Leuba) of fifty different attempts to define the concept of 'religion'. What this tells us, says Smith, is not that religion cannot be defined, but rather that 'it can be defined, with greater or lesser success, more than fifty ways' (1998: 281). This seems to be stating the obvious, but it is a profound point. The term 'religion' means many different things, and so there are many different ways in which we can say something is 'religious'. Or to put this another way, when the term 'religion' is used (and it is used a lot, by different types of people in diverse contexts), it is not clear what is actually being meant by the term. A person might think that its meaning is straightforward and simple, that religion is a 'thing' that is the same for everybody, but such a statement may be understood quite differently by another.

We must also bear in mind that scholars themselves are responsible for how the term 'religion' comes to mean certain things. Elsewhere Jonathan Z. Smith says, in a much quoted passage, that:

> Religion is solely the creation of the scholar's study. It is created for the scholar's analytic purposes by his [sic] imaginative acts of comparison and generalization. Religion has no independent existence apart from the academy.
>
> (Smith 1982: xi)

What he is suggesting is that the term religion is more useful as something that scholars think about, rather than something which exists in the 'outside world'. This is a useful comment, especially as in some cases the term is used to describe cultural concepts (such as *dharma*) which are not easily translatable as 'religion'. However, the word is frequently used well beyond academic life. It is commonly used within the popular culture and daily life of many (particularly English-speaking) people, along with other key words such as 'culture' itself. That is, most people who speak English tend to talk of 'my culture' and others' 'culture', and they may also talk about their own 'religion' as well as that of others.

And this is how I intend to talk about religion in this book: not because it has any distinct meaning, but because it is used in many ways in everyday life. So when I use the term, I intend to refer to the vast array of different things encompassed by this everyday usage of the word. I am not going to put my name to the list of definitions that Smith cites, to give a fifty-first (or rehash one that is already going). Definitions of religion can be a useful starting point, but they tend to narrow down options and often lead us to assume we 'know' our subject before we even start looking at it. I suggest that those who study religion and culture do not become bogged down in finding a definition, but instead work on the assumption that in many cultural contexts there is a field of cultural activity that is labelled as 'religion'. If we accept this as something that is given, then the purpose of our study is to see how the activities that go by this loose term are practised *as part of*, not separate from, the rest of cultural life.

Following this approach we do not have to single out any particular definition of religion. It is not necessary to say that religion has any particular essence (or basis), nor that it plays any particular role in social, cultural, or psychological life. There is no activity, no way of thinking or talking, and no particular type of place or text which is intrinsically religious. Instead religion is about a way of talking about the world, of perceiving differences and similarities with other types of activities.

My use of the terms 'religion' and 'religious' is based, therefore, on their common usage as a way of describing certain aspects of human activity. The terms are key cultural concepts, which have emerged in contemporary English out of a particular cultural and political history. At the same time, however, largely because of the spread of English language and western culture (and religion), the terms 'religion' and 'religious' are used widely across the world. Now many Hindus talk about their religion (using either the English word, or *dharma*). Similarly, many Muslims talk (in English) about their 'religion' (which corresponds to some degree with the Arabic word *din*). Controversial figures such as Osama bin Laden talk about their religion as a justification for the atrocities they commit – whilst other Muslims say that bin Laden's actions are against Islam and so against their religion. Religion is a term with a wide range of meanings, but it is used on a global scale for a variety of purposes and in many different, often contrasting and conflicting, ways.

In this way, the study of religion and culture helps us to make sense of the contemporary world. Not only does it tell us about the diversity of these discourses on religion (how and why people talk of what they do as religion), but also how such religion works as part of the lives and cultures of people in so many different contexts. In short, religion is not something mystical and detached from the human sphere – it is what people do, and how they talk about what they do.

Summary

- In this chapter I have argued that religion is something that humans do. The study of religion is concerned with people and culture.
- Religion is an ambiguous term, with a range of meanings and references. In particular, it refers both to specific religious traditions, and also to an aspect of human behaviour which is often assumed to be universal.
- We should remember that the term religion has a particular history. We need to be careful when applying it in non-English speaking contexts. But the word is often

> part of common usage in many contemporary cultures, and is a useful way of describe how people talk about their experiences.
> • Religion is part of everyday life, it is an aspect of culture.

Suggestions for further reading

The following books set out some useful introductions to the general study of religion, and are certainly worth consulting to get a sense of what scholars of religion have been saying in recent years: William Paden, *Religious Worlds* (1988); and Ninian Smart, *The World's Religions* (1989). A good overview of sociological studies of religion is provided by Malcolm Hamilton, *The Sociology of Religion* (1995, especially chapter 1). There are also two good introductions to anthropological approaches, that is John Bowen, *Religions in Practice* (1998); and Morton Klass, *Ordered Universes* (1995). For introductions to different religious traditions, see John Hinnells, *New Penguin Handbook of Living Religions* (1997); and Linda Woodhead *et al.*, *Religions in the Modern World* (2002).

On a more advanced level, the article I cite in this chapter by Jonathan Z. Smith. 'Religion, Religions, Religious', is in *Critical Terms for Religious Studies* (ed. Mark C. Taylor, 1998), along with a number of other very interesting essays, some of which I mention in later chapters. Also well worth a look is the *Guide to the Study of Religion* (ed. W. Braun and R. McCutcheon, 2000), particular the introductory chapter 'Religion' by Willi Braun, and the second chapter on 'Definition' by William Arnal.

Chapter 2

Culture

At the core of this book is the idea that the study of religion is the study of culture, and that religion is a fundamental aspect of culture. In this chapter, I will be exploring the various ways in which the term culture can be understood. However, somewhat like the term 'religion', the term 'culture' is not straightforward. For the writer Raymond Williams (1976), 'culture' is one of the three most complicated terms in the English language, referring to a variety of ideas and things. In this respect, as well as many others, there is considerable overlap between the terms 'culture' and 'religion'.

This chapter will introduce a broad range of scholarly ideas and approaches which are labelled as 'cultural studies'. What we think of as 'religious studies' is, in many ways, a form of cultural studies, or at least there is much in cultural studies that those in the study of religion need to be aware of. This might seem to be obvious, since the broad area of cultural studies is relevant to most aspects of human life: for example, work, play, adulthood,

21

youth, films, literature, sport, etc. But it is often the ignoring or avoidance of the idea of religion as part of culture that makes us treat religion as something special or set aside, to be understood 'on its own terms'. Over the next few pages I will introduce some of the key ideas in the study of culture, using where possible ideas from both the study of culture and the study of religion. It is worth remembering, however, that much of cultural studies developed outside of the study of religion, and so not all of the examples that I will use are explicitly concerned with religious aspects of culture.

Raymond Williams: three types of culture

The term 'culture' refers to a number of different types of activity. On one level, we all feel we have a culture, that we belong to and that makes us who we are (e.g., Scottish, Italian, Indian, etc.). There is also another form of culture which we do not possess, but with which we engage – that is, the sort of culture that is manifest in particular things, such as literature, art, and music. Thus, a book, or a film, or a piece of music, are considered as 'culture'. As the above-mentioned Raymond Williams (1961) has pointed out, there are three ways in which this category of culture can be used: as an *ideal*, in a *documentary* sense, and in a *social* sense. I will be examining the first two of these approaches to culture (ideal and documentary) in this present section, and will return to the idea of culture-as-social later in the chapter.

To take the first of these, culture is often seen as an *ideal*, in an elitist way. Not every book or piece of music is considered to be 'culture': the term is reserved for works of distinction, that contain or express something close to a state of human perfection. Thus children are often expected to imbibe such culture at school, for example by reading certain books: Shakespeare, Charles Dickens, Herman Melville, and so on. Certain types of music, particularly classical music, Mozart, Vivaldi, Bach, and so on, are seen to express this type of culture most particularly, as are certain types of drama, art, and architecture. From this perspective, one could pursue the study of culture as the study of the attempt by humans to reach perfection and civilisation through such expressions. Although possibly edifying and enjoyable, the study of culture in such a way is described by Williams as primarily a process of discovering and describing the peaks of human expression.

There are strong parallels here with some scholars of religion (particularly theologians and religious practitioners), who start with the expectation that religion, as well as culture, is about this high ideal and perfection. Following this line of thought, the study of religion then becomes a matter of describing and documenting such manifestations of perfection – religion through important people, thoughts, books, and so on. Indeed one could say there is a powerful overlap between these two approaches to the study of culture and the study of religion. After all, most scholars of elite culture would rank texts (such as the King James Bible, and John Milton's *Paradise Lost*) as not only pieces of 'high religion', but also 'high culture' (i.e. English literature).

But Williams does not wish to rest content with the study of culture on this elitist level, since this approach begs a number of questions about how certain expressions are given the significance that they appear to have. That is, why should a particular book or author be seen as 'culture' whilst another is not? While there are questions of artistic quality about any particular cultural expression (for example, artistic ability, writing style, aesthetics), there also needs to be a critical analysis of how the work itself relates to a wider field. This goes beyond merely saying that a book is good, or how good a book is, to asking how that book is good, and how it comes to be thought of as good.

In Williams' terms, these questions move us from the ideal to the *documentary* level of analysis. This shift makes it possible to include other forms of culture that are left out in studies of the ideal or perfect. Thus, in a critical study of culture one can include as subjects not only the 'great' works of art, literature, and music, but also the less great (or more popular). The focus is not only on Bach and Mozart, but also for example on the Beatles and Madonna, not just on Shakespeare, but on Stephen King and soap operas too. This is not meant in a flippant or disparaging sense – although accusations have been made that such an approach is flawed since it breaks down the 'quality barrier' between the great and lasting works of culture, and those that are bland and ephemeral.

Some might want to argue that, in terms of quality, Madonna is as good an artist as Mozart, and that in the ideal sense of culture, her work should be considered as one of the canons of perfection. Such a judgement really depends on how we rate the work of Madonna, or Mozart, and what criteria we may use for saying it is 'good'. But in this discussion of culture, the debate over which of these artists is better is not important. Indeed, we do not necessarily have to like or venerate either artist (Mozart or Madonna) to engage critically with their work. In contrast, the important questions to ask concern how particular expressions of culture work in different ways at different levels. A cultural study of either artist asks how they are doing what they are doing, within the context of their music, and also with reference to the particular traditions and societies where they are located.

These are broad questions that can be approached in many different ways. Indeed, there are many different forms of cultural studies. It is a diverse discipline, with a staggering range of theories and methodologies, assumptions, approaches, and areas of study. For example, the study of this type of culture may look not only at literature, art, music, and religion, but also film, television, commercials, newspapers, magazines, sport, the internet, science, geography, architecture, food, pornography – the list of things that are cultural in this sense is endless.

We can turn here, again, to revisit how such a study of culture is relevant to the study of religion. As I have said, some studies of religion are focused on what are taken as the 'best' and most sublime forms of culture. But the broadening out of the study of culture from this focus on the elite, looking also at other more popular types, mirrors the concerns of contemporary studies of religion and culture. To study Christians, one can of course study the Bible, high Christian art, and great Christian thinking, but that does not tell us everything about the traditions of Christianity. For many centuries Christian people have been practising their religions in other ways, through producing less 'great' works of art, music, and literature, which could also be studied as forms of Christian culture.

For example, the case of Madonna mentioned above gives a small reflection of this approach. Although this musician is not necessarily a 'Christian', much of her work, particularly in the late 1980s and early 1990s, did make very obvious use of the Christian ideas and symbols in which she, and most of her audience, were raised. This includes her choice of name (referring to a central Christian figure), her use of Christian imagery such as the cross in her videos, and other referents such as her song 'Like a Prayer' (see Hulsether 2000).

For some scholars, this analysis may be unsatisfactory, since it does not explore the issues of quality and perfection within the Christian tradition that are central to the elitist or ideal studies of culture. Instead, what we get from a study of Madonna, and indeed many other instances of contemporary popular culture, is a sense of the ways in which certain Christian practices and ideas are experienced in contemporary western culture. In fact, although most writers in cultural studies have been largely indifferent to specifically religious aspects of contemporary culture, there are many cases in which we can see culture as being integral to contemporary religion and vice versa (see Forbes and Mahan 2000). This is a point I will return to below, particularly with regard to the idea of popular religion and popular culture.

Stuart Hall: popular culture

This widening out of the concept of culture from the ideal or elitist to include other non-elite forms is often discussed in terms of the concept of 'popular culture'. That is, cultural studies is largely concerned with studies of non-elite or popular cultures, or at least the study of all aspects of culture as popular forms. In his exploration of this focus on 'popular' culture, Stuart Hall suggests there are three different ways in which we can talk of the 'popular'. That is: (a) popular as well liked by the masses; (b) popular as simply what people do; and (c) popular as being in contrast to the dominant (or elite) culture (Hall 1981).

Mass appeal and the business of culture

Popular in the first sense simply refers to anything that has *mass appeal*. Music artists with fans numbering millions, such as current idols like Britney Spears, Jennifer Lopez, and Eminem are, therefore, part of this popular culture, since their music (and their images) undoubtedly sell extremely well. Their popularity on this level does not need to be equated with aesthetic and technical achievement since popular music, or other culture, might not necessarily be 'good'. But more importantly for Hall, the critical issue with such mass appeal is bound up with consumer commercialism, and how cultural products become used in the popular domain. Music, books, films, and other forms of culture are rarely given out for free: they are distributed for the purposes of making money, not only money for the artist (the writer or singer), but also for the producer (the publisher or record company). Such culture therefore becomes popular through being *sold* to the public, with the sellers using marketing strategies to convince the public to buy.

Such a view of popular culture may seem to be relevant only to contemporary western societies, where consumerism is big business, and the selling of popular culture is dominated by a relatively small number of very powerful companies. If we look at other societies, in different parts of the world, and in different times of history, we might find that popular cultures come about through less capitalist means. It is true that there is a particular intensity within the early twenty-first century popular culture business in the west, but we cannot jump to the assumption that material considerations are going to be absent elsewhere. After all, cultural products are always material things – whether they be books, or CDs, or films – and somebody needs to invest some money into making them, and getting them to the public.

As a small example, in contemporary India films are very big business, just as in the USA, but there is a very different popular culture of films in India. The vast majority of films that are made in India come out of production studios based around the city of Mumbai (formerly called Bombay). These studios, labelled as 'Bollywood' (i.e. the 'Bombay Hollywood'), produce hundreds of films each year, in Hindi and other Indian languages, which are distributed on a very wide scale – across Asia, as well as Africa, Europe, and North America. Most Bollywood films are a mix of high and intense drama, stunning scenery, formulaic plots and fight scenes, and a number of song/dance routines. Film stars from Bollywood movies have a high status in Indian society, whilst the music from the film soundtracks is itself an important part of the Indian popular music industry. In short, in India one finds a very different popular culture, centring around Bollywood films and music, produced and marketed by a culture industry for the public.

With specific regard to religion and culture, it could be argued that there is no 'mass industry' of religious culture, in quite the same way as there is such a music or film industry. However, some global churches, and other religious organisations, work almost as such industries, producing religious cultures which are consumed on a popular level. The Catholic Church is probably the best and most successful example of an organisation working in this way. Further to this, however, religious cultures are engrained in and part of wider mass and popular cultures. The 'secular' industries of film, TV, music, and so on, all make use of religious ideas, images, and identities in their production of mass culture for consumption. Prime-time TV shows, such as the American series *Touched by an Angel*, are obvious examples of this.

Looking at this another way, popular cultures often have a profound impact on traditional religious groups. For example, in many contemporary cultures television has become the dominant medium through which individuals experience and interact with the world. It is hard to imagine any figure in popular culture having the impact they do without the medium of television to promote them, bringing them into the lives of millions. From the 1980s onwards many Christian churches in the USA, and elsewhere, began to make use of this medium, not only to promote their message but also to form congregations. Thus tele-evangelism – the broadcasting of church preaching and ministry through cable and network TV companies – has become a very significant business, as well as an important element of Christian ministry and practice.

Likewise, there is substantial overlap between religious traditions and the publishing industries. Each year there are thousands of best-selling books published with religious themes – some of which are explicitly Christian, and others less so. An example of a more generic (or post-Christian) best-seller is *The Celestine Prophecy* (Redfield 1994), a 'New Age' discussion of achieving better living and higher consciousness, which sold several million copies in the late 1990s. Such best-sellers are often dismissed as lesser, or more popular than the high culture of the dominant religion, and so are contrasted with established classics, such as the Bible, and 'serious' religious works such as Milton's *Paradise Lost* and Bunyan's *Pilgrim's Progress*. The distinction that is usually made between the two types of product is usually expressed in terms of quality – that is *Pilgrim's Progress* is held up as a piece of quality literature, whilst *The Celestine Prophecy* is dismissed as poor quality writing with spurious content. Even if this is the case, it cannot be denied that the wide circulation of *The Celestine Prophecy* has made it well known and quite influential, and so it is an important piece of popular culture (albeit in a different way to Britney Spears or Eminem).

The point I want to stress here is not how we identify a piece of culture (whether it is classed as religious or not religious, or as elite/'high' culture or popular culture), but in what ways it operates in the field of social relations. If we take *The Celestine Prophecy* as an influential cultural product, the questions then become: who is reading it, and why, and how is it shaping (and being shaped by) the religions and cultures of its readers? The answers to these questions may tell us something interesting about how large numbers of people practise (or at least think about) their religion at the beginning of the twenty-first century. I will come back to these issues in a later chapter, when I discuss the use of religious texts in particular.

Mass culture and the popular as 'what people do'

Returning to Stuart Hall's second form of popular culture, we can say that the term popular not only refers to mass appeal, but also to a more abstract concept of *'popular as what people do'*. This may, on face value, seem rather similar to the concept of mass appeal, but it is in fact more diffuse, and a little less subtle. If the popular is about what people do, then it will encompass practically anything – not only things which are popular with a lot of people, but absolutely *anything*.

Under this heading we can include not only artists with mass appeal such as Britney Spears, but also any other artists with a mass or a less limited following. For example, the children's writer J.K. Rowling is now a best-selling author with her *Harry Potter* series, and so is very much a mass-appeal part of popular culture (both adults' and children's). However, for the two years from 1997 to 1999 her books were well read but at a much smaller scale, selling in thousands rather than millions. Similarly, there are many musical artists and writers with more limited circulation and appeal than the Britneys and Rowlings, who are relatively unknown but still liked by many. If I mention the Scottish group *Capercaillie*, led by the singer Karen Mathieson, this name may or not be familiar. Likewise authors such as William Nicholson and Philip Pullman have published books that sell in large quantities to children, but have not achieved the status and sales of the *Harry Potter* series.

The point to note here is that the field of popular culture is almost unlimited. It is not only concerned with the best-selling of international best-sellers. Instead, anything that is in the popular domain is popular culture, and popular culture is anything that some people do. Whether it is engaged with by a few or by many, a piece of culture is in this respect part of popular culture. This may seem a rather unsatisfactory starting point for the analysis of culture and religion, but it does suggest that there are likewise no limits to what can be studied.

To give a brief example of this, the Hare Krishna movement (otherwise called ISKCON) has a relatively small number of followers in the west (around a few thousand full-time practitioners). It is a small religious group, popular with its own followers and a larger number of people (tens of thousands) who are interested in the ideas, philosophies, and practices associated with it. The Hare Krishnas are, however, part of a much wider popular culture, most particularly through the media of music and film. The music of the Hare Krishnas was heavily popularised in the early 1970s by the ex-Beatle George Harrison, when he helped some Krishna devotees to produce the chant 'Hare Krishna' as a pop single, which became number one in the UK charts. Harrison himself produced a Krishna-inspired song called 'My Sweet Lord', which became a best-seller in 1971, and again at the time of his death in 2001. In the area of film, images of the Hare Krishnas' public chanting on streets and airports figure very prominently in a number of contemporary films, in particular the 1980 spoof *Airplane*, where a number of visual jokes are made at the expense of this particular aspect of popular culture.

In taking Hall's first two points to distinguish the mass from what he considers to be popular culture, John Fiske (1995) describes this interaction between the popular and mass-appeal as 'mass culture'. Although, as we have already seen the 'cultural commodities of mass culture – films, TV shows, CDs, etc. – are produced and distributed by an industrialized system whose aim is to maximize profit' (Fiske 1995: 326), not every form of mass market 'culture' succeeds in this respect. He cites a failure figure of roughly 80 per cent – that is eight out of ten Hollywood films fail to make a profit at the box office, as happens also with new products such as TV shows, music, and print. What this shows is a process of interaction between the producers and consumers of culture, between those who are largely responsible for the industrial massification of culture (selling culture for profit), and the people who choose from the vast range what is interesting and relevant to their particular contexts.

This idea is in contrast to the more classical viewpoint put forward by Adorno and Horkheimer (1972 [1947]) that the process is more one way. Adorno and Horkheimer argued that the rise of a mass culture market was producing the end of popular or folk culture in its true sense. What was happening was an imposition of a standard mass culture which displaced the diversity of the various local cultures, and which in itself was driven by the capitalist needs of creating a compliant population who did not resist the powerful – that is those who produced the culture to which the masses were enslaved. Adorno and Horkheimer thus saw popular (or mass) culture as a form of ideology, in the sense that I will be discussing in the next chapter.

For Fiske, the process is more complex. The scale and the influence of the industry of mass culture is overwhelming. The twentieth century saw a phenomenal growth of both choice and commericialisation of culture at the popular level. But what has also happened is that the 'people' have been selective in which cultural products they make their own: not only through choosing certain artists, but also which particular elements of a cultural product become invested with meaning and significance.

Fiske uses the example of the popularity of old Hollywood western movies amongst certain Native Americans in the contemporary USA. What seems quite bizarre at first glance – Native Americans enjoying the stereotypical representations of conflict between 'Cowboys and Indians', becomes more complex when one learns that they choose to watch only the first halves of such films. He describes how they switch off 'at the point when the wagon train has been successfully attacked, the fort captured' and before the movie goes on to present the formulaic restoration of European white order and conquest (Fiske 1995: 327). Fiske goes on to cite further examples, of how the adaptation of such mass culture to the level of the popular is done by many different groups within society – as part of an interaction with and a resistance to the values that are being imposed by the producers of such culture.

> Popular culture, then, is not mass culture, though it is typically made from it ... The people constantly scan the repertoire produced by the cultural industries to find resources that they can use for their own cultural purposes. The industry similarly constantly scans the tastes and interests of the people to discover ones that it can commodify and turn to its own profit.
>
> (Fiske 1995: 331)

This possibly explains why a small religious group with a very limited appeal, such as the Hare Krishnas, may still become a frequently represented aspect of mass culture. In a similar way, and usually on a large scale, both people in general and culture industries in particular make use of and engage with aspects of Christian popular culture – in films, books, music, and many other areas of cultural practice.

Power and culture

Returning to Stuart Hall, there is a third concept of popular culture, so far not explored. The popular is not simply mass culture, nor is it simply what people do as culture, it is also in tension with and contrast to what is seen as 'proper' or elite culture.

This contrast is the one I noted earlier in this chapter, exemplified by the distinction between popular artists such as Madonna and the 'great people' of 'culture', such as Mozart or Shakespeare. Although the distinction is usually perceived as one of quality, for Hall what is primarily behind the distinct between popular and elite culture is the issue of power. That is, the dominant culture – those at the top of the social system – tell us there is a difference. If we talk of popular culture in terms of Hall's other two definitions of popular, that distinction is not so easy to see. The music of Britney Spears probably does sell more CDs than Mozart, but Mozart's music is still a best-seller. And people do still listen to Mozart, so it is popular in the sense of being used by people. Indeed, Mozart is used in many mass and popular culture ways, such as in films and TV commercials. The crucial difference that makes Britney Spears more a part of popular culture than Mozart is how their music is used, and in particular how this cultural product is part of relations of power.

In short, there is a power imbalance between those who usually listen to Britney and those who listen to Mozart. Mozart fans tend to be better off, have more job security, live in more expensive houses, invest in better education for their children, have better medical insurance, and more access to the channels of government than Britney fans. This is not because the former group listen to Mozart, rather their choice of culture reflects their social status and position. Of course, someone with wealth and power might like Britney too. But things that are called 'popular culture' are nearly always associated with mass consumption by a particular class who have relatively less power within society.

This point has been particularly observed by the French sociologist Pierre Bourdieu (1984), who has highlighted how cultural taste and social class mark each other out. A person's reading and experience of a particular form of culture is dependent on who they are, which in turn helps to determine what they know, and what they have been taught to see. Thus, it is people of a particular wealthy class who are more likely to visit art galleries and operas, who are able see the distinction between, for example, a dead animal and Damien Hirst's works of art. And so although the distinction between high and popular culture usually refers to issues of aesthetics and quality – 'proper' art is 'good', whilst popular culture is more 'trashy' – it is actually based on something more political, that is on who has the power to say what is good and bad. Thus we can talk about the cultural politics of aesthetics – the question of quality can never be judged from a neutral position. If I say something is good or bad, I say it because of who I am, and where I am in society. Whatever is taken to be 'good' (whether that be beauty, or refinement, or art) is determined by culture and cultural difference, which are determined by social relations of power.

Following this line of argument can be quite challenging, since it suggests there are no rules for determining quality. It suggests that I (or anybody else) will think a piece of music or a book is good because I am from a particular class or group, but in the end no one and everyone is right. This is what is often called the 'problem of relativism': it is problematic because it says all claims are equal, no claim is more correct than any other. Living in such a relativist world we may think (for ourselves) that some writers, such as Virginia Woolf, or Ernest Hemingway, are good, but we have to concede that this is our own perspective. Someone, perhaps of a different social class, who thinks Stephen

King is better than Woolf is equally right. This is a dilemma that is hard to resolve, since indeed the basis of our desire to say that one is better than the other is because of our need to assert a social distinction.

Likewise, the ways in which particular forms of religious practice are evaluated can be equally relativised. Whether it be styles of worship, texts, symbols, art forms, or language, this seems to suggest that every religious culture is as good as any other. Indeed, for some it suggests that the questions of truth which some religions themselves premise as central to their practices can themselves be relativised. Although this is certainly a conclusion that can be drawn from this approach, it is not the central concern here. What is more important to emphasise is not so much whether one set of practices (or truth claims) is better than any others, but rather what political relations are in place that create such claims.

Culture and resistance

Returning to Stuart Hall, the politics of differentiating between popular culture and the dominant culture can be played out in more subversive and challenging ways. Power differences do not go unchallenged, rather they produce tensions between groups. Those who exert power may seek to find ways to make those they control more amenable to being controlled, whilst those with less power will resist such attempts to control them. Such conflicts and tensions are often played out in the area of popular culture. That is, popular culture may often be a place in which relationships of power within society are established and resisted. (I will discuss this issue of power and resistance in more depth, particularly with relation to Antonio Gramsci, in the next chapter.)

As an example of the former, the idea of equal opportunity for all is a central concept in US society, which is somewhat belied by the real relationships of inequality between groups. Stories of how economically disadvantaged individuals have achieved success against the odds have been a basic theme of TV movies and Hollywood films for years. Although they can be experienced as entertaining and potentially inspirational, these stories also create an idea that differences between those in power and those outside of power are a matter of personal choice and ability, rather than being created by economic, political, and social structures. In contrast to this, however, there is much within popular culture that resists such a view, and that resists the power differences within society. An obvious example of this is black rap music, in its various forms, including white forms of black rap, such as Eminem. Popular culture may, therefore, often challenge and resist the ways things are, even if the basic relations are not necessarily changed. And for Stuart Hall, this is what the study of popular culture is about: how it is that popular culture is used as a site for power struggles. That is, it is not so much about the actual content of the cultural product (who sings what, and in what ways), but how it is used in a wider set of relations.

Thus the study of popular religious cultures is not simply a quaint addition to the overall field of religious studies. Rather it is about looking at the diverse alternative forms of practice that exist alongside, and often in tension with more official and elitist religious cultures. Such popular religions are thus non-mainstream and even subversive practices, often frowned upon by those in control. Thus, for example, Roman Catholicism has given rise to many forms of popular Catholic culture. These range from the brightly coloured pop art of sacred hearts and Madonnas (which are officially sanctioned by the church elite), to less orthodox forms such as the filmic visualisations of Catholic ideas in works such as Kevin Smith's *Dogma*, the critique of church secrecy and doctrine in *Stigmata*, and the bizarre humour of the Irish *Father Ted* TV series.

In some cases, the popular culture of resistance may in turn give rise to a new organisation, and a new church (and social) structure – as happened at the beginning of the twentieth century with the rise of Pentecostalism from disaffected (mainly black) congregations in the USA. As so often happens with popular culture, the forms that at one point are challenging and subversive towards the dominant tradition may themselves be moulded to become dominant forms in their own right. In this way a popular culture of resistance may get to be reworked as something less radical, and more compliant with social structures.

I have described above some of the features of popular culture within the context of India. As in the west, there are some very significant areas of crossover between popular culture and popular religion, and in many ways the two cannot be disconnected (see Beckerlegge 2002). Many Bollywood films have explicitly religious themes, and indeed there is one classic case in which a mass produced film – called *Jai Santoshi Ma* – led to the worship of a new goddess (of the same name). In the early 1990s, prime-time Indian TV was dominated by two networked series, made by the main TV station Doordarshan. These were adaptations of the books called the *Ramayana* and the *Mahabharat*, both ancient religious texts, telling (among other themes) the stories of the deities Rama and Krishna for a new contemporary audience: the mass market of the Hindu Indian population. The success of these series was phenomenal, with life in India coming to a standstill on Sunday mornings when the programmes were broadcast. Indeed, the interaction between popular culture, religion, and the wider social sphere became even more apparent when actors from the series achieved prominence in national politics. It is even argued that the rise of Hindu nationalism in India in the 1990s (which I will discuss in the final chapter) was partly a by-product of the growth of this Indian-wide popular Hinduism through the medium of television.

Religion, culture, and society

My discussion has moved somewhat away from the specifics of Raymond Williams' analysis, but I wish to return now to the classification he makes between different approaches to the study of culture. That is, in this section I will discuss his third view of culture: as *social*, or as a 'way of life'. In this sense, the study of culture is concerned with all aspects of what people do – thus, things such as language, food, worldviews, and everyday life are all aspects of culture. Williams (1977) talks about this idea of culture as a 'structure of feeling', whilst it has been discussed in numerous other ways by anthropologists: for example, Pierre Bourdieu (1977, 1992) has given it the fairly abstract term 'habitus'. However, the most accessible proponent of this idea of culture is the American anthropologist Clifford Geertz (1973), in his work on 'religion as a cultural system', which I will discuss below.

Probably the most influential attempt to relate religion to a social context in this respect was made by the French sociologist Emile Durkheim, writing at the beginning of the twentieth century. Although there are few people who would wholeheartedly agree with his ideas today, Durkheim's (1964 [1915]) idea of religion as the basis for society has been taught to generations of students in introductory courses on sociology and religion.

Durkheim saw his project as looking for the basic origins of religion: where it was that religion came from, and what role it had for people living in the present day. In his book *The Elementary Forms of the Religious Life* (1964 [1915]), he suggested that we can look at cultures which are very different to our own (specifically Native Australians), to see how religion operates in its most basic and elementary form. Writing when he did nearly a hundred years ago, this idea did not seem as problematic as it does now: the assumption that Native Australians are any closer to an 'elementary' or 'primitive' form of society or religion is not easily justified. Although the groups he discusses in *Elementary Forms* (which he never encountered first hand, but simply read about through others' writings) are very different to western cultures, they are still the results of complex histories of development, and are not 'stuck' in some rudimentary 'evolutionary' backwater. Durkheim was assuming that Native Australians could be seen as living fossils, to be examined under a theoretical microscope to demonstrate 'natural' laws of social behaviour.

To cut a long story short, Durkheim argued that these cases demonstrated a close correlation between religious activities and social organisation. It was through religion – particularly large-scale ritual ceremonies – that people came together into social groups. In fact, for Durkheim religion had two very important functions: first, it made people get together, and so was a form of social glue that created social solidarity. And second, it gave people a way of understanding and seeing society, since it was through religious identities that people came to have social identities. A person belonged to a group because her or his religious emblem was shared by others within that same group. Together these two functions of religion made society possible. At one level, he was arguing that religion is merely society perceiving itself, misunderstanding that the sacred basis of the group is simply the sum of the social whole. Or in Durkheim's terms, religion is a form of collective consciousness that actively (through rituals) keeps society together.

The strength and weakness of this argument depends, to a large extent, on what Durkheim meant by society and how he saw religion fitting into the social group. On the first point, he seemed to make his task easier by concentrating on what he took to be 'elementary' societies. There has been considerable debate on how his ideas relate to other social groups – such as in contemporary Europe and north America – where the term 'society' can refer to groups as small as local communities as well as large nation-states. Which of these levels of society is it that religion binds together?

The theory also seems to leave a blind spot with regard to social division and conflict. In Northern Ireland, and in many other contexts, we can point to obvious ways in which religious practices and organisations help to create social cohesion in communities (among Protestants, and among Catholics). But at the same time, the 'wider society' is pulled apart by religious differences – and so one could say that religion not only binds society, it can also create division. This does not necessarily disprove Durkheim's idea, what it does is show that it is not quite so good an 'explanation' for religion as Durkheim thought it was.

Despite these limitations, Durkheim did put on the agenda two fundamental ideas: that religion has a very direct relationship with social and cultural factors, and that to understand religion one does not merely look at the content of religion (what people do), but how religion functions and is practised in a wider social and cultural context. These ideas were taken up by later writers on religion and society in a cultural context, particularly Clifford Geertz.

Clifford Geertz: religion as a cultural system

Writing in the 1960s and '70s, Clifford Geertz (1973) suggested that the study of all human activity, including religion, needs to be related to the ways in which people are bound together in the symbolic 'webs of significance' that they themselves spin. The study of culture then becomes an attempt to understand these humanly created webs of meaning that humans find themselves suspended within.

For Geertz such culture is summed up in the phrase 'historically transmitted patterns of meaning' (Geertz 1973: 89), which each person experiences as something outside of themselves, and it is given to them by their community/society. It is usually in the process of growing up – through education and general childhood rearing – that a person comes to have a culture. Meanwhile, everything that a person does interacts with their culture: the systems of meanings that they share with others within their group.

Lying behind this idea of culture is a much earlier definition, proposed at the end of the nineteenth century by the writer Edward Tylor. Tylor's approach was very different from Geertz's, but in his book *Primitive Culture* he set out his understanding that culture 'is that complex whole which includes knowledge, belief, art, morals, law, custom, and any other capabilities and habits acquired by man [humans] as a member of society' (Tylor 1871: 1). Each different group has its own culture, a complicated collection that adds up to more than the sum of its parts. To understand differences between humans (both women and men) we assume it is culture that makes one group different from another.

This culture concept – a concept of difference – has been the main concern of the discipline of anthropology since the beginning of the twentieth century. By looking at people in non-western contexts (such as Africa, Asia, Australasia and

South America) which are quite different from those in the west, anthropologists argued that such cultures should be learnt about and understood in their own terms. In more recent decades, anthropologists have also looked within western contexts, at new cultural groups formed by migration, as well as turning the 'anthropological lens' on to western cultures to examine in depth their own particular cultural locations.

An important aspect of cultural difference for many anthropologists has been religious differences, which often seem to present the greatest challenges (from a western perspective). Perhaps this could be put another way: when westerners encounter exotic cultural practices which they don't understand, they often assume that the difference is a matter of *religion*. For example, if there is no obvious rational explanation for some behaviour which appears bizarre, it is given the label of religion (or ritual). In this sense, religion is often at the heart of the symbolic webs of meanings, and to get a proper sense of another culture's religion the anthropologist must find some way of interpreting these meanings. Why do people do what they do, especially when it is so obviously different from what 'we' do?

Geertz's attempt to answer this question – which he pursued in a number of contexts, including Java, Bali and Morocco – was to propose a theory of religion as a cultural system. He argued that we should understand religion as a 'system of symbols, which acts to establish powerful, pervasive, and long lasting moods and motivations in men [humans] by formulating conceptions of a general order of existence and clothing those conceptions with such an aura of factuality that the moods and motivations seem uniquely realistic' (Geertz 1973: 90). Relating this to his concept of culture, what he was suggesting was that the types of things that we see religion as doing are similar, in many respects, to what culture does as a whole.

Thus a religion relies on symbols – most usually physical objects that are understood to have a particular meaning (or meanings) associated with them that goes beyond their obvious physical properties (a point to which I will return in Chapter 6). We all live in a world saturated by symbols, both religious and non-religious, and they are indeed the basis of the webs of significance that Geertz sees as culture. But some symbols are more important and powerful than others, some help to establish 'long lasting moods and motivations', affecting how we feel and how we relate to the world.

For Geertz, then, religion involves symbols, actions (rituals and other practices), and a conceptual framework of belief and knowledge that together constitute a 'cultural system', which powerfully effects the ways in which people see and live in their particular worlds. It is not clear from reading Geertz whether or not all aspects of culture that work in this way are 'religious', although he does suggest we separate out the religious perspective from common-sense and aesthetic perspectives.

This understanding of culture – as a way of life, and a framework for how a person behaves and sees the world – does not necessarily contrast with the other idea of culture as a product. When we talk of culture we frequently mean both, often at the same time, so that a piece of culture (for example a book) comes from a particular cultural context. Any book or piece of music needs to be understood and analysed from within the cultural context in which it is found: both the culture of the author or composer, and also the culture in which one finds it being used. Thus the music of Mozart came out of the central European culture of late-eighteenth-century Austria, where it was also first performed and disseminated. If I listen to this composer now, I experience his work through my own cultural experiences, which are distinct from those in which Mozart lived.

This does not mean that Mozart (or his music) transcends culture, or exists beyond it in some disembodied way as an elitist form of 'high culture'. After all, much the same can be said about Madonna, whose music has travelled culturally far beyond her New York roots to diverse cultures across the globe. That is, the same cultural product can go beyond the limits of the culture that produced it into another, different culture. But in doing so, we have to pay attention to how it is received and experienced in each new context. A Papua New Guinea highlander, listening to a Madonna CD in a rural village, will probably experience and relate to the music in a very different way to someone listening in rural Midwest America. The 'meaning' of the music is determined as much by the cultural location of the person listening as by the music itself, in a similar way to the Native Americans mentioned earlier who watch and interpret western films from within their own particular cultural perspectives.

The problem of culture

Whilst Stuart Hall and Raymond Williams give us a perspective on culture that emphasises issues of power relations, Geertz's idea of culture seems to be rather disconnected to such issues. However, there is a significant imbalance of power within the field of cross-cultural interaction, not least because anthropology itself emerged from the practice of colonial Europeans observing and writing about subordinate non-Europeans. When discussing culture in these terms, we also need to be aware of the complex issues of power relations and differences of power, both between cultures (or cultural groups), and also within cultures. I will be discussing both of these issues in later chapters. In particular, however, it is necessary to ask how symbols, religion, and culture as a whole get worked to create power differences.

One way of viewing this is to break down the rather restricting concept of culture that Geertz presents. Geertz's idea of culture has similar limitations to Durkheim's idea of society as a wide-ranging (or totalising) entity. This term culture can refer to the shared system of meaning (or way of life, or even the social group) at a varied number of levels, ranging from nations to the very local. There is no real consensus about what sort of scale there is to the concept of culture – we can talk of western, or Arab, or Asian culture in the same breath as much smaller-scale groups such as Arrernte, or Yoruba, or Glaswegian culture. But this point is not only important in terms of size – the idea of 'culture-as-a-system' tends to ignore the political, and other, differences within such cultures. That is, cultures themselves have cultural divisions *within* them, and each culture is made up of various sub-cultures.

This idea of sub-cultures is particularly associated with the writers Dick Hebdige (1979), and others in the Birmingham

Centre for Cultural Studies (such as Clarke *et al.* 1976). The idea of sub-cultures places particular emphasis on the existence of smaller units within the larger 'culture', very often reflecting power differences. Using the work of Gramsci (who I will discuss in the next chapter), Hebdige suggested that sub-cultures do not simply exist in themselves, but are articulations of resistance to the prevailing dominant culture. He uses examples of sub-cultures in contemporary western contexts – such as groups organised on the basis of age (youth sub-cultures) and/or ethnicity (black sub-cultures). Such groups will often use 'culture' – in the sense of cultural products, such as music, dress-style and ways of speech – to express a collective 'sub-culture' of resistance. Religious groups may themselves be formed as this type of sub-cultural resistance, for example the Nation of Islam as a form of African American resistance in the USA, and the various Christian churches in the former Soviet Union and communist Eastern Europe.

In recent years, there has in fact been a strong questioning by anthropologists of the culture concept associated with Geertz. Not only does the idea of culture as system tend to disregard issues of sub-cultural diversity, it also makes us view such cultures in rather absolute terms. It is all too easy to use Geertz to say that a person is how they are because of their 'culture' (because they are Russian, or Arab, or American). In this view, the culture makes a person, and the culture explains what they do. Roger Keesing (1994), for example, criticises such a view, saying that it treats 'cultures' in too rigid a sense, as things which act for themselves, indeed in much the way that 'religions' are often seen to work. This makes us see cultures as having 'the kind of history coral reefs have: the cumulated accretion of minute deposits' (1994: 301). Instead he argues for a study of which looks not for such deposited or fossilised entities, but rather at culture as a dynamic process, in which differences – for example, gender, age, ethnicity, and access to wealth – are the basis of how people live out and relate to their 'culture'. Such culture is expressed, in one form, in the cultural products (books, music, etc.) that they make from their particular cultural or sub-cultural location.

Cultural hybridity and religious syncretism

One implication of this changing perspective is a movement towards looking not so much at cultures, but rather at the spaces between cultures. This is what the literary critic Homi Bhabha (1994) calls 'the third space', and Gloria Anzaldúa (1999 [1987]) calls 'borderlands'. In the contemporary world, it becomes increasingly hard to find any 'pure' or 'pristine' cultures, which are untouched by outside and other cultural influences. Indeed, it is questionable whether any such 'pure cultures' have *ever* existed. Instead, most people now live within these borderlands, across and between cultures. This is not only true for those who are of a minority ethnic status (for example, Latino/as and African Americans in the USA, Asians and Blacks in the UK, etc.), but also for those of the 'mainstream' cultures. Thus to be 'British' in the present day is to be subject to many different cultural influences, including very powerful forces of Americanisation (through the culture of diverse popular artists, and through McDonalds, films, TV shows, and so on). Such external influences have been present for a long time, to the extent that one politician described Englishness as a 'mongrel' culture.

But *all* cultures are 'mongrel' in this sense, being practised within such borderlands of cultural change and external influences. Culture is about hybridity, mixing up different elements, as well as about defining a particular way of life. The study of culture is, then, a study of such hybridity, and how the different elements of a cultural group work together and also against each other. Much of this hybridity is often expressed through cultural products: books, art, and music are often deliberately hybrid, as is perhaps most clearly shown through the success of the white rap artist Eminem.

Against this, it is often assumed that religions are far less open to cultural mixing and hybridity than cultures. For many, religion is a 'given', with religions such as Christianity and Islam being viewed as static, eternal, and essentially beyond human culture. In practice, however, religious organisations and religious cultures are as subject to change and influence as any other human activity. As I have outlined in the first chapter, there are many different cultural forms of Christianity – both across the contemporary world, and through the two millennia of Christian history. The same can be said about other major religious traditions – Islam, and Buddhism, Hinduism, and so on. Each of these traditions contains within itself a very wide range of religious cultures in particular contexts.

But that is not to say that people, individually and collectively, do not resist such changes, both within the wider sphere of culture, or with particular respect to religion. Words such as hybridity, mongrel, or syncretism (which refers to religious mixing) are often considered to be offensive and insulting, implying a process of 'watering down' or even 'bastardisation'. When anthropologists and other cultural analysts describe such processes of hybridity they are not implying that the mixing is a problem, rather they are trying to describe a reality that they perceive. That is, cultures and religions are rarely as 'pure' and unmixed as their members would like to think they are. This is what Rosalind Shaw and Charles Stewart (1994) describe, in the context of religion, as the antithesis between 'syncretism' and 'anti-syncretism'. Thus they argue that 'all religions have composite origins and are continually reconstructed through ongoing processes of synthesis and erasure' (Shaw and Stewart 1994: 7). This happens all the time, and any religion, whether it is Baptist Christianity in the USA, or Hinduism in India, is particular and unique: made up of specific historical and cultural processes that make it distinct from other religious cultures, even of the same religion.

So in this sense, all religious cultures are syncretic, and there is no such thing as a non-syncretic religion. Even so, this does not mean that a particular religious tradition cannot also be authentic, since for Shaw and Stewart

> 'authenticity' or 'originality' do not necessarily depend on purity ... What makes [a tradition] 'authentic' and valuable is a separate issue, a discursive matter involving power, rhetoric and persuasion. Thus both putatively pure *and* putatively

> syncretic traditions can be 'authentic' if people claim that these traditions are unique.
>
> (Shaw and Stewart 1994: 7)

Such claims to 'purity' and 'authenticity' are usually directed at sources seen as existing beyond human culture – in particular to the authority of sacred texts, and to an idea of god (or some other deity or deities). Indeed, this is what they mean by the term 'anti-syncretism', referring not so much to non-syncretic traditions, but rather to the processes by which people make claims for being pure and authentic. Obvious examples of this are the many cases of religious 'fundamentalism' or 'revivalism', in which a group makes claim to a pristine and authentic set of practices. Other practices, which are considered to be 'cultural' and syncretic, are particularly targeted in the claim for true authenticity. For example, the outlawing of Christmas by various Christian groups, such as Oliver Cromwell's Puritans in seventeenth-century England and in Calvinist Scotland.

This view makes the assumption that there is a tangible distinction between 'culture' and 'religion'. That is, claims for fundamentalism or anti-syncretism assume that culture is human-derived, whilst religion is something that comes from beyond humans (at least in its purest form). The academic study of religion cannot prove or refute this claim. Instead, scholars of religion analyse both cultures and religions as aspects of human life, and any assumption that religion is beyond the cultural (or human) is a theological or faith-based perspective.

Summary

- Religion can be understood as a form of culture, and the study of religion is a form of cultural studies. However, this does not necessarily make the study any easier, since the idea of culture is a multifaceted albeit useful tool for analysis.
- The term culture usually refers to two quite distinct areas of life: (a) culture as cultural products, i.e. what people

do in literature, art, music and so on; and (b) culture as a shared system or way of life.

- But these two ideas of culture are related, a group which shares a culture will identify with particular cultural products, and religion may act to unite the two (for example, the English as a culture share not only Shakespeare, but also the King James Bible).

- The study of religion and cultural products needs to pay attention not only to popular and mass culture, but also to the relations of power within a cultural group – whether those power relations be articulated in terms of 'high/popular' culture, or mainstream and sub-cultures, or majority and minority cultures.

- Every culture (and religion) is not a fixed or static entity, the study of culture and religion requires us to understand that all cultures are hybrid and all religions are syncretic. Such hybridity is at the centre of the study of religion and culture.

Suggestions for further reading

Two very useful collections of readings on the range of approaches to the study of culture are: John Storey, *Cultural Theory and Popular Culture: A Reader* (1997); and Simon During, *The Cultural Studies Reader* (1999).

For a broad introduction to the study of culture, there is John Storey's *Introduction to Cultural Theory and Popular Culture* (2000), which is a companion book to his reader. His short book *What is Cultural Studies* (1996) is also useful. Specifically on popular culture there are John Fiske's short article 'Popular Culture' (in *Critical Terms for Literary Studies*, 2nd edition, Chicago: University of Chicago Press, 1995), and his book *Understanding Popular Culture* (1989b).

On the relationships between the study of religion and cultural studies see: Mark Hulsether, 'New Approaches to the

Study of Religion and Culture' (forthcoming 2003); Bruce Lincoln, 'Culture' (2000); Tomoko Masuzawa, 'Culture' (1998); and Timothy Fitzgerald, 'Religious Studies as Cultural Studies' (1995). Also well worth looking at is Bruce Forbes and Jeffery Mahan (eds), *Religion and Popular Culture in America* (2000). There is also the journal *Culture and Religion* (published by Routledge), and the internet-based *Journal of Film and Religion* (http://www.unomaha.edu/~wwwjrf/).

Chapter 3

Power

The South African anti-apartheid campaigner
Desmond Tutu is reported as saying in the 1980s
that if someone suggests 'there is no connection
between religion and politics, then they must be
reading a different Bible' to his own. Although this
is a comment specifically directed at Christians
(after all Tutu was the Anglican archbishop of
Cape Town), there is still much poignancy in what
he says. There is a commonly held idea that
somehow the cultural spheres of religion and politics are separate – a view that is somewhat at odds
with the many ways in which religions are bound
up with systems of power. At a different end of the
spectrum to this, perhaps, is the view that all religions are only about the operation of power. This
is expressed particularly in the idea that religion is
a means for those in power to keep their power,
most famously associated with the analysis of the
philosopher and activist Karl Marx.

In this chapter, I will be exploring some of the
ways in which we can talk about religion in terms
of power, and vice versa, looking in particular at

the work of Max Weber, Antonio Gramsci, Louis Althusser, and Michel Foucault. I take as a basic assumption that religion and power are not separate and at odds, but instead are closely bound up with each other, and are both ways in which we can talk about culture.

Karl Marx: religion as ideology

Karl Marx wrote on the study of religion as part of a much wider project on the relationship between social division and the material world. To understand Marx's (*not* necessarily the 'marxist') view on religion, it is first important to understand how he viewed the basis of social relations and the operation of power.

For Marx, contemporary (i.e. for him, nineteenth-century) society was determined by economic relations: it was based on profound inequalities between those who controlled economic resources, and those who did not. The phrase that Marx used for this was 'access to the means of production', referring to the fact that control over material products (food, clothing, goods, etc.) is the most significant social source for empowerment or disempowerment. To control the means of production is to have control over others, and in present day capitalist society, those who work (the working class) have their labours exploited as they produce wealth for the ruling class. This overall system is called the 'mode of production', hence Marx lived (as we do now) in the capitalist mode of production.

This analysis, therefore, highlights the importance of social division, and that the two main classes of society – the working and the ruling classes – are in conflict, because of the economic and political control of the former by the latter. Of course, Marx's analysis also recommended a prescription for change – in the *Communist Manifesto* he called on the working classes to take back control of the means of production, and so to remedy the political imbalance (Marx and Engels 1986 [1888]). And in an early piece of writing (*Theses on Feuerbach*), Marx argued that 'philosophers have only interpreted the world: the point, however, is to change it' (Marx 1986 [1888]). These ideas in themselves have had a profound impact on twentieth-century history in various ways, although in this chapter I will be focusing more on Marx's own theories, and the wider implications of his approach.

In particular, Marx's approach to the analysis of class and political differences makes a significant contribution to discussions of religion and culture, not only in what he says, but also in how he has influenced later thinkers. Marx saw religion as having a particular role within the processes of oppression and exploitation. He argued that religion (and here he had in mind particularly Christianity and Judaism) was not in itself a bad thing, but that it helped to facilitate the processes of exploitation. It did this through masking the harsh economic and political realities of life with a warmer, more comfortable glow. If it were not for religion, the working classes would see their exploitation more clearly. As such, the ideology of religion is a false consciousness, representing reality in a distorted way. And because so many religions tend to present a world in which existing social relations are not only 'natural' but also 'god-given' (or divinely ordained), religion does the dirty work of keeping the oppressed content with their oppression.

Central to this was the concept of *ideology*, and in particular that religion often operates in ideological ways. At its most basic, ideology here refers to the political uses of religion, to describe how religious perspectives and practices are inevitably part of power relations. For Marx, however, as well as later writers, the term ideology is used to describe the politically obscuring aspect of religion: that is, religion is ideology when it masks and legitimates inequality. Such a concept of ideology may describe contexts that are not specifically religious, referring to any cultural perspective that gives legitimacy to a set of power relations, and makes the rule by one group over another appear 'natural' and unquestionable.

It is on this basis that Marx described religion as the 'sigh of the oppressed creature, the heart of a heartless world ... It is the opium of the people' (Marx and Engels 1957: 37). In these terms, religion is not the actual cause of social and economic suffering, it is not harmful in itself. Rather, religion is a symptom of a sick social system, which is used by both the ruling class and the exploited workers as a means of obscuring the root problems of economic and political inequality. For example, if I have a cold, then blowing my nose (to remove the mucus) will not cure the cold, likewise banning or attacking religion will not create social or economic equality. It is only when things change, when the means of production comes under the control of the people who produce capital through their labour, that religion and ideology will inevitably disappear.

When put in these terms, there is a lot about Marx's approach to religion that is useful, but yet at the same time it seems rather simplistic. For one thing, it is rather reductive, in that it suggests there is only one way of analysing religious practices, as ideology. And although this concept of religion as ideology is very important, the complexities of religion in the contemporary world, and in historical perspectives, cannot be so easily summed up in the ways this theory suggests. After all, Marx did have in mind particular cultural examples of religion – Christianity and Judaism in Europe – so it cannot be assumed that what he says works equally well in other parts of the world, and with other religious cultures.

This basic Marx-derived idea of religion as ideology also gives a rather simplistic view of social difference, one that has also been continually discussed by later commentators on Marx's writings. Even if we follow his assumption that all social relations are based on the economic infrastructure (coming from groups' access to and control over the means of production), is it enough to consider this simply in terms of those at the top and bottom of the system? For example, how do relations of power between women and men fit into the analysis? How do men exploit women? Indeed, how do women (and men) of the ruling class exploit working-class men (and women)? And how does religion work as an ideology for this exploitation? I will come back to this point later, but it is important to note that the operation of power and control works in a number of ways, including (but not only) class differences. And what the theory suggests, but does not explain, is the question of whether such ideology is produced deliberately or not – do groups in power create religions as ideologies to legitimate their power over others, or is it simply inevitable that religious practices will work in this way?

In sum, Marx's concept of religion as ideology is a useful, although limited, way of analysing political roles of religion. It is more simplistic than it needs to be, and yet it is a powerful means of thinking about ways in which religious teachings and practices, ritual actions, and religious organisations can all be part of the political justification and legitimation of unequal relationships. But there are other ways in which we can say that religious activities work in the political sphere – sometimes to challenge power differences as well as support them.

Antonio Gramsci and the concept of hegemony

The Italian marxist Antonio Gramsci, writing in the 1930s (but not published in English until 1971), suggests a more nuanced perspective on the ways in which ideology can work in the struggles between classes. For Gramsci (1971) the relationship between power differences and cultural forms (particularly language, but much of what he has to say can be applied to the study of religion) is more subtle than simply arguing that power is legitimated by ideology. Like Marx, Gramsci took as his basis for analysis the fact that social groups are divided, and that most societies comprise a small ruling elite group who exert power and control over others. This power may be based on some sort of brute force, and may well have an economic (and hence exploitative) base. However, this requires consent, and this is achieved by making power relations appear 'natural' – as part of the day-to-day practice of culture.

The key concept for Gramsci in this power dynamic is *hegemony*, referring to the complex means by which those who are ruled over come to accept and feel they have a stake in the powers that are exploiting and controlling them. How hegemony works, therefore, is that particular forms of culture are imposed by the ruling elite, as the 'preferred' or dominant form. But this happens through a process of consent – the ruled-over classes tend to internalise the ideology/dominant culture and behave as if that culture is their own. Alternative forms will exist alongside this dominant and dominating culture, but are regarded as having lower status. What happens, therefore, is not so much a straightforward 'top down' imposition of ideological domination by the ruling class or elite group, although the end result may in fact be this. Instead, the hegemony concept suggests that political relations are a process of struggle, through which the ruling group have to negotiate with and impose – by force and by other means, such as through education – their particular cultural views, standards, and practices.

Within this struggle, however, those who are ruled over (the phrase *subaltern* is often used for such groups) can resist and challenge the hegemonical culture of the ruling group, asserting their own culture – albeit in a field in which it is devalued and derided. What also happens, however, is that subaltern groups (outside of the ruling elite) seek to engage with the hegemonical culture and make it their own, to the extent that it may become *their* culture. By taking on the cultural trappings of the powerful they attempt to get some of that power for themselves. In this sense, then, hegemonical culture becomes ideological in a way that is fairly similar to Marx. Those with power use culture as a means of exerting that power, and those who are ruled begin to participate in their own exploitation through becoming immersed in the hegemonical culture.

For example, in colonial nineteenth-century India, Britishness and British culture became the cultural practice of certain sections of Indian society, those in the social groups that gained most from British colonial rule. Likewise, in the contemporary world Americanisation is not simply about cultural diffusion and sharing across the globe, but is itself the process by which less powerful groups and nations internalise the culture of the dominant superpower. As Gramsci showed, this happens particularly with language, where in both cases the language of the powerful, English, has become hegemonic, dominating and in some cases displacing local languages. This is not to say, however, that in each case such hegemony has not been resisted, both at the level of language, and of culture more generally.

The practice of religion in the contemporary world can be understood in these terms also. The spread of American influence and power has seen the globalisation of various Christian churches too, as previously occurred with earlier European colonialism by the British and others. This happened not only through the migration of Christians to non-European countries, but also by the widespread adoption of Christianity by people in numerous non-western communities. Christianity is part of the culture of power, and so is hegemonic. Although alternatives exist and struggle against its power, Christianity is taken up as a means by which individuals and groups may engage with the powerful in various ways.

On the other hand, as Gramsci argues, the imposition of ideology often implies a concept of struggle – or in other words, hegemony can produce counter-hegemony. The power exerted by the powerful may be resisted by those being controlled. At the local level there may be reactions against the use of English (in favour of the local language, or languages), and also against the hegemonic power of Christianity. In a very broad sense we can see this happening with the assertion of Islam as a counter-ideology against Christianity in the Middle East and elsewhere. By asserting Islam as a non-western religion and culture, some Muslims may engage with alternative religious identities to resist the unequal relations of power within the global sphere between the USA and Middle Eastern countries.

Of course, these processes do not only work at the global level, we can also see something similar happening at national, and indeed more local levels. All nation-states define a certain culture as hegemonic, which is imposed upon and taken up by the various groups within that nation. So, for example, most nation-states privilege certain forms of religion. Until relatively recently the Church of England was the dominant religious form in England and was the only means by which a person could achieve power. For example, until the nineteenth century a person who was not a member of the church could not be in parliament, or study at university. However, there have been continual struggles against this, ever since the reformation, not only from Catholics but also Protestant dissenters. In the latter part of the twentieth century the exclusivist power of the Church of England had changed to a more inclusive attitude, allowing a certain degree of tolerance and acceptance of diversity. But even so, this more ecumenical (religiously inclusive) model has itself become hegemonic, being the dominating form of British Christianity.

In the USA the situation has been somewhat different since, from the time of the Pilgrim Fathers on the Mayflower, there has been a political rejection of a single state religion. This was, of course, a part of the resistance to British hegemony – with its state church – which led to the founding of the independent republic of the United States of America. Thus, in the USA there is no single religion which is exclusively privileged by the state, and to protect against this there is a carefully maintained 'wall of separation' between church and state. However, in practice there is still a hegemonic religious culture: although no single religious group has a monopoly in the state, Protestant Christianity is a very powerful and dominating force within the whole of American culture and society. All other religious groups, that is those who are not Protestant, or even Christian, need to adapt to make themselves compatible with Protestantism. Otherwise, they may become seen as antithetical to what it means to be American, as could be said to have happened with Muslims.

More particularly, however, the idea of a general shared Protestantism is itself hegemonic, and has not only arisen out of history through the post-reformation era, but has a strong ideological force. The idea of a generic Protestantism allows particular groups to become representative of the whole: the Church of England for other Protestants in the UK, and Southern Baptists and certain Presbyterian groups in the USA. This then requires less influential groups to either accept their place within the Protestant fold, and therefore align themselves with the religious majority, or otherwise to mark themselves out as separate from it, and so become counter-hegemonic. The clearly political dimensions of this hegemony become most apparent in actual religious–political movements, such as the

Moral Majority movement in the USA in the 1980s and onwards. Hegemony is therefore not only working between religious organisations (such as churches), but also within organisations as particular groups attempt to become dominant by asserting their position.

Gramsci's idea of hegemony is, therefore, a way of analysing the struggles of religion and ideology within a cultural and political context. It highlights the use of various forms of culture (including religion) as a means of both asserting and resisting control, and also as a part of the exercise of power. Like ideology, hegemony can become the means by which those who are controlled become content with the relations of inequality, but the concept also draws attention to the ideological challenges made by less powerful, subaltern groups.

Indeed, much of the discussion of hegemony relates back to ideas discussed in the previous chapter, when I looked at the relationships between popular and 'high' culture. The concept of a 'high' or elite culture (and indeed religion) is itself hegemonic: it is a means of controlling and asserting power relations. Certain forms of culture become ideologically charged, since they are associated with power, and social position is related to an engagement with such hegemonic 'high' culture. However, as I showed, popular cultures are often counter-hegemonic, resisting the dominant culture, even though powerful group interests may themselves be represented in such culture (such as the economic interests of the music industry). Furthermore, although popular culture may be resistant of the dominant culture, there may also be other power relations asserted and acting hegemonically within it. For example, although black rap is a popular cultural form that resists white cultural and political dominance, it can also assert certain forms of black culture hegemonically over others, in particular male over female.

Althusser and ideological apparatus

The French marxist writer Louis Althusser (1971), writing in the late 1960s, presented a similarly sophisticated model for developing Marx's concept of ideology. His contribution to the discussion focused on two particular aspects of ideology: first how the ruling order is imposed, and second how such ideology works at the level of the individual person. For Althusser, ideology is a way of seeing other realities. That is, it is an illusion, although it makes allusion to reality. From this assumption, he explores the circumstances through which people are happy to participate in such an illusion, even though it helps to produce their subjugation and oppression, without them realising that it is doing so.

Althusser's starting point is to argue that there are two forms of *state apparatus* that enable the ruling group to exercise power over the population. These are: (a) the *repressive status apparatus* (including the army, police, prisons, courts, and government itself), which together act through force, violence, or the threat of violence; and (b) the *ideological state apparatus*, which is more diffuse and heterogeneous. As examples of forms of ideological state apparatus, he lists education (i.e. schools), the family, the media, arts and literature, and also the churches. Thus for Althusser, organised religious organisations are one means, out of a number, by which the ideological dominance of the state is internalised.

This does not mean that churches intentionally subjugate their members, but the end result is that they help to do so. It is possible to see this demonstrated in obvious ways – historically churches in Europe have been active participants in the ideological suppression of nations. The fact many states have had established churches, integrated into the administration of the state (for example, in the UK) makes clear how churches can provide some of the ideological apparatus through which power is legitimated. Indeed, examples such as the Inquisition in various eras of Catholic history demonstrate how the churches can also be involved in the repressive apparatus of the state – physically and violently enforcing the rule of law.

Similarly, one can also point to the example of the Taliban government in 1990s Afghanistan, where the religious ideology (of a certain form of Islam) was very much integrated into the regime of power. The Taliban's form of Islamic law was not only an apparatus of ideology, it was also a crucial part of the way in which power was exercised by the state, through the use, and threat, of violence against any that resisted. Thus the role of this particular practice of religion in Afghanistan involved not solely the use of Islam as an ideological part of the state apparatus, but also its integration into the basic coercive mechanics of maintaining state power. This perhaps shows limitations in Althusser's distinction between repressive and ideological state apparatus: they are sides of the same coin, requiring the other for effective order. Although violence is usually the prerogative of repressive status organisations, this will not always exclude religious organisations in the way that Althusser assumes. After all, his argument is based primarily on a European concept of religion and religious organisations modelled on certain forms of Christianity, with a view that religions will be separated out from the basic mechanics of state. Although it works fairly effectively for liberal democracies (such as France, the UK, and the USA), his placing of churches and other religious organisations as an apparatus for ideology may blind us to the fact that in some cases religious organisations may themselves be part of the mechanism through which coercion by the state (through violence) occurs.

Althusser goes on to argue that this ideology (through ideological state apparatuses) works through a process of *interpellation*. That is, the people who are subjugated through such ideology are freely acting, even though they are being exploited in doing so. Thus, Althusser describes how

> [a person] behaves in such and such a way, adopts such and such a practical attitude, and ... participates in certain regular practices which are those of the ideological apparatus [such as the church] on which 'depend' the ideas which [s/he] has in all consciousness freely chosen as a subject.
>
> (Althusser 1971 [1994: 156])

Unlike Marx's concept of ideology, this concept of interpellation suggests that the person is not a dupe participating in a false consciousness. S/he is still acting on an illusion (based on a representation of the imaginary relationship of individuals to their real conditions of existence), but one which s/he feels has been 'freely chosen'. For Althusser, interpellation is the process by which people act under ideology without realising that their seemingly 'free' actions are so controlled.

This is how ideology tends to work, by making people act in an obvious way: 'ideology ... imposes ... obviousness as obviousness, which we cannot fail to recognize' (Althusser 1971 [1994: 159]). He reminds us that we are not simply talking about other people, living in other systems. It is impossible for anyone to escape such conditions: we are all immersed in an ideology that traps us into such interpellation. He points out that 'the author and the reader of these lines both live "spontaneously" or "naturally" in ideology' (1971 [1994: 159]). If this sounds depressing, it is meant to. For Althusser there is little room to escape the power that ideology has on creating people who think they act freely but are in fact trapped into an ideology that tells them they are free.

Put together with Gramsci's notion of hegemony, however, Althusser's ideas do not sound quite so deterministic. If we can talk about hegemony as somewhat similar to ideology, since both act to instil a worldview into subjects who then make that worldview their own, then we can pull from Gramsci the idea that ideology is never completely successful. An ideology, no matter how powerfully it is transmitted through religious organisations, or schools, or other media, is always going to exist alongside alternatives – counter-hegemonies which may resist the power of the ruling class. Sometimes such a counter-hegemony, and counter ideology, may exist as a secular (non-religious) opposition to the power of the dominant religion, but in other cases it may be framed as religious. For example, the growth of liberation theology as a form of Catholicism for the poor and oppressed within Latin America (and many other parts of the world), was a counter-hegemonic resistance to the mainstream Catholic church, who were effectively giving ideological justification to capitalist exploitation of developing countries.

Two further points may be taken from Althusser. First, for Althusser, ideology is not simply a matter of disembodied or abstract ideas. Ideology has a 'material existence' (1971 [1994: 156]), not necessarily in the same way as a 'paving-stone or a rifle', but it is 'in the last instance' rooted in materiality. That is, ideology is a form of concrete reality in itself. The existence of ideas and ideology 'is inscribed in the actions of practices governed by rituals, defined in the last instance by an ideological apparatus [e.g. a church]' (1971 [1994: 158]).

Thus the power of ideology works in a circular way: an ideology which is propagated by a state apparatus produces material practices such as rituals, which require people to actually do them, by taking part, and through so doing a personal and internalised ideology is created. The ideology is embodied through the practice, and is lived out in the people who are interpellated by the ideology. That is, the ideology of state apparatus becomes embodied and inscribed on, and practised by, the person. I will be looking at these ideas later (in Chapter 5), when I relate them to Pierre Bourdieu's (1977, 1992) idea of habitus.

The second point to take from Althusser concerns the way in which ideology is perceived with regard to social and economic forces. In this regard, Althusser suggests a very different conclusion from Marx's idea of ideology as a by-product of economic forces. Althusser's contention is that 'man is an ideological animal by nature' (1971 [1994: 159]), since a person cannot act without an ideology and there cannot be an ideology without people. One may wish to rephrase his comment in a less gender-exclusive way, perhaps to say that being ideological is a part of human nature.

On one level this seems obvious – after all, it is hard to imagine a society which does not have ideology, or indeed which does not have political division. Even if the marxist dream of a utopian society of the proletariat ruling as a class by and for themselves could ever be realised in practice, it is still hard to believe that ideology would disappear in the way Marx himself expected. In the meantime, however, we are left with a multitude of religions and cultures in which there are significant economic inequalities, but in which too the experience of those economic conditions is created by the ideological system. Marx's famous phrase, inspired by the German philosopher Feuerbach, that 'religion does not make man, man makes religion' (Marx and Engels 1957: 37) can still be affirmed, in the sense that the study of religion is the study of human activity. But on the other hand, if we follow Althusser in assuming that to be human is to be ideological, then other aspects of human experience can be produced by this ideological inclination. Religion, as a form of ideology, does help to create other human experiences, such as economic and power relations, as do these other experiences help to create religious practices.

Max Weber: religious ideology and economic change

It is this idea that comes out very strongly in the work of another German writer, Max Weber, who put forward a famously subtle argument about the rise of modern capitalism. Weber (1930) carefully examined the social, ideological, and material conditions that were in place – particularly in north America and parts of north-western Europe – in the sixteenth to eighteenth centuries, when the modern capitalist system first took form. One of a number of factors that gave rise to this 'spirit of capitalism', he argued, was the predominance of certain forms of post-reformation Protestant Christianity, particularly those deriving from ascetic Calvinism. This Protestantism encouraged a high level of personal self-discipline amongst its followers, with a valorisation of thrift and hard work, and a requirement to demonstrate one's salvation (or calling) through material achievement. These factors amounted to a religious ideology that was both emerging from social and economic relations, but at the same time encouraging the development of a new social and economic system, of capitalism.

The subtlety of this argument is sometimes hard to grasp. Critics of Weber's thesis have pointed to the rise of capitalist activity in non-Protestant, particularly Catholic, European countries, indicating that it could happen without the ascetic religious culture of Calvinism. And likewise, there were largely-Calvinistic countries where capitalism was slow to take off, such as Scotland. But Weber was not necessarily saying that ascetic Protestantism created capitalism, in the sense of a religious tradition producing an economic system. Instead, ascetic Protestantism was a *factor* in a profound social, cultural, and economic change, and not merely a *product* of such change. In a sense this appears to turn Marx's idea of ideology on its head, with religion seeming to give rise to economics, whilst for Marx it was other way around. Instead, Weber was making a case for the role of ideology as a means by which social change can come about – not by determining or forcing that change, but as one out of a number of influences.

In fact, we can take from Weber the idea that it is nearly impossible to say where the distinction lies between religion and economics, politics, or culture. There is not a 'purely' political or economic domain that gives rise to particular religions and cultures, but instead a complex social fabric in which there are a number of interrelated factors, which we broadly label as 'religion', 'politics', 'economics', and so on. The problem in our analysis often comes when we try to isolate 'religion' off too much from other cultural activities. In fact all religious practices can have a political dimension (e.g. being used as an ideology), and this is also the case the other way around. As Weber suggests, religious ideologies and practices can also be a part of the engine of social and economic change.

Michel Foucault: religion, discourse, and power/knowledge

One of the most profoundly influential thinkers of the second half of the twentieth century, the French philosopher and social theorist Michel Foucault, said relatively little with regard to the specific analysis of 'religion'. Unlike Marx, for example, Foucault made no attempt to theorise or explain religion as a social phenomenon. However, the breadth of his writings, which covered a range of ideas and institutions – including bodies, sexuality, prisons, armies, hospitals, and the history (or archaeology) of knowledge – provides a range of perspectives that have a very concrete relevance to the study of religion and culture. Foucault's approach cannot be so easily distilled into simple formulae, as for example Marx into economics and ideology, or Gramsci into hegemony. Indeed, one commentator on his work,

Gayatri Spivak, suggests that the application of Foucault's approach is rather like being 'assembled at a race where the point is to stay on a bicycle at as slow a speed as possible' (Spivak 1996: 158). The complexity and deep probing issues of his thinking can be so easily lost by a simple application of elements of his writings, and there has been a strong temptation for writers to take off in certain directions and 'pedal along' too fast.

This being said, I will take here several ideas from Foucault and show how we can expand on this concept of religion as ideology, or more broadly religion and power. In particular, Foucault's writings on the concept of power take us in quite different directions from those already explored in Marx, Gramsci, and Althusser. For although Marx had a strong influence on Foucault's work, Foucault himself was far less interested in class divisions than any of these other writers. That is, Foucault pursued an analysis of power as a diffuse force operating in all social contexts, and at all levels of society. Thus, in his highly influential introduction to his work *The History of Sexuality* (Foucault 1981) he set out his fundamental approach to the concept of power:

> By power, I do not mean 'Power' as a group of institutions and mechanisms that ensure the subservience of the citizens of a given state ... [nor] a general system of domination exerted by one group over another ... It seems to me that *power must be understood in the first instance as the multiplicity of force relations immanent in the sphere in which they operate* and which constitute their own organization; as the process which, through ceaseless struggles and confrontations, transforms, strengthens, or reverses them ... Power is everywhere; not because it embraces everything, but because it comes from everywhere.
>
> (Foucault 1981: 92; emphasis added)

This view is quite different from an idea of power being exerted by one group over another, and so it is not simply a matter of looking for the ways in which a ruling class exerts power over another class. Such a 'binary and all-encompassing opposition' (1981: 93) needs to be understood within a much wider matrix of power relations. This being the case, the concept of ideology as a tool (or mask) of power relations becomes considerably more complicated.

The diffuseness of this concept of power is most clearly illustrated by Foucault's (1977) discussion of the concept of the *panopticon*, a model for a prison designed in the late eighteenth century by the English philosopher Jeremy Bentham. The panopticon had a circular structure, with cells arranged on the outside of the circle, and an office for the prison guard in the centre. From this room, the prison guard could look through a small window into each of the prison cells, without himself being seen. The effect was that the prisoners (or other detainees, such as patients, workers, or madmen) could be easily and discretely observed at all times. What is more, the observation was not in itself observed by the prisoners, so they never know when the prison guard was watching them. The result was the potential for permanent observation, or at least that was how it was experienced by the prisoners – they acted and behaved as though they were being constantly watched.

This idea took another turn two hundred years later, with the rise of the concept of the *Big Brother* TV game show. In this a group of people are confined in a house fitted with a multitude of cameras, which silently observe (and broadcast through TV and web media) everything that they do. (Foucault himself died in 1984, and so never had the perhaps dubious opportunity to see the panopticon be transformed so dramatically to the popular entertainment genre of 'reality TV'.) Indeed, as I will discuss below, the idea also has resonances with the Christian idea of an ever-watchful deity, who knows both the actions and thoughts of all humans.

The power of the panopticon, Foucault argued, was not so much in the potential labour saving it provided, but rather the way in which the principle of constant surveillance produces a profound internalisation of power and subjugation. The prisoner has to behave as though s/he is being permanently watched

– even when there is no one looking – and so the prisoner effectively participates in the system which is controlling and containing him/her. Prisoners have to watch their own actions, because they know they are/might be being watched. In this sense, they internalise the surveillance of their actions, and become their own jailers.

The historical continuity between Bentham's panopticon and *Big Brother* is not an accident. Instead, Foucault argues, the idiom of surveillance as a means of exerting control over subjects has become a predominant force within modern times. Such surveillance works at many different levels – for example, the use by the state of a police force, the growth of security cameras in public places as a deterrent against crime, through to the development of clinical professions such as psychology and psychiatry. Indeed it is no accident that the great ideology of the current era – that is science, and the scientific method – is itself based on the methodology of *observation*. This Foucault contrasts with the dominance of a different idiom in the Middle Ages, when power and control was manifest more overtly in the practice of spectacle rather than surveillance.

What Foucault appears to be describing, therefore, is a basis for the mechanisms of ideology – a means by which power is exerted within the field of social relationships. Such power is not merely the power of the state over the subjugated individual – although this can be one form of power relationship – but also how a wide nebula of relationships are experienced and controlled in a variety of contexts. For example, when I walk through the grounds of my children's school, I am aware of the security cameras that are constantly 'on watch'. But it would be simplistic to explain or analyse such surveillance as ideologically the same as the cameras trained on me at my local shopping mall, or the police helicopters that fly over student demonstrations taking photos of the participants. All are different forms of surveillance, with different consequences – working in different (although perhaps related) fields of power relations.

It could be argued (and has been by a number of polemicists) that the Catholic practice of confession has this very effect. The intimate confession of sins by the penitent to the priest exposes the former to the gaze of the church in a way that one can equate with other agents of power, such as psychiatrists, teachers, doctors, and parole officers. A similar argument could also be made with regard to social control among Protestant groups: although there is no priest or confession, the surveillance of good conduct still occurs (or is felt to occur). This is either through a sense of an almighty god, who sees and knows everything, judging a person's heart and faith, or through the perhaps more tangible role of the church community and elders constantly scrutinising each other and maintaining order. In each of these cases we can analyse religious traditions or practices not as a special or unique type of ideology, but as one out of many means by which power is exercised in the field of social relations through the internalisation of surveillance.

What this model does is to take the grand explanatory framework of Marx's concept of ideology and make it work at a much more subtle level. There is still plenty of room within Foucault's argument to see religion as an ideological form of oppression – either in terms of Althusser's ideological apparatus and the practice of ideology, or in more general terms of writing social relations in a more abstract and mystical framework. Foucault's concept of surveillance suggests – like both Gramsci and Althusser – that the subject person (on the individual level) is complicit and compliant in the forces of domination. Power and control is exerted through surveillance by making the subject accept the terms of control – by becoming their own jailer. In Foucault's later writings (particularly volumes 2 and 3 of *The History of Sexuality* (1992 [1984], 1990 [1984]), this concept is described as governmentality. This refers not simply to the actions of states and governments, but the many diffuse ways in which people (as individual subjects) are involved on a subjective level with the power forces that control their lives.

Foucault's ideas can be taken further than this, however. Much of the discussion of his work has centred on the three concepts of *power*, *knowledge*, and *discourse*. At its most basic, for Foucault there was a simple equation that could be made: knowledge is power. But this statement is not as simple as it looks, because his concern was not so much with the idea of true knowledge, but rather the way in which what is taken to be 'knowledge' (or as 'truth') is used in political ways, to exert control over others. But this also works the other way around: what is taken to be knowledge is itself the product of power. Knowledge gives power and is derived from power. Thus we can ask a question deriving from this, posed by Talal Asad: 'how does (religious) power create (religious) truth?' (Asad 1993: 33).

This is where discourse comes in – discourses are a way of talking about the world, a verbal means of describing how reality is seen. Such discourses are crucial, since humans rely on language to communicate and to think, and thus to engage with 'the world' beyond them. Discourses do not simply describe our sense of reality, they give us the means by which we experience it. Thus on a simple level if I use the word 'table' to describe (or name) a piece of wood, I might feel inclined to eat my dinner off it. If I use another word, for example 'altar', then it might seem inappropriate to use that same piece of wood for eating. Discourses work on this principle: they shape the world, and make people act through their power. But discourses do not have the power in themselves, they are instead a means by which power relationships are expressed and constructed. Power relationships produce discourses, which act – in Foucault's phrase – as 'regimes of truth'. Existing within such a regime makes it difficult to accept any other truth than that which is given by the dominant discourse.

Thus power shapes discourses, and through these discourses knowledge is constructed. As a simple example, for centuries during the Middle Ages most people in European society talked about (engaged in a discourse) the sun as part of the heavenly sphere, which circulated above the world (the earth). This was not simply a way of talking – it was, for priests, kings, and peasants, taken to be the truth. Certain events led this discourse to be questioned and challenged, so in contemporary Europe there is a quite different way of talking about the position of the earth *vis-à-vis* the sun. But we cannot assume that the present discourse is less politically charged than the Medieval Catholic one. Rather we are more immersed in it, and so it is less easy to see the connections between the power and the knowledge that is produced.

To take a different example, the contemporary ways of talking about warfare rely on a quite different discourse. Modern forms of warfare, particularly as waged by the dominant superpower of the USA, rely on highly technological long-range attacks at high altitude, through aerial bombing and computer-guided missiles. Like most other forms of warfare, however, the result is to produce death, injury, and destruction on a large scale. Often this violence is against 'legitimate targets' (soldiers and other military personnel, who are themselves defined as 'targets' because they are the 'perpetrators' of violence). But the technology of killing and violence is not completely accurate, and others may also be hit by the bombs and missiles. To justify such innocent killing, which in other circumstances may be considered immoral, the discourse of power uses phrases such as 'collateral damage' (for example, in the killing of thousands of non-Taliban Afghans in 2001). Thus power can define discourse, and in doing so define truth (or at least the truth as it is perceived by those who engage in that discourse). Of course, the same happens the other way around, as certain Muslim religious fighters have themselves asserted their own power and discourse in the fight against the 'infidel unbeliever' (*kafr*) and decadent Christian west.

The concept of discourse should, however, be taken in a much broader sense than an abstract understanding of 'false consciousness', as indeed Althusser argued for the concept of ideology. For one thing, discourse – like ideology – is not a non-material activity: discourse is about action and practice as well as words. Words, and discourses, do not only exist as exhaled air or words on a page, they are inscribed in activities and written on to bodies. The power of discourse is made most clear in the punishments of those who challenge the discourse (and the power relations behind the discourse): through beheadings, mutilations, bombings, and torture. But discourses can be written on bodies in more subtle and less painful ways, through clothes, body markings (such as tattoos, make up, hair cutting and shaving), and ritual mutilations (such as circumcision).

They are also acted out by bodies, as rituals (or ritual actions), which I will be discussing in Chapter 6. Practice and action are, therefore, discursive, and discourses are not merely talk, but a type of action too.

Following from this, also, we should not assume that the stress on discourse entails a notion of falsity. The analysis of discourse (and in a similar way of ideology) needs to put aside the basic question of whether it is true or not, since the assumption of truth is itself a function of the power of the discourse. Althusser's summary of this as the 'obviousness of obviousness' sums this up quite well – truth is seen as truth because that is how the discourse is framed through the power relations, and that is how it is lived in (and internalised). On this level, we have to return again to the basic assumptions in the study of religion: there may be some ultimate truth out there (who knows?), but our analysis is concerned with how the idea and ideology of such truth works out in discourse.

Summary

- There are many means by which religion and politics interact *in power relations*, often described through the concept of ideology.
- Marx's analysis sees religion (as ideology) as a by-product of economic relations of inequality, which it legitimates and helps to mask. It is not difficult to find examples of situations where religion is used as a means of articulating and obscuring relations of power.
- In contrast, Weber made a case for perceiving religious ideology and practice as an element of social relations (and social change), so that religion can produce economics as well as vice versa.
- Gramsci and Althusser both point out the ways in which relations of power are internalised by those without power as ideologies, whether through participation in hegemony (for Gramsci), or through interpellation (for Althusser).

- Religion (and ideology) can create power, and can itself be part of a discourse that is constructed through power relations. This can operate on both a large-scale level, for example between social-economic classes, and throughout all aspects of social and cultural relations in 'everyday life'.
- Religious ideologies, as a set of both ideas and practices, may be part of the justification and imposition of power relations, and also the means by which power is challenged and resisted.

Suggestions for further reading

There are numerous books, particularly by sociologists, that give introductions to the writings of Karl Marx and Max Weber on religion. One of the most recent is the second edition (Routledge, 2001) of the useful Malcolm Hamilton, *The Sociology of Religion: Theoretical and Comparative Perspectives* (1995).

On Marx and religion, see Clarke and Byrne, *Religion Defined, and Explained* (1993); and Daniel Pals, *Seven Theories of Religion* (1996). On Weber, see Frank Parkin, *Max Weber* (1982); Bryan S. Turner, *Max Weber: From History to Modernity* (1992); and Stephen Turner (ed.), *Cambridge Companion to Weber* (2000). On Gramsci, see Bruce Lincoln, 'Culture' (2000). On Foucault and religion, the article by Talal Asad, 'The Construction of Religion as an Anthropological Category', is an excellent starting point, as is the volume in which it is published, *Genealogies of Religion* (1993). There are also two recent books by Jeremy Carrette: *Religion and Culture by Michel Foucault* (1999) provides a collection of papers by Foucault which touch on issues of religion; whilst *Foucault and Religion* (2000) seeks to explore what he calls 'the religion question' in the work of Foucault in a largely theological way.

For various readings on religion and ideology, see Robert Bocock and Kenneth Thompson (eds), *Religion and Ideology: A*

Reader (1985). John Storey's *Cultural Theory and Popular Culture: A Reader* (1994) contains extracts from Foucault, Gramsci, and Althusser on power and ideology. Some good general essays on religion and ideology include Gary Lease, 'Ideology' (*Guide to the Study of Religion*, Continuum 2000); and Bruce Lincoln, 'Conflict' (*Critical Terms for Religious Studies*, Chicago UP 1998). For a recent article on religion and politics, using some interesting case studies, see Jeffrey Haynes, 'Religion and politics' (*Religions in the Modern World*, Routledge 2002).

Chapter 4

Gender

A dissident in Cold War Poland once wrote that 'under capitalism man oppresses man, whilst under communism this is reversed'. I have shown in the previous chapter that what we think of as religion is often integral to such power relations, as an ideology or discourse on truth and difference. What the cynical and ironic observation I have quoted is silent about, however, is the significance of gender as a basic element of such difference. If man is oppressing man, what is happening with (and to) women? In what ways do religious traditions and ideologies create gender relations, and exert forces of power?

Despite decades of debate about feminist (and post-feminist) theory and practice, the study of religion, culture, and gender is still relatively 'new' and 'innovative'. As Darlene Juschka (2001: 1) has recently argued, 'whatever the reasons, it is evident that some fields of study are less receptive to feminist perspectives ... The study of religion has been one of those disciplines-' There has, however, been much good feminist research – some of which I will

be discussing in this chapter – but unfortunately many feminist writers on religion 'have tended to be ignored or superficially acknowledged; never seriously engaged by androcentric scholars' (Juschka 2001: 1).

A fundamental problem here, which the study of religion shares with a number of other humanities subjects, is the pervasiveness of androcentrism (see, for example, Gross 1977). Androcentrism is the assumption that male-ness, the male perspective, and men's experiences are the central and most important point of reference. Such androcentrism can work in all aspects of life: from having buildings with more toilets for men than women, to education and career systems that favour men's working patterns, to the writings and ideas of male academics on their view of what religion is and how it should be understood. Challenging such androcentrism does not necessarily mean that men are wrong or unimportant, rather the point is that there are other perspectives too, which might not be the same as what is considered to be the normative male-centred one.

Decent scholarship, in trying to understand the world as it really is, therefore needs to be nuanced and sensitive to the politics of gender differences. The ways in which religions and cultures are practised and thought about are very profoundly affected, in many ways, by gender differences. Indeed, we can follow the historian Joan Scott by assuming that 'gender is a primary field within which or by which means of power are articulated', and while it is not the only such field, gender 'seems to have been a persistent and recurring way of enabling the signification of power in the West, in Judaeo-Christian as well as Islamic traditions' (Scott 1986: 1069).

Gender as a basis for analysis

This may well seem like common sense so far, but in practice how can such a gender-aware (or gender-critical) perspective be applied to the study of religion? It can be a matter of asking basic questions: How do women and men experience and participate in religions? In what ways do religions contribute to or challenge power differences between women and men? And indeed – the most frequently asked question – is (male-dominated) religion good or bad for women?

There are numerous examples of the ways in which women have come off rather badly in religious cultures: the denigration of women as 'daughters of Eve' and progenitors of sin in many Christian traditions; the veiling and separation of women amongst Muslim cultures, violence against women in practices of female genital mutilation within the context of religious circumcision in North Africa; and the notorious burning of widows at their husband's death (*sati*) which is associated with certain strands of Hindu tradition. This list is not exhaustive, and has indeed been used by a number of feminist writers (mainly writing from a European, culturally Christian background) to make the point that religion (as a global human system) is always profoundly oppressive and harmful to women – whether that religion be Christianity, Islam, Hinduism, or another. The most vocal example of such a view is Mary Daly, who argues that the concept of belief in a male deity leads to profound sexual inequalities.

But the gender-aware study of religion is not solely about religion and women (a point made by Warne 2000, among many others). The focus on women by many scholars in the field has been predominantly to redress an obvious imbalance – since most pre-feminist studies of religion were, in fact, studies of men's religion. There is, of course, nothing wrong with studies that are specifically men/male focused, just as there is much to be gained from studies that are women/female focused. However, it is intellectually dishonest, and also incomplete, to assume that what is being said from talking mainly to men, or reading texts written predominantly by men about male experiences, is somehow representative in an inclusive way of both men and women. In fact, what has emerged through the development of religion and gender studies has been an examination of not only women and religion, but also men and religion. That is, how do religious cultures construct ideas of maleness and masculinity? And from this, how are such ideologically constructed ideas of maleness presented as politically normative (see Boyarin 1998)?

We have to start by assuming that what goes for men is not the same as for women within a particular context (and vice versa). Indeed, because so much writing on religion (and by religious practitioners) has shown so much male bias and androcentricism, Elisabeth Schüssler Fiorenza (1984) has argued that any study of religion should be based on a 'feminist hermeneutics of suspicion'. That is, any text (whether written by an academic, a religious practitioner, or both) should not be taken at face value. The interpretation of it (its hermeneutics) should lead us to read it assuming a male–female power imbalance, in which women's voices and experiences have been ignored or excluded. We should be 'suspicious' that what is being presented as 'normal', 'inclusive', and 'representative' is in fact a male-centred perspective that marginalises women.

Sex, gender, and sexuality

However, gender studies has also pointed out an essential conundrum. That is, there is no clear consensus among scholars (feminist or non-feminist) on what is meant by the concepts of 'gender', 'female/male', or even 'women/men'. Most people have a sense of what they mean by the women–man distinction. In western cultural contexts it is extremely hard to go about the everyday practice of life without making this distinction, and most people are either one or the other. One of the complicating questions is, though, what is the difference? What makes gender, or what makes a person either a female or a male?

Part of the answer to this has been the issue of anatomy, or bodies. That is, a distinction is often made between two elements of difference: between *sex* and *gender*. In this distinction, sex is the biological 'given', the 'obvious' anatomical difference. However, there are a host of other differences which are not so biologically determined, and are in fact culturally defined – these are labelled as gender. Such gender is not 'natural' or universal, it is something that is produced by specific cultural circumstances which vary according to which particular culture one is referring to. Thus what is considered to be normal female or male behaviour is culture-dependent. There is no essential basis for gender – instead gender is dependent on what each particular culture holds gender to be. In this sense, culture (and religion) makes man and woman.

Thus to make a statement such as 'women tend to be more religious than men', or that 'men make more effective leaders', or that 'only men should be religious leaders', is to talk in terms of gender rather than sex differences. Having a penis or a uterus does not necessarily make someone behave in certain ways. Behaviour is shaped by culture more than such 'natural' givens, and so the cultural study of differences between women and men has tended to focus much more on differences in terms of (cultural) gender, rather than (biological) sex. In particular, the prime focus of study is the ways in which such gender differences are perceived and practised within cultural contexts (and particularly across cultural contexts).

This being said, however, there are problems with this sex–gender distinction, particularly associated with the criticisms of Judith Butler (1990) and Christine Delphy (1993). That is, although it is helpful to move away from the assumption that male-ness and female-ness are 'biologically given', this does not really go far enough. For Butler, gender is a powerful discourse which creates the sense by which we define and understand the bodies we live in. And as, following Foucault, discourse defines reality, we cannot say that gender ends at a particular point, leaving the 'basic' sex- (or anatomical-) based difference. Biology does not exist 'in the raw', but is itself a product of culture. What this argument suggests is that Butler is reversing the biology-creates-behaviour argument. Instead of a person's gender behaviour being determined by their biology (a woman behaving in a certain way because of her anatomy), Butler is saying that the biology itself is constructed by practice and discourse. Being a woman is inscribed or written, onto certain bodies – a process that begins at birth when genital anatomy is scrutinised to determine whether the new-born baby is a 'boy' or a 'girl'.

What this argument can lead to is an idea of gender voluntarism. If bodies are made by discourse, it is possible to challenge accepted and expected gendered behaviour. Thus transsexuality, or transgendering (popularly labelled as a range of activities from 'cross-dressing' to 'sex-changes' and 'gender-bending'), offer examples of ways in which a person's gender can be challenged by individuals beyond what is 'given' to them by their culture. As Henrietta Moore (1999: 158) shows, Butler herself does not wish to argue too strong a case for such voluntarism, but her ideas do leave this open as one way of analysing (and challenging) cultural constructions of gender. However, Butler's argument can be read as a critique both of biological determinism of gender, and also 'straightforward' gender polarism as *either* male or female.

This element of Butler's work makes her a key writer in the area of study known as Queer Theory, in which gender is not only a matter of sex and gender, but also of *sexuality*. How a person lives her or his gender, and to a large degree how they see their 'sex' (as a gendered body) is bound up with their sexuality. The 'basic division' of sex difference presumes sexual complementarity: the 'usual norm' is an expectation of heterosexuality, that men and women engage in sexual activities with (and are inclined towards) each other. However, if we take the assumption that gender is culturally constructed, then one could also argue that sexuality is too, and that there is nothing more 'natural' about heterosexuality than homosexuality. In fact, the distinction between the two has powerful consequences, and the concept (and derogation) of homosexuality is used in numerous political ways through which cultures and religions construct regimes of power and order (see Comstock and Henking 1997; see also Blackwood and Wieringa 1999).

Indeed, the 'normality' of heterosexuality tends to be created in hegemonic ways, by creating a sense of both order (those who are 'right') and difference (those who are abnormal, or 'bent'). Thus many Christian and Muslim traditions take strong stances on the rightness or *righteousness* of heterosexuality, and conversely the 'sin' or 'disgrace' of 'unnatural' and immoral homosexuality. Such statements are not only ways of commenting on a person's sexual orientation (and practice). They are also an important cultural and religious means of defining correct gender behaviour (that is, what men and women should be), and through that of regulating social and cultural practices.

Religion and ideologies of gender

Taking some of the ideas from the previous chapter, it is worth exploring how we can analyse religion as an ideology in terms of gender (rather than class) difference. Michel Foucault's argument that power works within all social relationships, not simply from the top (ruling class) down, suggests that power is an element of gender division. In contemporary western cultures, such as the USA and Britain, as well as many non-western societies, there is a clear difference in power relations between women and men.

Patriarchy, the organisation of societies so that men tend to exert a large degree of control and power over women, is fairly ubiquitous. A large part of the agenda of contemporary feminist movements is to make a political, economic, and cultural challenge to patriarchy – at the level of both the state, and individual people's lives (hence the well-known phrase 'the personal is the political'). One means by which the power imbalance can be challenged, and changed, is through an understanding of how such power works – how it is justified, as well as its social and economic underpinnings.

As I have mentioned above, some feminist writers – such as Mary Daly (1973) have singled out religion as a basic element of patriarchy, since many religions seem to give women a particularly hard time. A Marx-derived perspective argues that the image of god is used by those in power as a misrepresentation of the struggle of class against class. This can be reworked as a feminist argument that the male creator god (of Christianity and other religions) is a tool of the oppression of women – gender against gender, rather than class against class. Such a god is no more than a matter of men writing their political dominance on to 'heaven', and the institutions which men produce for such a god, particularly churches, are key tools for controlling women.

Therefore, the ideology of a male god works to legitimate the economic and political subordination of women. For Daly, women suffer under male control, and suffer through worshipping a male god that men have forced on them. In doing so, women's participation in religious practices and beliefs is a matter of them participating in their own exploitation and oppression. From this Daly argues that all notions of god are produced by men for these purposes. Thus, religion is androcentric (male-centred) and phallocentric (phallus-centred), and the only place given to women within these systems is as silent participants coerced by ideology and forced into exploitation. God is no more than this projection of power relations, there is no reality beyond that, and so god (as an object of belief) can be reduced to patriarchal oppression.

Daly's response to this ideology, however, is not the same as Marx's, for whom religion will disappear, as ideologies do, when social and economic equality is achieved. Daly argues, however, for a change in religious practice as a means of working to reject patriarchy, in particular through her famous phrase that we must 'castrate the maleness from our conceptualisation of god' (Daly 1973: 13). This does not, necessarily require a total rejection of god, but rather a rejection of the male patriarchal god of Christianity who is implicated in the excesses of patriarchal Christian culture. Indeed, Daly suggests a de-masculinised deity, who we learn to think of differently, in terms of a verb rather than a noun, as a 'Be-ing' process (1973: 28–33).

Luce Irigaray and Grace Jantzen

This idea bears similarities with the work of French feminist philosopher Luce Irigaray, particularly her idea of 'divine becoming' (Irigaray 1985a [1974], 1985b [1977], 1987; Jantzen 1998; Magee 1995: 102–6). Irigaray, however, brings a very different theoretical view to the critique of patriarchy, focusing instead on psychoanalytic-derived concepts associated with the writings of Sigmund Freud and Jacques Lacan. This concerns the creation of human personhood, how a person is formed (as a 'subject') – and through that, a person's understanding of who they are (their 'subjectivity').

Psychoanalytic theory suggests that 'persons are not ready-made souls inserted in bodies by God. Rather, human personhood is *achieved* ... at considerable cost' (Jantzen 1998: 8). This occurs primarily through the repression of the person's many conflicting desires, and it is religion that has traditionally 'been the source of some of the most effective ... strategies of control' (1998: 8). For Lacan, however, this repression of desire comes about for a boy when he enters into 'the symbolic', a term he uses 'to designate the broad conceptual patterns of civilization' (Jantzen 1998: 10). It is only by entering this symbolic – by developing language, and overall cultural competence – that a person becomes a unified self with her or his own subjectivity. However, Lacan's symbolic is a decidedly male domain, it exists by and for men, with women being marginalised. Indeed, for Lacan, women are so much outside of the symbolic that they are 'the Other', the thing against which the male subject defines itself. However, for women to achieve subjectivity, they must also enter into the symbolic.

This amounts, in a sense, to the same bind outlined by a Marx-derived view of ideology and religion. The symbolic, which is broadly both culture and religion, is a male construction which women must enter into. In fact, Lacan suggested that the symbolic is so much a male domain, that language itself is exclusively male. This then leaves for him a problem of how women can speak: if language (and more broadly the symbolic) is male, then women must either remain silent, or otherwise participate in a psycho-social framework that is not their own. For Irigaray it is not so simple: this is not a problem for women using language, but of psychoanalytic theorists failing to listen to women. Lacan and Freud 'were first consigning women to silence by defining language as masculine, and then complaining that women had nothing to say' (Jantzen 1998: 11). Instead, Irigaray argues, women do not lack language and the symbolic, rather they use it in different ways to men.

For women to develop a women-centred symbolic they must disrupt the male symbolic, 'displacing its masculinist stuctures by a new imaginary ... based ... on new ways of conceiving and being which enable women to be subjects *as women*' (Jantzen 1998: 12). This is achieved through the idea of the 'divine'. The symbolic includes not only language and culture, but also religion, which Irigaray describes as the 'linchpin of the western symbolic' (Jantzen 1998: 12). The women's symbolic is achieved by transforming rather than rejecting religion.

In short, the divine provides a 'horizon of becoming', which serves as the 'ideal of perfection, the place of the absolute for us, its path, the hope of its fulfillment' (Irigaray 1987: 63). That is, divinity as part of the female symbolic 'is what we need to become free, autonomous, sovereign' (1987: 62). But this divine is not an 'all-powerful super-being in a timeless realm' (Jantzen 1998: 12), nor is it an 'absolute Presence' or an 'absolute Absence' (Magee 1995: 106). Rather it is part of the process of female subjectivity, through which women experience the female symbolic, and so 'discover, affirm, achieve certain ends' (Irigaray 1987: 67).

In many respects, this is a theological perspective on gender inequality. Unlike Marx's idea that religion would disappear with social change, instead social change comes through reconstruction of female subjectivity as reimaging the divine. Even so, Irigaray's god is not an absolute external force, instead s/he is embedded within the psychocultural processes of subjectivity, and may not need to exist for all time (Irigaray 1987: 62). In this respect, therefore, Irigaray's ideas can be read as both a theological exploration, and also as a theory for describing (and prescribing) social, cultural, and theological change in religious traditions.

Gender and Christianity

An important ambiguity in both these writers, however, is the slippage that can easily occur between describing patriarchy and religion, and describing patriarchy and Christianity. As Daly and many other feminist writers have shown Christian traditions through the centuries have often been oppressive for women. Many Christian traditions maintain some very strong (for some people offensive) ideological representations of gender difference. Christian texts suggest an ambiguity about the natural construction of women and men. Hence the book of Genesis describes the creation of woman/Eve in two conflicting ways: as *both* at the same time as man/Adam (Genesis 1.27), *and* also as after, and from, man (Genesis 2.18–25). Based around this latter account – and largely ignoring the first, more gender-balanced, Genesis account – there are long traditions of misogyny and exclusion for women within the various churches.

Through Christian history, prominent (male) Christian theologians have written essays on the question of whether or not women are 'properly' human. And, of course, it is women in particular who are associated with what most Christian theologies see as the basic flaw of humankind: that is, sin, and in particular the original sin that came from the actions of the first woman and man eating the apple of knowledge and 'falling' (that is, leaving the Garden of Eden). Despite comments in the Christian foundational books (the New Testament) about potential equality between women and men (e.g. Paul's comment that 'in Christ there is no male or female' (Galatians 4.28)), there are equally strong instructions for women to take a deferential role in church and in Christian community. What is more, the presence of a significant element of female-oriented worship in one particular Christian tradition, that of Mary amongst Catholics, is itself ambiguous, focusing women ideologically on a figure who combines the contradictory status of both mother and also pure virginal woman (without 'sin').

Many women in the past century have concluded from this that being a woman in Christian traditions can be difficult, if not impossible. Much of what has been taught and practised by the various churches has been largely based on a principle of male control and superiority over women. What is more, the political challenge by women of exclusive male political hierarchies and organisational control (such as the various movements to admit women into priesthood, other ministries, and into bishoprics) has most often met with strong opposition from the men who dominate these positions. Changes have been made in some Christian churches in recent decades, for example, some Anglican, Methodist, Baptist, and Presbyterian churches now have female priests/ministers. But there remains the uncomfortable question of why women still wish to stick around in traditions that have disadvantaged them so much in the past two millennia?

The response that there are many women who choose to remain Christians, despite these problems, may lead us to conclude that such women are effectively participating in their own oppression. Christian traditions do appear to provide a Lacanian male symbolic. There is a deep vein of androcentrism and phallocentrism in Christian ideologies where a male human–divine figure (Jesus), acting on the wishes of a male creator God, offers hope and promise of a better world, along with truth, wisdom, and salvation for both women and men. Access to this better world can only come, for most Christians, through acceptance of a political organisation that is dominated by men and male-centred values.

A more sophisticated analysis of ideology, deriving from writers such as Althusser or Gramsci, suggests some interesting readings we can make of the role of Christian religious traditions within the construction and maintenance of gender politics. In Gramscian terms, we can argue that male hegemonic culture has been largely internalised by women who, throughout Christian history, have participated in its practices. In terms of Althusser's notion of interpellation, women as subjects have become Christians through male ideological apparatuses (such as the churches, but also through institutions such as the family, schools, etc.), and in doing so have participated in an ideology which oppresses them.

Is this the case? Many Christian women may argue otherwise, that Christianity is not an ideology, but is in fact the way to the (ultimate) truth and so goes beyond such categories. In response one could argue that 'they would say that wouldn't they?' Someone in the grip of an ideology, or who has internalised a hegemony, is not able to step outside of it, indeed Althusser gives a rigid perspective in which it is almost impossible to step out of one's subject position. There are throughout the world (including in the USA and the UK) many millions of women who are happy to accept what could be called 'traditional' Christianity, including many of the androcentric and women-exclusive elements that I have mentioned. It might be possible to argue that such women are trapped in a male-dominated ideology, which they have internalised and which traps them into gender inequality which impacts on many other areas of their lives.

For example, such women, and their husbands/fathers/brothers, may consider that a Christian woman's role in life should primarily focus on providing for the needs of her husband, bearing and raising his children, maintaining his household, etc., and thus being economically dependent on him. If this is combined with a religious injunction against effective contraception, the result will be Christian women spending large parts of their lives bearing and looking after many children, immersed physically and economically in a system which favours their husbands and their male relatives far more than them.

Against this, however, there are also now (since the second half of the twentieth century in particular), many women who have challenged such patriarchal assumptions. In particular feminist Christians have questioned the ideological basics of various Christian traditions, in many different ways. These include the maleness of God, the link between Jesus' maleness and priesthood/leadership, and in particular the link between traditional Christian models of social and family organisation and the opportunities (and gender politics) of the contemporary world. Despite conventional interpretations of Paul's and Jesus' teachings that designate women's 'place' as within the domestic sphere and predominantly motherhood, many contemporary women see no contradiction in being married, having a career, and deferring parenthood to a time that suits their interests (or forgoing it altogether), whilst also being a practising Christian. So, inasmuch as the various Christian traditions produce an ideology and hegemony that can be oppressive to women, there are definitely, at least in recent times, counter-hegemonic forms of feminist Christianity that profoundly challenge that ideology.

In line, however, with perspectives akin to Daly's and Irigaray's there are growing numbers of women (and men) in contemporary western cultures who are rejecting what they see as the inescapable patriarchy of Christian traditions, but still remaining religious. That is, although they accept that a feminist critique can (and should) be made of Christian androcentrism, this does not necessarily mean that the critique should be

extended as a blanket universal criticism of all religious traditions. This view tends to argue that it is traditional Christianity
(and perhaps Judaism and Islam) which has constructed an
ideology based on an oppressive father deity. But what they see
as the reality behind the deity may be quite different from this.
God as father may create patriarchy, but if women (and men) see
god as mother, and more generally as female, then it is argued
that this more inclusive deity becomes more accessible. As both
Daly and Irigaray and many goddess worshippers also argue, the
replacement of male god imagery with a female deity entails also
the potential for a decline in the political oppression of women.

A remodelling of such goddess worship is a key component
of the contemporary Neo-Pagan movement in a number of
European countries (Harvey 1997; Salomonsen 2001). In these
cases, inclusive goddess worship has been developed as a deliberate attempt to recreate a religion which is non-patriarchal and
so is more socially and culturally egalitarian. This raises,
however, the question of whether or not a goddess-centred type
of religiosity is less patriarchal or androcentric than those which
focus on images of singular male deities. Against this, case
studies of Hinduism suggest that the worship of female deities
(of whom there are many within the various Hindu traditions)
does not necessarily create any more favourable economic,
social, or cultural conditions for Hindu women (Erndl 1993).
Indeed the notorious (and extremely rare) ideology of *sati*
among certain Hindus is in fact tied (at one level) to women's
devotion to a female deity (Hawley 1994; Harlan 1992).

Religion, gender, and agency

Some of these issues can be viewed from a different angle, using
the concept of agency. That is, how individuals behave in spite
of, and also because of, the social, cultural, and religious forces
that act upon them. If someone is brought up in a rigorously
religious background (for example, Baptist Christian, Orthodox
Jewish, or otherwise), that does not necessarily mean they will
themselves be religious in the same way as their family. Acting
on their own individual agency a person can make choices – to

act in ways for which they have not been culturally pre-programmed.

At this simple level it appears commonsensical: cultures and religions do not produce clones. Individuals have a role in shaping how they live out and practise the cultures (and religions) into which they have been raised. George W. Bush may not have grown up to be a Republican like his father, it was through his own agency that he made the decisions that finally led to him becoming the US President. Of course, there were many other larger forces at work too, such as the immense wealth of his family, the constraints of the cultural and party-political tradition which he had imbibed through his family, and other pressures from friends, colleagues, family, and from his own expectations of himself. There were many aspects of his own self-interest (in terms of personal, political, and economic gain) that encouraged him to choose the options that he did. But what the concept of agency does is to give room for under-standing why not all people who grow up as sons of US Presidents themselves become Presidents. In contrast, one might ask a different set of questions about Chelsea Clinton. Whether or not she ever becomes president will also depend not only on her own agency – would she want to be a president or not – but also whether the social and cultural system will make it possible, when there has never been a woman president of the USA.

These examples suggest that ideology, and the cultures that produce that ideology, are not all-pervasive – they can be challenged on the individual basis. The existence of an ideology, through a particular religious tradition and culture, may not necessarily mean the acceptance of that ideology (and oppression) by the women in its influence. Structures, and ideologies, are there to be resisted – as Foucault argues: 'where there is power, there is resistance' (Foucault 1981). But is this simply wishful thinking? Is the idea of agency simply a product of the contemporary western idea of freedom of choice?

At its most simple, the idea of agency seems to be based on a loose assumption that, as Talal Asad puts it: 'power is external to and repressive of the agent, that it 'subjects' her, and that nevertheless the agent as 'active subject' has both the desire to oppose power and the responsibility to become more powerful' (Asad 2000: 32). For Asad, this idea romanticises the idea of resistance, as something which is the 'natural' reaction for those oppressed by social and cultural forces.

Thus the agency concept is rather limited if it builds in an expectation of resistance: for example, that George W. should see the folly of his father's policies and become a Democrat, or that a girl raised in a restrictive Christian household can and should rebel and find a life path with which she is satisfied. Such expectations are often confounded by actual examples, such as the cases of women who do not challenge patriarchal religious groups, or of women who were brought up in liberal feminist families actively choosing to join 'traditional' or orthodox traditions in which their gender roles become much more narrowly defined (see, for example Kaufman 1991 on women converts to traditional Judaism, and Palmer 1994 on women joining traditional 'new religions'). The concept of agency should be useful to explain such choices too.

The tricky and unresolved balance depends on whether there is such a thing as a 'free choice', of whether any person can ever step completely outside of the culture, worldview, and religious ideology in which they were raised. There are genuine cases of conversion, when one worldview and lifestyle is exchanged for another, but even so there is still the idea that 'once a Catholic, always a Catholic'. The traditions, cultures, religions, and general social and political forces that one lives within have extremely powerful influences on us as individuals which are very hard to escape. Therefore, agency itself may not simply be a matter of free choice. A person's agency, how they relate to and act out the possibilities that are offered to them, is itself determined by the cultural and religious world in which they live. Culture and religion create a person's agency, and so agency is not a matter of stepping out of the culture – it is more of a matter of living for oneself within the confines of it.

The question of agency also raises another problem, particularly with regard to how we can understand the agency of the actions of people who are not usually listened to, such as women. The Indian post-colonial theorist Gayatri Spivak (1993, 1999) describes this in terms of 'can the subaltern speak?' (the term 'subaltern' meaning here a group who are marginalised or excluded). That is, social organisation and academic study have tended to be so androcentric that it is nearly impossible to find a way of hearing the voices of women in the past, particularly women without power. Historical records, literary sources, religious texts, and oral traditions all seem to speak volumes in their silence about women and women's experiences in the past. The descriptions of women in such texts often present them one-dimensionally (as people who are acted upon, rather than people who act, with agency) and without any voice of their own (usually a male narrator speaking for them, or neglecting to report their speech). Indeed, writing on reconstructing the experiences of women in colonial India, Spivak argues that in the end the subaltern cannot speak, or what she might have said (being passed on to us through history) cannot be heard. At the very least, we need to find new ways of listening to what she (or he) may be saying (Spivak 1999).

From this develops, then, the difficult question of how we listen to women's (and other marginal groups' and individuals') voices within the study of religion and culture? If women and men are active participants in, and against, the ideologies and religious practices of their cultures, then in what ways does this agency help to shape, and resist, cultures and religions? There are, of course, no straightforward answers to these questions. What they give are means to try to understand the particularities of specific cases. In fact, the concept of agency versus ideology and tradition should make us sensitive to the fact that generalisations are always going to be difficult. It then becomes difficult to say something general such as 'religion is bad for women', or 'Muslim (or Christian or Hindu) women are oppressed'. What becomes more important is *how* a religious culture may play a significant role in subjugating and oppressing women (and others) in a *particular* context.

'Veiled' Muslim women

Of the many examples used in studies of women and religion, the one that raises most discussion is the question of women's social and political roles within Muslim traditions. There is a very commonly held assumption that Islam is oppressive of women – as evidenced by specific practices, such as the covering of women's heads, faces, and bodies, and the usually strict social separation between women and men in Muslim daily life. To highlight this, examples can be taken – particularly of the Taliban in Afghanistan, as well as a number of other Muslim states and societies – which clearly show that the strict application of certain Muslim teachings can work in very close parallel with repressive patriarchy.

Even so, it is very easy to over-generalise and so to miss some important local and historical details that are important to the particular context. To start with, there are important distinctions to be made between clothes that almost totally cover both face and head (such as the *burqa* in Afghanistan, and the *niqab* in Saudi Arabia), to the headscarf (*hijab*) that is a much more common form of dress for Muslim women (see Roald 2001: 254–94). Furthermore, it is possible to argue an alternative (or complementary) view that the wearing of either a scarf (*hijab*) or veil (*niqab*) can be a counter-hegemonic strategy, as a means of women's resistance against patriarchy rather than, or as well as, being subjected to it. In this sense, perhaps we can say that these clothes sometimes create a space for women. Although the 'veil', and what it stands for, is in some respects defined in terms of men's values what it actually creates is also largely outside of male control.

Looking at arguments in the specific context of Egypt, Leila Ahmed (1992) points out some of the issues behind why western observers choose to focus on the veil and Islam. Thus the first criticisms of the veil as the symbol of oppression were raised at the time of British colonial rule in the late nineteenth and early twentieth centuries, by figures who could hardly be called 'feminists'. Ahmed singles out in particular Lord Cromer, British consul general in Egypt, who argued that the degradation of women in the East is a canker that begins its destructive work early in childhood, and has eaten into the whole system of Islam ... [The practice of veiling] a baneful effect ... The arguments in the case are, indeed, so commonplace that it is unnecessary to dwell on them.

(Lord Cromer, *Modern Egypt* (1908),
quoted in Ahmed 1992: 152–3)

As Ahmed points out, however, this same would-be emancipator of Muslim women in Egypt was also, at home in Britain, one of the principal agitators *against* women's suffrage (that is, against extending voting rights to women). Cromer did, in fact, pursue policies in Egypt that prevented the expansion of women's education, and discouraged the training of women doctors. What Ahmed concludes is that colonialists such as Cromer (and subsequent generations) were using their critique of the veil as a means to substitute 'the garb of Islamic-style male dominance for that of Western-style male dominance' (1992: 161). Thus she argues:

The idea (which still often informs discussions about women in Arab and Muslim cultures ...) that improving the status of women entails abandoning native customs [such as wearing the veil] was the product of a particular historical moment [of British colonialism] and was constructed by an androcentric colonial establishment committed to male dominance.

(Ahmed 1992: 165)

What this brief historical example suggests, perhaps, is that there are varied and complex reasons why the veil in particular is emphasised by westerners. Although it can be an expression of patriarchal social relations, a critique of the veil may be motivated by equally androcentric factors, especially one that says Muslim women should give up the veil along with other aspects of their culture.

In the context of Egypt in the late twentieth century, Hala Shukrallah (1994) explores the possible reasons why Muslim women do 'still' wear the veil, or more correctly the *hijab* head-scarf. First, she notes that women are often given the task of symbolically representing traditional values. That is, women rather than men have the responsibility for upholding decency, Islamic values, and morals in times of rapid social, economic, and cultural change. Hence, 'decent' behaviour by women, such as the wearing of 'proper' and modest Islamic dress, becomes imperative not only for the women themselves, but for the sake of society as a whole, both women and men.

Despite this, critics such as Cromer, as well as Egyptian feminists, led to many Egyptian (particularly middle-class) women rejecting the veil. However, in more recent years (particularly the last two decades) analysts have observed that *hijab* has again become very prominent among such women. It cannot simply be argued that the renewed popularity of *hijab* is a sign of increased traditionalisation of women, nor of greater exploitation or subordination of Egyptian women. On the contrary, there are now *more* women working in paid employment, earning their own incomes, as well as women participating in higher education at college and university level. In fact, the wearing of *hijab* by many women has been in direct response to the challenges entailed by their increased participation in the public (non-domestic) sphere. Thus, Shukrallah points out, the previously traditional distinction between women as home-makers and keepers in the private sphere, and men as those who enter the public domain for work, has somewhat broken down. Increasingly large numbers of women are now in the previously male-dominated public domain.

It is this fundamental social change that has prompted the increased wearing of *hijab*. On one level, by covering themselves women have made it easier to enter the male/public domain without engendering conflict. *Hijab* minimises the conflict, but does not completely prevent it. There are still many male religious leaders who resist this greater prominence of women in public roles, even though in doing so the women have taken up the symbols of traditional gender relations. For the women, however, *hijab* has also been largely used to resist another element of male political control – as a means of protecting themselves from the potential of male sexual harassment. Covering the head may publicly show a woman to be modest and Islamic, whilst its absence means the woman is exposed to the male gaze as an object of sexual desire.

For Shukrallah, therefore, the increased use of *hijab* in modern Egypt is serving a number of gender political functions. It has become a specific cultural (and religious) option to facilitate women's adaptations to cultural changes – changes of their own making, such as working outside the home in greater numbers. It has also been used as a strategy within the complex gender dynamics specific to the area and the culture, providing a means of resisting and also participating in male attempts to control them. As she concludes, Egyptian 'women have, by donning the new veil, made a statement that both expresses protest and consent at the same time' (Shukrallah 1994 [2001: 195]).

Of course, we must remember that this does not explain 'why' many Muslim women wear *hijab* (beyond the specific context of the women in Egypt discussed by Shukrallah). Nor does it fully explore the ways in which head covering, and the religious ideas and practices associated with it, are produced by the gender political relations between women and men in various Muslim cultures. The wearing of *hijab* by Muslim women in the USA or the UK may be for very different reasons. For example, in this context *hijab* may not only express a challenge of Muslim male control of their activities, as in the Egyptian case, but it may also be used as a form of resistance to the dominant (hegemonic) non-Muslim American or British culture.

Writing on British Muslim women, Myfanwy Franks (2001) suggests that the argument over whether *hijab* is oppressive or not misses the point. Instead, she encourages us 'to recognize that women can and do make subversive and feminist readings of patriarchal discourses', and that 'what is collusion in one context may be viewed as resistance in another' (Franks 2001: 130). In fact, there are various levels of ambiguity in the use of *hijab* which are not easily resolved. For example, head covering makes a clear public statement that its wearer is a good Muslim, even to the extent – as one woman told Franks – that she is 'more Islamic than her husband' (2001: 143). On the other hand, *hijab* marks out its wearer for attention among non-Muslims, attention which can go as far as abuse and violence against the Muslim woman 'for not revealing enough of her body' (2001: 138). In this respect, the covering then becomes a critique of non-Muslim gender relations. Indeed, if we return to Foucault's idea of power as surveillance (as discussed in the previous chapter), we can argue that a woman who wears both *hijab* and a face-veil is challenging the everyday panoptical power of the male, patriarchal gaze. This male gaze (of power) cannot see past 'the veil', and instead the Muslim woman becomes the only one who can survey, rather than being under surveillance.

I have raised these interpretations of women and *hijab* in Islam in order to demonstrate the limitations of any particular explanation. Head covering, as a part of the cultural apparatus of many Muslims, does not necessarily create or reflect any single and particular form of power relations. Although there is a strong element of the wearing of *hijab* by Muslim women that comes out of patriarchal, male-dominated gender relations, the act of wearing may equally be charged with a challenge to such patriarchy. A gender-critical analysis of this particular form of religious practice helps us to understand that there are considerable ambiguities about the *hijab*'s use and meaning.

Gender-nuanced studies of religion and culture

A gender-critical perspective is not only about looking at how religions and cultures act in oppressive ways upon women. The relatively recent development of feminist and gender-critical scholarship means that serious questions can be asked about the ways in which 'traditional' studies have been carried out. For example, what sorts of expectations have been made in previous studies that have concentrated on male viewpoints and activities, and left out or marginalised women? What sorts of things have been said about religion and religions in general, which more particularly relate to the activities of a few powerful men? And to develop this further, how should more gender-critical studies of religion be done?

In the next three chapters I will be developing some of these ideas, to show some of the strengths and weaknesses of focusing studies of religion on belief, rituals, and texts. Indeed, so much research and debate has been conducted on religious beliefs and texts, that it seems there has been little time taken by previous generations of scholars to point out how texts are often profoundly androcentric. After all, the books of the Bible were all written by men, have been translated into English by men, and are usually publicly interpreted by men also. The books contain stories and accounts of various women's (as well as men's) lives, and have been used, in many ways, by women over the millennia. A study of a religion, however, that concentrates solely on the texts themselves and how the text should be understood in terms of its authors and its intended meaning is seriously in danger of missing the point. That is, the ways in which the text is used within the religious and cultural lives of women, as well as men, cannot be reconstructed and understood so easily. Instead, such a text tells us something of the religious practices and concerns of certain men, but that is about it.

In contrast then, studies of religion have to look in different places for the broad range of activities that could be designated as 'religious' within any particular context. A focus on beliefs, and other types of texts (not only 'sacred texts', but also more 'popular' or informal ones) may help us find readings and perspectives of women as well as men. Susan Starr Sered's (1994) discussion of prominent women figures in several religious traditions also draws attention to a number of areas in which women's religious traditions are located. Her focus is on women's particular experiences, whatever they may be, as sources for the development of religious ideas and practices. This may be through domestic experiences, particular life-cycles, or women-focused social networks.

From the perspective of mainstream religious institutions, such as churches, these experiences and networks may produce practices and discourses which are not orthodox or 'proper'. Indeed, in some cases religious cultures associated with women may provide a counter-hegemonic challenge for 'orthodoxy' or mainstream religious practice, but in other cases they may be part of such orthodoxy. An example of the latter can be found in Callum Brown's (2001) analysis of female piety as the mainstay of Protestantism in Britain in the nineteenth and early twentieth centuries (which I will discuss in more detail in Chapter 8). Indeed, for Brown the collapse of such female religious practice in the 1960s has led to an overall decline of cultural Christian practice and ideology in contemporary Britain.

Finally, however, I would like to return to the point made by Joan Scott (1986) that I quoted at the beginning of this chapter. As I have shown, gender is a very important category of analysis for the study of religion and culture. Alongside this, however, we should not lose sight of the fact that, as Scott herself argues, there are other categories of difference as well as gender – such as race, class, ethnicity, age, and sexuality – which cross-cut the lines of difference set up by the male–female distinction (see Maynard 1994).

One small illustration of this is the problems raised by the application of feminist thinking beyond western cultural locations. It is possible to argue that western feminism has imposed an idea of 'women' on to non-western cultures, and then faced problems with the perspectives that such an imposition produces. The case of Muslim women is a good example of this – it could be argued that western feminists do not really know 'what to do' with Muslim women who are happy with their cultural and religious traditions. There are indeed many feminist Muslim women, who engage as feminists with women in western countries and elsewhere. But they are outnumbered by others who consider their religious (e.g. Muslim) and cultural (e.g. Arabic, or South Asian, etc.) identities as more important than their gender.

One response to this is the development of *womanism* rather than feminism – a theoretical and political stance that extends to 'women of colour', beyond the confines of what is otherwise a politically (and economically) elite group of white women in rich western countries (see, for example Walker 1983; hooks 1982). Such a distinction raises two further categories of difference:

race or ethnicity, and class. Much womanism in north America is directed at the 'colour blindness' of white feminists, who fail to see the important issues of racial and economic disadvantage as well as issues of gender.

What was often known as 'third wave' feminism in the 1990s has led to a re-evaluation of some of the complexities of these issues. 'First wave' feminism saw a small number of elite women in the west begin to challenge the dominance of patriarchy in the nineteenth century, and 'second wave' feminism was the much wider explosion of feminist scholarship and activism in the west, and elsewhere, in the 1960s and 1970s (see Juschka 2001: 3–9). Although it could be said that 'second wave' feminism is still in the process of developing, it has been largely superseded by the 'third wave' that offers a more cross-cultural set of perspectives that place the category of gender within the framework of other categories of differences. Gender is an important aspect of cultural and religious practice, but so also are differences based on class, race, power, age, sexuality, and location. Studies of religion and culture require a broad-based approach which assumes this premise of diversity – that religions are products of the politics of such differences, and are experienced through the particular lenses of people who are shaped (in their different ways) by their own particular combinations of identities.

Summary

- Studies of religion need to be gender critical. Indeed, gender is a very important category of difference, as a key element of the practice and ideology of power differences in many cultures.
- Gender critical studies need to look at how religious cultures are constructed and practised around both women *and* men. However, a central problematic about the study of religion and culture remains focused on questions of women's experiences of religion.

> • Western perceptions of women in other religions – such as women in Islam – require a subtle and carefully examined exploration of the politics of religious behaviour, such as the wearing of *hijab*, i.e. 'the veil'.
> • Such an analysis also needs to recognise other aspects of difference, such as 'race', class, ethnicity, age, and sexuality, which are all important social elements that affect religious and cultural practices.

Suggestions for further reading

An excellent starting point for the study of religion and gender is the recent reader edited by Darlene Juschka called *Feminism in the Study of Religion: A Reader* (2001). It contains a wide range of essays, a number of which are mentioned in this chapter. Juschka's introduction sets out the history of feminist thinking very concisely and covers the main issues in the growth of feminist studies of religion. Another good collection of articles is Ursula King, *Religion and Gender* (1995), which also has a very useful introduction.

Other recent articles on the field of gender and religion are: Daniel Boyarin, 'Gender' (1998); and Randi Warne, 'Gender' (2000). Mary Keller's *The Hammer and the Flute: Women, Power, and Spirit Possession* (2002) provides some excellent discussion on contemporary issues in the study of religion, gender, and agency. See also Linda Woodhead, 'Women and Religion' (*Religions in the Modern World*, Routledge 2002). On issues of religion and gender in a post-colonial context see Laura E. Donaldson and Kwok Pui-Lan, *Postcolonialism, Feminism, and Religious Discourse* (2002).

For a very useful discussion of the complexities of contemporary debates on gender, sex, and sexuality, see Henrietta Moore, 'Whatever happened to women and men? Gender and other crises in anthropology' (*Anthropological Theory Today* 1999). Christine Delphy's article on 'Rethinking Sex and Gender'

(1993) is reprinted in the Darlene Juschka *Reader*, whilst for the very strong-hearted, Judith Butler's *Gender Trouble* (1990) makes a very challenging read (in more ways than one). The volume edited by Gary David Comstock and Susan E. Henking, *Que(e)rying religion: A Critical Anthology* (1997) provides some good articles on issues arising from the application of queer theory to the study of religion and culture.

For studies of religion and gender with regard to specific religious traditions, some useful starting points are: on Islam, Anne-Sofie Roald, *Women in Islam* (2001); and Leila Ahmed, *Women and Gender in Islam* (1992). On Hinduism, Julia Leslie, *Roles and Rituals for Hindu Women* (1991). On Buddhism, Rita Gross, *Buddhism after Patriarchy* (1993). And on New/Alternative Religions, Elizabeth Puttick, *Women and New Religions* (1997); and Susan Palmer, *Moon Sisters, Krishna Mothers, Rajneesh Lovers: Women's Roles in New Religions* (1994).

Chapter 5

Belief

For many Christians, a defining element of their religiosity is the statement called the creed (or *credo*), which begins 'I believe in one God, the father almighty'. The creed is based on a form of words agreed by 218 (male) bishops at the seminal Council of Nicea in 325 CE. From this there is a widespread expectation that to be a Christian *is* to believe: not only in a general sense (of believing in anything), but specifically believing in *something* (in the Christian trinity god). Along with accepting the centrality of a particular book (that is, the Bible), it is this concept of belief which is seen to define Christianity. Christians may believe in many different interpretations of the trinity, and may be organised into many different institutions and groups, but they are all supposed to believe in a god who combines the status of father, son, and spirit.

The study of Christianity traditions, therefore, requires us to take this concept of belief seriously. Very often that may entail an examination of the historical and cultural differences between (Christian) believers, as well as the historical

formulations of particular belief statements. At its most simple, this may entail an examination of how Martin Luther's statements on his beliefs differ from other significant Christian figures, such as Calvin, Wesley, Aquinas, St Paul, Martin Luther King, Hans Küng, and many others. This may be taken further, by looking at how each of these individuals came to develop and to present their beliefs within their particular social and cultural contexts. It may also look at the range of ways in which these beliefs were practised as a part of a much larger dynamic of social and cultural life. In this respect, Max Weber's subtle analysis of the development of modern capitalism from Calvinistic beliefs in pre-destination is a good example.

The centrality of belief within Christian traditions is not, however, universal. That is, the ways in which Christians have understood the practice of believing has varied considerably. After all, one of the chief arguments of the Protestant Reformation in the fifteenth century was to establish the prominence of individual faith (or belief) over what Protestants saw as the suffocating and corrupt hegemony of the Catholic Church. There is an immense difference between contemporary twenty-first century ideas of belief as a matter of internal resolution of certain concepts about reality, and medieval European Christian assumptions that belief comes through recitation of certain words. Neither is intrinsically a 'better' or 'truer' form of belief, they are instead two very different Christian perspectives on what religious belief is meant to be.

So far my discussion of religion and belief has focused exclusively on belief as an aspect of Christian traditions. We are, however, used to applying the concept of belief to other religions than Christianity, and indeed to make it central to our assumptions on the general 'nature' of religion. After all, do not Muslims also believe in Allah, Hindus in Vishnu, Shiva and other deities, Jews in Yahweh, and so on? And is it not obvious that *all* religious traditions must have some form of belief – for if there were no beliefs then there would be no religion? This idea is summed up particularly succinctly by the nineteenth-century anthropologist Edward Tylor, who gave a famous definition of religion as 'the belief in spiritual beings' (Tylor 1871: 8).

Problems with 'belief'

The focus on belief in the study of religion, and as the means of trying to 'explain' or 'interpret' religion, is by no means as straightforward as Tylor's comments seem to suggest. As Malcolm Ruel (1982) argues in his article on 'Christians as believers', there are considerable problems in applying the term 'belief' to Muslim, Jewish, and Buddhist traditions. Part of this problem lies in translation: there are no words in Arabic, Hebrew, or Pali (or Sinhala) that can be effectively translated into the English word 'belief' – a point made very effectively in other contexts by Rodney Needham (1972). But this is not merely a problem of finding the right (or wrong) word to translate, it reflects an even deeper problem. First, in assuming that religion is concerned with belief we are taking a primarily Christian concept and making it the basis for a universal concept of what religion is meant to be about. And second, the practice of religiosity in non-Christian contexts may emphasise other aspects of behaviour than belief, such as ritual.

As Talal Asad argues, it was only in the relatively recent era of western, mainly Protestant Christian thinkers that 'religion' was regarded as having an element of 'belief' by necessity, 'as part of a wider change in the modern language of power and knowledge' (Asad 1993: 43). It became necessary to have a religious theory which discussed 'belief' to uncover 'a correct reading of the mute ritual hieroglyphics of others, for reducing their practices to texts' (1993: 43). Asad suggests that thinkers on religion needed to find in other traditions 'something that exists beyond the observed practices, the heard utterances, the written words', and hence it was necessary to assume religious beliefs, a basis for religion which was 'essentially cognitive' (1993: 44).

Christianity in western Europe and north America has been largely dominated by Protestant traditions, where there is a strong emphasis on *faith*. This goes back particularly to the division of western European Christianity resulting from the Reformation. On the one hand were Catholics who argued for the traditional view: that a person's religion was primarily about what s/he did (through 'works'). On the other were Protestants who criticised what they saw as the simplicity and superstition of this view and argued instead (in various ways) that 'true religion' was first and foremost a matter of what one thought and believed in. This was a fundamental division which was expressed in many ways – not only through the creation of many new religious organisations (churches), and wars between societies and groups who fought to establish their religious (and political) positions. In European countries that developed influential intellectual and academic traditions (particularly Britain, Germany, and the USA), it was Protestant assumptions and culture that generally predominated. And it was very often deeply religious Protestant thinkers who had the strongest influences on the development of these traditions.

Belief and reductionism

I do not mean to suggest here that the study of religion is dominated by Christian theologians, but rather that a number of assumptions in the study of religion have in the past come specifically out of Christian traditions. One particular critique of this has been what is broadly labelled reductionism, which argues that the object of beliefs (deities, or superhuman entities) are nothing more than human constructions that can be 'reduced' to human basics. That is, the assumptions of Christians, and by extension people of other religions, are held to be groundless, since they have no reality in themselves. This approach is also called a naturalist argument – that is, our understanding of deities (or super-human beings) can only be understood in terms of the natural world in which we live. This naturalistic approach is the basis of science, which has given us phenomenal power in understanding (and putting to our use) the natural world, and so there are very good reasons to apply such a theory and methodology to understanding religion and religious beliefs.

This reductionist approach to religious belief can be found in writers such as Marx and Freud, discussed in earlier chapters. Both were strongly influenced by the German philosopher Ludwig Feuerbach, who argued that 'the divine being is nothing else than the human being, or, rather, the human nature purified

... All the attributes of the divine nature are, therefore, attributes of the human nature' (Feuerbach 1974 [1841]: 14). Thus humankind 'unconsciously and involuntarily creates God in his [*sic*.] own image' (Feuerbach 1974 [1841]: 118). Indeed this point was itself noted amongst ancient Greeks, when the writer Xenophanes commented that

> Ethiopians make their gods black with turned up noses, Thracians make them with red hair and blue eyes ... [If animals] had hands and could draw ..., horses would draw the shapes of the gods like horses, oxen like oxen.
>
> (quoted in Hick 1989: 7)

According to this line of interpretation, what is taken as 'divine reality' is in fact a human reality. God is, then, merely what humans want him/her/it to be, a projection of one or more aspects of human nature, and humans make up images of gods for human purposes.

I began this book with saying that the study of religion is about the study of humans. In this respect, there is a measure of overlap between my approach and such reductionism. However, I do not agree with the view that the study of religion is a matter of 'explaining' beliefs in this way. To study religion in a cultural as well as a naturalistic perspective is to look at the broader context of how people come to talk and think (and believe) in the ways in which they do. In order to do this, one not only looks at the content of beliefs (for example, that Christians believe in god), but at the specific contexts of such statements. That is, the study of Christian traditions does not begin or end with a theoretical analysis of whether belief in god is a human projection or a manifestation of a divine reality. Or rather, I would prefer to leave such questions to theologians.

Hick and Eliade: non-reductionist views on religion

Two recent writers in the study of religion have presented arguments which return us to the question of a non-reducible reality

– these are John Hick and Mircea Eliade. In quite different ways, they have attempted to argue that religion is universally based on a belief in and experience of something that exists beyond humanity. For Hick this is called the Real, and for Eliade this is the sacred. Both have sought to find some basis for understanding and contrasting the diversity of religious experiences across the world, and in particular to demonstrate that there is a common 'essence' or basis of all religions.

For John Hick (1989) this is discussed in terms of the problem of pluralism. He assumes that all religions are concerned with a divine entity (in some form or other), and asks if this entity is real, then is it singular or plural? That is, as Christians believe in God, Muslims in Allah, and so on, are *all* these deities equally real? Or indeed, do all deities represent a single reality that lies behind human interpretations of this reality? Hick's answer is the latter: religion is primarily about experience of, and belief in a transcendent reality which he calls 'the Real' (or the Real *an sich* – in itself), that is known in particular cultural contexts as specific manifestations (the Real as thought-and-experienced). In some cases, the Real is known theistically as *personae* (as a deity, or deities). But in others the Real is thought-and-experienced non-theistically or as metaphysical *impersonae* (that is, as a more abstract force, such as the Hindu concept of Brahman).

This distinction between the Real *an sich* as an Ultimate reality, and the plurality of humanly experienced *personae* and *impersonae* is, therefore, Hick's way of resolving the philosophical problem of differences of religious beliefs (1989: 233–51). In this sense, all religious beliefs are expressions of the Real (perhaps some more than others), since they are all 'drawing from the same well'. The main criterion that Hick uses to make distinctions between the various *personae* and *impersonae* is soteriology (1989: 309), that is, the extent to which particular religions are based on 'the transformation of human existence which is called salvation or liberation'. And because of the preponderance of this idea of salvation he argues that 'the major world religions' are 'at least to some extent in alignment with' the Real (1989: 300).

In some ways his argument is circular: he assumes the Real exists because so many traditions talk about it, and by extension so many people experience the Real through *personae* and *impersonae*. Such experiences in themselves give substance to the reality of the Real, not as conclusive evidence but through their persistence and widespread occurrence. In many ways, this appears to leave the idea of the Real as a matter of faith – it exists because it is believed in and experienced. On to put this another way, either one accepts his argument for the Real, or one doesn't.

Much the same can also be said about the *phenomenological* (history of religions) approach to the study of religion, associated particularly with the Romanian scholar Mircea Eliade (1963). Working in Chicago in the mid- to late twentieth century, Eliade's 'history of religions' has had a profound impact on certain branches of European and north American scholarship. Eliade's basic assumption was, like Hick, that there is a 'really-real' entity towards which humans are inclined. For Eliade this was 'the sacred', which exists in and of itself, and which is experienced by humans through particular (and partial) manifestations. All religions (and so all cultures), according to Eliade, attempt to get back to the uniqueness of this sacred. But the sacred exists beyond time and place, whilst also being manifest in time and place.

The project of religious studies, from this Eliadean perspective, is to compare and contrast the various ways in which the sacred is manifest in particular times, places, and cultures. In pursuit of understanding the sacred in other, mainly non-western cultures, Eliade explored and discussed different religious traditions and experiences which he glossed as 'shamanism', 'yoga', and 'cosmogonic' myths ('myths of return' to a sacred origin). In using ethnographies and other descriptions of what he called 'archaic' cultures, it is clear in retrospect that Eliade chose to write of details that suited his theories and leave out what did not. Sam Gill (1998) in particular shows – through his contemporary research among Arrernte Native Australians – that Eliade's understanding of the 'sacred' in this particular people's religious and cultural practices is based as much on wishful thinking as on serious analysis.

In many respects Eliade's argument about the sacred is open to similar criticisms of Hick's concept of 'the Real'. Either one buys into such a largely theological argument, or one doesn't (see, for example, Idinopolous and Yonan 1994). As with Hick, the divine/sacred basis of religion is entrenched as a given by this theory – not only as an object of study but as an element of human nature and the natural world. As such, it appears to be an extension of Christian theological reflection into the supposedly non-theological discipline of religious studies (cf. Fitzgerald 1999).

A further problem with Eliade's methodology for studying religion is his rejection of reductionism in favour of what has been called a *sui generis* approach to religion. That is, for Eliade religious phenomena must be understood on their 'own level ... as something religious' (Eliade 1963: xiii). Thus he makes a distinction between his phenomenological, and non-reductionist approach, and other disciplinary approaches, such as 'psychology, sociology, economics, linguistics or any other study', which he considers 'false' since they analyse religion exclusively as human rather than sacred activity. That is, Eliade argues they 'miss the one unique and irreducible element of [religion] – the sacred', which exists 'on its own level', as unique. This uniqueness is what is referred to as the '*sui generis*' approach, that religion is a distinct element of human activity, that can be explained in solely human terms.

The *sui generis* argument for the uniqueness of religion has been subject to intense criticism in recent years, in particular by Donald Wiebe (1981, 1999) and Russell McCutcheon (1997). They both contest the assumption that sacred-ness is a universal element of all religion, and they also refute the idea that the purpose of studying religion is to describe and analyse this 'thing' (such as the Real, or the sacred) as something distinct from any other aspect of human and cultural life. For both Wiebe and McCutcheon, the existence of a distinct religious category of the sacred is a theological assumption, based on a particular form of faith, which can be neither proved nor disproved. Instead they argue that the study of religion is primarily about doing what Eliade refutes: studying religion as a human activity.

By placing Hick and Eliade side-by-side here in this way, it is not too unreasonable to conclude that both are reading into their respective religious traditions concepts of 'belief in the transcendent' (Hick 1989: 5–6) that they wish to find. Hick in particular is presenting an argument for the reality of the Real which fits in well with his own Protestant Christian perspective. It is not, of course, exclusively Christian, as he uses a broad range of examples from Hindu, Buddhist, and other non-Christian texts. In many ways, the idea of an ultimate inclusive reality that transcends particular beliefs in particular gods is one that derives strongly from certain strands of Hindu religious philosophy, as shown by Hick's own use of the ancient Vedic saying that truth (or 'the Real') 'is one – sages name it variously' (1989: 252).

However, the premises of Hick's discussion depend on two main assumptions that: (a) comparisons and contrasts between religious traditions are largely about how those traditions articulate (through texts) their beliefs about the transcendent; and (b) the 'interpretation of religion', as a universal aspect of human life, can be pursued most effectively by trying to articulate a single, ultimate basis for belief, through the concept of the Real. Both of these assumptions are in many ways merely an extension of Protestant Christian theological thinking to the study of other non-Christian religions.

Belief and the absence of 'religion'

Another important foundation for the contemporary concept of religion as belief emerged from the encounters between the west and non-western cultures during the colonial era. In particular, European colonialism brought Protestant Christians into close contact with cultures and religious traditions very different from their own forms. Such encounters raised one particular problem for scholars: in what ways could they try to comprehend and make sense of these different traditions and peoples? The first obvious question was whether or not these were 'religions' in the same way that their own 'true religion' of Christianity was. In one particular case, this led to the emergence of the idea that the people of India generally shared a 'religion' akin to Christianity, and this religion went under the name of 'Hinduism'.

However, there were other groups who did not seem to fit into this scheme quite so well. There are numerous examples of Europeans in the sixteenth to nineteenth centuries assuming that the non-Europeans they came across had 'no religion' (see Chidester 2000: 428–30), For example, the native people of Australia ('Aborigines' or 'Blackfellows' – now often called Native Australians, or First Nation Australians) had no 'obvious' religiosity, seeming so radically 'primitive' to European colonialists that it was inconceivable that they could possibly have developed anything as sophisticated as, what western Europeans considered, religion (see Swain and Trompf 1995). Likewise, a European traveller in southern Africa in 1811 proposed that the Xhosa people's 'superstition, their belief in magic or enchantment, and in omens and prognostics, is in proportion to their want of religious feelings' (quoted in Chidester 2000: 428).

As this quote shows, an important criterion used by Europeans to determine the presence (or absence) of 'religion' was the concept of belief. As the Europeans' own Protestant traditions led them to expect religion to be a matter of faith, or belief, they rather unsurprisingly applied that to the people and cultures they encountered. And in those cases where the 'faith' or 'belief' appeared strange and unexpected, this was designated as 'more simple' or 'primitive', and was labelled as mere superstition and magic.

So the means of understanding a religion, of understanding the differences between religions, and of determining if a group actually had a religion or not was largely a matter of looking at what sort of beliefs that *other* group had. Hindus were a very diverse group of people, but at one level – particularly within their religious texts – they were seen as having clearly elaborated ideas of what their gods were, and so had a fairly systematised set of religious 'beliefs'. In contrast, however, the many different Native Australian and African groups were seen in a different light. They had cultures, but Europeans perceived these cultures as so primitive and backward that it was assumed they were 'survivals' from a distant evolutionary age. And the absence of any clear beliefs or doctrines on god suggested to the Europeans that such people were so 'primitive' that they had not even 'evolved' to the stage of religion. The natural and civilised thing to do, of course, was to help such 'savages' pull themselves up the evolutionary ladder by converting them to a 'true faith' in Christian traditions.

This concept of belief was, therefore, inevitably going to be used as one of the ways that scholars in western contexts tried to make sense of (and classify) 'other' religious traditions. However, the term can be used in a variety of ways, to mean quite different ways of thinking. Thus, for example, writing on Sri Lankan Theravadan Buddhist practice Richard Gombrich (1971) describes a distinction he found between two quite different types of 'belief'. This was between *cognitive* beliefs (which are what people 'say about their beliefs and practices'), and *affective* beliefs (which are what people actually do). It is the former of these, the cognitive, that scholars of religion have tended to emphasise, since they are what people *should* be believing. We should not, though, be too surprised to find a mismatch between the cognitive and affective, nor indeed to find that the affective can be equally as important as the cognitive. In illustration of this, he uses the common example of Catholic Christians 'believing' in ghosts, despite the lack of textual support for such ideas within Catholic traditions.

Malcolm Ruel, however, makes a different type of distinction: between a 'weak' and a 'strong' meaning for the term belief (Ruel 1982 [2002: 110]). A weak meaning refers to a presupposition or expectation for oneself (for example, 'I believe that I can do it'), or an assumption on the part of others ('she believes the train will come on time'). The strong sense refers to a more definite assertion, such as 'I believe in God', which emerges in particular ways in different cultural contexts. The problem arises, however, when the strong meaning is taken from the specifically Christian context and imposed incongruously on to others as a definition or categorisation – for example, 'Muslims believe in Allah'.

What is happening here is, in fact, that this idea of belief is being used not merely as a definition, but as an explanation. That is, religious belief becomes an explanation in itself: our absence of understanding of what a person from another religion is doing or thinking leads us to fall back on our basic knowledge of their beliefs. Thus we assume that a Hindu is acting in a certain way because s/he 'believes' in reincarnation, and a Muslim in another way because s/he believes in Allah. Such an explanation may or may not be correct – but what it does is rule out a number of other possible explanations. Thus, we may think a Hindu has avoided stamping on a spider because she believes in reincarnation, when her action could more easily be explained by the fact she has a sore foot.

In using the concept of belief to describe and categorise others' behaviour we are also making a basic assumption that such belief is 'fundamentally an interior state, a psychological condition' (Ruel 1982 [2002: 111]). The internal wrangle that I mentioned as being at the heart of contemporary Protestant Christian notions of belief ('do I believe?', 'do I believe strongly enough?', etc.) is not necessarily experienced in the same way by people in non-Christian religious cultures. In fact, what a Muslim may feel and think about Allah may be better described as 'knowledge' rather than 'belief' (Needham 1972). Or otherwise, there may not actually be a core of 'beliefs' to easily identify and define as the substance of the particular religion.

Thus, for example, the anthropologist Deborah Tooker spent some time in a highland area of Northern Thailand with some Akha-speaking people (Tooker 1992). She found that amongst this group there was a strong gap between 'being religious' and 'believing'. They were influenced by a number of religious cultural traditions which had come into the area, including European Christianity, and Chinese traditional religions, and certain people in the area had 'converted' to these traditions. For the main part, however, these people followed traditional religious practices which had been labelled in the early twentieth century as 'animism', that is focusing on beliefs in spirits. However, for Tooker this categorisation of Akhan religion and culture in such terms was erroneous. Their religion and their culture seemed to have very little to do with any such form of belief.

Instead, their religion was manifest and lived out through their ethno-religious identity and tradition, which distinguished being Akhan from being anything else (such as Christian). The idiom they used for describing this Akhan identity and culture was the term *zan*. This *zan*, according to Tooker, was maintained through the action of carrying: that is 'carrying tradition' in a manner similar to the carrying of rice in a basket on their backs. When asked by Tooker about their 'beliefs', individual Akha people gave a confusing and inconsistent variety of statements, but there was a strong element of conformity when it came to deciding what was right practice, or *zan*. Thus Tooker comments, 'as far as I know, no family has been excluded or exiled from an Akha village because of heretical statements, that is because of their 'beliefs'. However, there were exclusions because people did not do *zan*' (Tooker 1992: 815).

This is a similar point to one made by Ruel: the concept of belief as it is usually understood, particularly in its 'strong' sense, is not helpful to understand the religious practices of some cultural and religious groups. In particular, she rejects the theoretical assumption that 'religion' is always based on a body of beliefs, and that these beliefs are statements about the 'order of things' which are internalised by people on the basis of being either true or false. This may be the case in certain religious and cultural traditions (such as contemporary Protestant Christianity in Europe and North America), but may not work in other contexts.

Tooker argues that the term belief 'is a particular and histori-cally specific western cultural idiom for expressing the relationship to tradition, an idiom that emphasizes the interi-ority of ethno-religious identity' (Tooker 1992: 816). In the case of Akha society, the idiom may differ so that 'ethno-religious identity takes an exteriorised form', as *zan*, which is carried (1992: 816). However, she does stress that in arguing this, she is not suggesting a simple distinction between western and non-western religions and cultures, in which non-western cultures have exteriorised forms of religion, while religion is interiorised (as belief) in western cultures. Instead she argues that cultural and religious practice will vary: that 'the psychologistic idiom of interiorisation is strong in the West, and that people in other parts of the world may or may not emphasise that kind of idiom' (1992: 815).

Belief, doctrine, and common-sense

To be religious, therefore, is not always a matter of belief, even though we tend to expect that the two depend on each other. Mary Keller puts this very well, when she says: 'If I say that I am not religious but that my sister is, one is likely to get the sense that my sister has a bubble in her brain where she cultivates her belief ... Religiousness is construed as a mental activity' (Keller 2002: 6). Thus, people such as the Akha, appear to manage without the 'bubble', or at least carry the bubble in a basket on their backs rather than inside their heads.

The problem goes further than this, however, since we also tend to assume that there are other bubbles, or ways of thinking, that exist alongside (and often in contrast to) believing. In particular, we assume there is a difference between (religious) belief and (non-religious) common-sense. This is put most forcefully by the anthropologist Edmund Leach in his essay on how and why certain people 'believe in' the concept of 'virgin birth' (Leach 1969). Of course, the term refers in particular to a Christian idea of how Jesus came to be conceived and born – without any sexual contact between his mother and father. This idea in fact forms part of the Creed, mentioned above, as one of the bases of Christian thinking (and belief).

The idea of virgin birth is not, however, exclusive to Christian contexts. It has (like the term belief) also been applied by western scholars to other cultures. The most notorious examples of this were in Australasia, in particular amongst certain Native Australian groups, and amongst a group of people on the island of Kiriwina, which lies in the Melanesian Trobriand Islands, just off Papua New Guinea (studied by the influential anthropologist Bronislaw Malinowski 1932: 140–78). In these cases, late-nineteenth-century travellers and anthropologists had found an apparent lack of knowledge (or ignorance) of the seemingly obvious fact that human reproduction, and particularly conception, requires heterosexual intercourse. Malinowski himself concluded, however, that the Kiriwinan people simply did not 'know' these facts, and that instead they believed that humans are incarnations of spirits that enter women when they bathe in the sea. Interestingly, however, the phrase 'virgin birth' was not particularly relevant to the particularities of Kiriwinan ideas of conception, since they made a strong assertion to Malinowski that conception could not occur in this way if a woman was a virgin.

Leach himself did not conduct any first-hand research in Australian or Melanesia, and so based his argument against this conclusion on Malinowski's (and others') work. For Leach, it appeared outrageous and blatantly racist to assume that such people were ignorant of such universally obvious 'facts of life'. According to Leach, Malinowski was failing to recognise a basic distinction between types of thinking, or types of knowledge. That is, between 'common-sense' or practical knowledge which he argued was quite different from (and superior to) sacred or religious knowledge, or 'dogma' (Leach 1969: 93, 107–108).

Thus, Leach argued, Kiriwinans *knew* – as all other humans know through common-sense – that a woman cannot conceive without having sex with a man. But their religious and social dogmas (or beliefs) told them something different: that every person comes into being at birth as a fully fledged member of their kinship group (*dala*), which is passed on to them through the mother's line. So long as the two forms of knowledge were kept separate, then the Kiriwinans would be happy. But if an outsider, such as an inquisitive anthropologist from Europe, tried to juxtapose the two discourses then there was inevitable trouble: dogmas would be asserted over common-sense.

In a similar way, Clifford Geertz (1973: 111–12, 119–22) also presented a rather more sophisticated distinction between what he called 'the religious perspective' from both 'common-sensical' and 'scientific' perspectives, as well as from the 'aesthetic' perspective. Thus for Geertz, the key elements of the religious perspective, which make it different from common-sense, are that

> [the religious perspective] moves beyond the realities of
> everyday life to wider ones which correct and compete with
> them, and its defining concern is not action upon those wider
> realities but acceptance of them, faith in them ... It is this
> sense of the 'really real' upon which the religious perspective
> rests.
>
> (Geertz 1973: 112)

This distinction between common-sense versus religious
knowledge (or dogma) may appear very reasonable at first view.
But is it correct to assume common-sense is any more universal
than the idea of belief, and are the two always *separate*? In some
cultural and religious contexts the two may well be seen as
connected and indeed the same, particularly at the level of experience. That is, the religious perspective is not necessarily distinct
from what is taken as common-sense. As Talal Asad points out
(1993: 52), this distinction assumes that there is a *universal*
common-sense view, of the world as it actually is, whilst the religious view is more specifically *culture*-bound and so varies. What
is more, there is a paradox in that for Geertz (if not for Leach)
the religious viewpoint can also affect the common-sense view,
which itself becomes culture-bound. In this sense, neither is
wholly straightforward or given, since both play between the
ideas of the 'real' and the 'really real'.

To return to the specific example of 'virgin birth': the anthropologist Robert Tonkinson (1978) found himself confused when
he tried to apply Leach's distinction between dogma and
common-sense in the context of his fieldwork among a Native
Australian group called the Jigalong mob in the Western Desert.
In fact, he found the distinction unnecessarily simplified a
complex picture. Whatever may have been the case among the
Jigalong in the millennia before contact with Europeans, in the
contemporary situation there was intense interplay between
European ways of thinking and specifically Jigalong discourses
on human conception. That is, it was fairly common knowledge,
particularly among Jigalong youth, that white European
Australians believed in a link between sex and pregnancy – this

was what the whites would tell the 'ignorant Aborigines' at every possible occasion.

Jigalong ideas in this post-contact era were, however, not so clear-cut. Tonkinson found that the elder men of the group were adamant that talk of semen and menstrual blood was 'dirty talk'. It was offensive to mention such things in relation to human conception – something that came about through the incarnation of dreaming 'spirit' beings within humans. This amounted to a definite rejection of western knowledge (based on physiological accounts of conception) in favour of their own Jigalong way of knowing. Such a conflict of religious and cultural perspectives came about largely because of the unequal power relations between white European and Native Australians.

But it could also have been accounted for in terms of an incommensurability (that is a lack of fit) between two quite different ways of knowing the world. Unlike Leach's distinction between common-sense (real knowledge) and sacred dogma (religious belief), what Tonkinson saw in the Jigalong scenario was an alternative religious knowledge. Such knowledge was based on and coming out of personal experiences, and was equally as common-sensical to those who knew (rather than believed in) it as those put forward by white Europeans.

Belief and practice

The emphasis on belief in this discussion, and in particular on interiorisation of belief (that is, asking the question 'do the Kiriwinans/Jigalong 'really' know or believe?'), is therefore rather unhelpful. Leach's explanation of 'dogmatic' religious assertion over common-sense knowledge somewhat obscures an important point: for those involved belief is not an issue. Instead, if we wish to use the term 'religion' here at all, then the 'religious' aspect of this discussion does not rely on a simple idea of Kiriwinans and Jigalong having beliefs about 'spirit children' creating life. Rather it should be focused on the *practising* of such religious concepts within and through *bodies* – in this case women's bodies in particular, as they conceive human foetuses and then bring them to birth.

Religious ideas and assumptions, in forms similar to what might be called knowledge or common-sense, shape these experiences of conception and pregnancy, and are done through the bodies of Kiriwinan women in ways which cannot be said to separate out the 'religious beliefs' from the bodily experiences. At the same time, the Kiriwinans' (men's and women's) concepts of bodies are different from 'our' concepts (what Leach took to be universal common-sense conceptions), and can only be understood through religious formulations. In sum, what we may choose to call 'religion' here *is* the body, or otherwise, how people use and perceive their own (and others') bodies. In this sense, then, religious belief is more than simply a 'bubble in the brain', it is something that permeates the whole of a person's body.

This point returns us to a number of the issues raised in previous chapters. In particular, the concept of subjectivity discussed by writers such as Irigaray (Chapter 4) describes such embodied experience. The process of 'becoming divine' for Irigaray is likewise not an abstract cerebral experience, but is located within women's specific cultural and embodied subjectivities. We can also return to Louis Althusser's perspective (Chapter 3), that ideology (including religious ideology) has a 'material existence' that is like and unlike the materiality of 'a paving-stone or a rifle' (Althusser 1971 [1994: 156]). He goes on to argue that for a person (a 'subject') 'the existence of his [or her] belief is material in that his ideas are his material actions inserted into material practices governed by material rituals which are themselves defined by the material ideological apparatus from which derive the ideas of that subject' (1971 [1994: 157]). There are differences between each of these different forms of materiality, thus

the materialities of ... going to Mass, of kneeling down, of the gesture of the sign of the cross, or of the *mea culpa*, of a sentence, of a prayer, or an act of contrition, of a gaze, of a handshake, of an external verbal discourse or an 'internal' verbal discourse (consciousness), are not one and the same materiality.

(Althusser 1971 [1994: 157])

In sum, there is a complex interaction between 'believing' and doing: the two aspects of behaviour cannot be separated.

Catherine Bell, Pierre Bourdieu, and habitus

Catherine Bell criticises what appears to be the simple theoretical assumption of a distinction between what is said and what is done – between thought and practice, or as it is otherwise put, between belief and ritual. Not only does this make what she considers an unhelpful distinction, it also tends to emphasise thought over practice, with the former prior to the latter (Bell 1992: 30–54). She points out the common assumption that ritual is the acting out (or performance) of world-views or beliefs. The problem with this approach, according to Bell, is that it encourages us to view 'ritual' as a thing in itself which does something (such as mediating or integrating oppositions), and so 'primarily serves to solve the problems posed for scholars by their reliance on a distinction between thought and action' (1992: 48).

This distinction is not neutral, since within it there is a fundamental privileging of thought over action: 'it differentiates a "thinking" subject from an "acting" object – or, when pushed to its logical conclusion, a "thinking" subject from a "nonthinking" object' (Bell 1992: 47). Such an approach is readily observed by the strong tendency within traditional studies of religion to look to religious texts and beliefs/doctrines as the basis of 'religions' (as I will discuss in Chapter 7). But as Bell shows, this is only partially overcome by an alternative focus on ritual as a mediator or expresser of thought through action.

According to Bell, a way of resolving this issue is to use the work of the French sociologist Pierre Bourdieu (1977, 1992), whose approach is labelled as 'practice theory'. Bourdieu's writing on this subject is notoriously difficult to read, but the basis of this practice theory is his concept of *habitus*, which broadly refers to the cultural context in which people live and practise their lives. Thus, for Bell habitus refers to 'the set of habitual dispositions through which people "give shape and form to social conventions" ... and the matrix in which objective structures are realized within the (subjective) dispositions that produce practices' (Bell 1992: 79). In Bourdieu's own words, habitus is described as 'systems of durable, transposable dispositions, structured structures predisposed to function as structuring structures, that is, as principles which generate and organize practices and representations' (Bourdieu 1992: 53).

As these quotes indicate, habitus is not an easy idea to convey. But it is one worth thinking about, particularly for belief within the context of the study of religion. For Bell, the concept of habitus helps to break down the unhelpful distinction between thought and action. Rather than being distinct, we should see action as a form of embodied or practised thought. Similarly, a thought can only be understood in terms of the action or practices in which it is embodied. The habitus describes and outlines the context in which such thought–action practice occurs, it is the actual cultural place (and places) in which people do their cultural and religious lives.

Much of this discussion is connected to the issues of agency that I mentioned in the previous chapter: when I act I do not do so solely as a distinct individual. My actions (and thoughts) come from being within a particular culture, having particular cultural and religious influences on my general 'dispositions'. These influences help to shape what I do, although as a subjective individual I act through my own agency and volition (I am not preprogrammed or brainwashed). It is the interaction between all these actions and influences, the 'field' or space in which all this occurs, that is called the habitus.

So to return specifically to the idea of religious belief: if a religious tradition does place emphasis on the interiorisation of assumptions or beliefs (as occurs within many Christian traditions), these beliefs need to be understood within the broader context of the particular habitus in which they are found. At its most simple, perhaps, this indicates that we do not really learn very much by being told 'Christians believe in the trinitarian god'. Such a statement makes much more sense when related to a particular context (for example, a group of Catholics in New Jersey), and the ways in which such a (belief) statement is worked out in that context.

So, for example, in some cases the belief statement may be understood with reference to (among other things) the sanctity of all forms of human life, including unborn children. So a New Jersey Catholic may inhabit a habitus where the practice of the belief is founded on a principled rejection of abortion. Within a different habitus, however, in the same town or street, the belief may be practised in a quite different way. That is, not in terms of the rights of the unborn child, but rather the sanctity of human (and particularly women's) rights to avoid the oppression of a social system based on profound gender inequalities. Within either habitus, the agency of the particular people involved is shaped by their beliefs, and their interaction with others who have their own beliefs and practices. And the actions they take come out of these complex networks and webs of social and cultural forces.

Summary

- Belief is often assumed to be a central and defining element of the study of religions. However the concept carries a lot of theoretical and ideological baggage since it applies a predominantly Protestant Christian concept in often inappropriate ways to non-Christian contexts.
- Many studies of religion may be classed as either reductionist or phenomenological, and both remain focused on the idea of religion as belief. Reductionists tend to assume religion as 'false', whilst phenomenologists seek to treat it as a thing in itself, as '*sui generis*'.
- 'Belief' is such an ambiguous term that it is hard to know if it can be applied to the religious practices of other people – an alternative term such as 'knowledge' might be equally appropriate.

- In order to study beliefs we must locate them within a much wider context, within a particular habitus, or cultural context, and across different contexts, rather than looking at belief statements as abstract words or propositions.
- The beliefs that Christians (and others) may hold cannot simply be reduced to mere 'bubbles in the brain', they are practised and done as much as they are thought out.

Suggestions for further reading

The essay by Malcolm Ruel on 'Christians as believers' (1982; reprinted in *A Reader in the Anthropology of Religion*, 2002) is a good starting point for looking at how contemporary anthropologists are talking about the issue of belief. There is also some useful discussion of the history and meaning of the term belief in W.C. Smith's classic work *The Meaning and End of Religion* (1978). Talal Asad's article 'The Construction of Religion as an Anthropological Category' (in *Genealogies of Religion*, 1993; also in the *Reader in the Anthropology of Religion*, 2002) is more challenging, but is certainly worth the effort.

For Hick, see his book *An Interpretation of Religion: Human Responses to the Transcendent* (1989), which systematically presents his argument on the Real. His subtitle is something of a give-away with respect to his theological expectations. Mircea Eliade's writings are difficult to summarise, but *Patterns in Comparative Religion* (1963) is a good starting point. For an excellent critique of Eliade, see Russell McCutcheon's *Manufacturing Religion* (1997); and Donald Wiebe's *The Politics of Religious Studies* (1999). Timothy Fitzgerald's similarly named *The Ideology of Religious Studies* (1999) gives a good critique of some of the theological assumptions lying behind this attempt to apply the concept of 'belief' as a central category of the study of religion. David Chidester's paper 'Colonialism' (*Guide to the Study of Religion*, Cassell 2000) gives a very good summary of the ways in which ideas of religion have been applied to non-Europeans through the history of colonial contact.

There are as yet no easy ways into Catherine Bell's use of practice theory – see *Ritual Theory, Ritual Practice* (1992); and also *Ritual: Perspectives and Dimensions* (1997). Mary Keller's *The Hammer and the Flute* (2002) has some useful discussion of her work. You might also like to look at my own essay 'Religion, post-religionism, and religioning: religious studies and contemporary cultural debates' (Nye 2000). On Bourdieu, see Richard Jenkins, *Pierre Bourdieu* (1991); and Jeremy Lane, *Pierre Bourdieu: A Critical Introduction* (2000).

Chapter 6

Ritual

The previous chapter ended on the point that it is unhelpful to make a distinction between religious belief and religious practice. Being religious is not simply a matter of holding certain ideas in the head – it also involves doing things. Most obviously, religion is done through rituals, or ritual actions (although not all rituals are necessarily religious), and I will examine below the many ways we can try to understand and interpret ritual. But the practice of religion is not only to be found in rituals, rituals are just one particular type of bodily place in which religiosity is practised. More generally religion is practised in the lives people lead, their daily activities, and in how they interact with other material things, such as texts, objects, and places.

Ritual and ritualising

As we have found with many of the other basic terms in the study of religion, the term 'ritual' is not as straightforward as it may seem. For a start,

there is the tricky boundary between religion and ritual – something may be a ritual, but might not necessarily be religious, and possibly vice versa too. Of the two terms, 'ritual' does sometimes win out over 'religion', since it covers a more immediate and less abstract concept than 'religion'. Indeed, some writers, such as the anthropologist Maurice Bloch (1985), suggest that the study of religion would be better framed as the study of ritual. This might be a useful alternative to the problems involved in the term 'religion', so long as we have a reasonable sense of what we mean by the term ritual. Where the term ritual is helpful, however, is in the emphasis it puts on the *practice* of religion, the things that people do, which the more traditional focus in the study of religion (on texts and beliefs) has tended to obscure.

However, there remain significant problems with the term 'ritual' raised in the work of Catherine Bell, who I have discussed in part in the previous chapter. In two very influential books written in the 1990s (*Ritual Theory, Ritual Practice* and *Ritual*) she argued that the term ritual is itself misleading. That is, by talking of 'ritual' we are suggesting that 'it' is a 'thing' with a nature of its own. Indeed, 'ritual' is used to describe very varied types of behaviour, helping us try to understand things (activities) that other people are doing. In many ways, this is the same problem that we have encountered (in Chapter 1) with the term 'religion'. Both religion and ritual are not 'things' in a conventional sense, instead they are terms that refer to a diverse range of ways in which people behave and act in the world. Rituals are not 'things', nor do they do things: people do rituals. To encourage scholars to think differently about rituals, to emphasise their practicality, Bell suggests we avoid the term 'ritual' if we can (although she herself has been unable to do so in the titles of both of her books!). In place of the 'r-word', she suggests the alternative of 'ritualisation', or more specifically to talk of ritual behaviour as forms of activity (or practice) that are done with a 'sense of ritualisation'.

This is not simply a matter of splitting academic hairs. Indeed it is much easier just to say 'ritual', and get on with talking about ritual and rituals in practice. And of course 'ritualisation' is a bit of a mouthful. But if we think carefully about how the word 'ritual' is used, we find that a substitution of the idea of ritualisation (or even ritualising) makes us see the process in a rather different light. When we look through Bell's lens at ritual actions, we focus less on the 'rituals' in themselves (as pre-given actions with a life of their own), and more on the way in which those doing rituals are making certain things happen. That is, actions labelled rituals are 'rituals' because they are a means of creating and using a sense of ritualisation.

This being said, however, it does not really answer the basic questions we might have about what the term ritual refers to, nor why rituals (or ritualisation) are such a fundamental element of the study of religion.

What is ritual?

Let's start with some attempts to define rituals. Ronald Grimes, in his book *Beginnings in Ritual Studies*, suggests that 'ritualizing transpires as animated persons enact formative gestures in the face of receptivity during crucial times in founded places' (Grimes 1982: 55). For Felicia Hughes-Freeland, 'ritual generally refers to human experience and perception in forms which are complicated by the imagination, making reality more complex and unnatural than more mundane instrumental spheres of human experience assume' (Hughes-Freeland 1998: 2). Catherine Bell (*Ritual Theory, Ritual Practice*) argues that 'ritualization is a matter of various culturally specific strategies for setting some activities off from others, for creating and privileging a qualitative distinction between the "sacred" and the "profane", and for ascribing such distinctions to realities thought to transcend the powers of human actors' (Bell 1992: 74). While for Victor Turner, ritual is 'formal behaviour prescribed for occasions not given over to technological routine that have reference to beliefs in mystical (or non-empirical) beings or powers' (Turner 1982: 79).

Most of these writers agree that rituals are a matter of doing something, performing actions, particular types of behaviour, and engaging in that behaviour in certain ways. However, as with definitions of religion, we are probably wise not to try to create any definitive definition – indeed writers such as Bell suggest that there cannot be any universal definition of the subject, since what ritual is depends to a large degree on the local context.

It is fairly clear that ritual behaviour is a very important element of cultural life – it is, in fact, impossible to think of a culture where there are no rituals. However, most ritual behaviour is done unreflectively, out of habit without even thinking about whether there is any meaning and purpose behind the action. Sometimes, in fact, it is the automatic-ness of such ritual action that encourages us to call it ritual, in the sense of ritual behaviour being unthinking and meaningless. So, for example, if we greet a friend in the street we do not reflect on the significance of the greeting, we merely behave as we are expected to behave – we say 'hello', wave or shake hands, and ask 'how are you?'. However, not every ritual action is performed in this unthinking way – some may be performed more solemnly. Worshippers taking communion in a Christian church are usually expected to be serious, and to reflect on the significance of the ritual they are participating in. In this case, it is perceived that the ritual action has a meaning, and those taking part should try to understand that meaning.

There is, however, no single aspect of ritual that such activity can be boiled down to. Ritual actions 'do' many things, in different ways, and of course are experienced in very different ways by those who participate in them. If I attend a particular ritual event – for example, a friend's wedding or funeral – the meaning, purpose, and experience of that event will be rather different for me than for anyone else who is present. We need to bear this in mind as we talk of rituals and ritual action: the purpose of studying and analysing rituals is to try to understand the many ways in which ritual activity is performed and experienced, and the many things that are going on as a person (or a group of people) participates in a certain type of actions.

To map out some of these diverse aspects of ritual activity, and also to see how various writers have sought to interpret ritual, we can concentrate on eight particular ways of looking at rituals. These are: (a) meaning; (b) symbolism; (c) communication; (d) performance; (e) society; (f) repetition; (g) transformation; and (h) power. The degree to which each of these elements is emphasised in any particular ritual may vary greatly, but they are all significant to a certain degree.

In sum, the types of action we call ritual can be any type of behaviour: both those that are obviously religious, and also actions which have seemingly little to do with what we expect 'religion' to be about. Ritual behaviour can range from something as simple as saying hello, or visiting a bank manager, to elaborate ritual and religious activities such as marriages, circumcisions, funerals, and even national events such as presidential inaugurations, memorials, or coronations. Ronald Grimes suggests that there are sixteen different categories of ritual action (including rites of passage, marriage rites, pilgrimage, and worship among others), whilst Catherine Bell breaks it down into four (rites of passage, calendrical rites, rites of exchange and communion, and rites of affliction). Whether we choose one or other of these schemes, the term ritual is intended to refer to a variety of activities. In most, if not all, cases any action which is described as a ritual involves some special behaviour and special ideas and symbols, which mark the action as being ritualistic.

Rituals and meaning

A basic assumption about ritual action is that it has some sense of meaning and purpose, even if that meaning is not immediately obvious. For example, the greeting of a friend is not merely functional, it expresses the relationship that exists between two people, and the type of greeting (and how it is performed) demonstrates the intensity of the relationship. For example, we may hug our mother, shake hands with a friend, kiss a lover, or merely say 'hello' to our tutor. Furthermore, the performance of the greeting demonstrates that we are acting correctly according to our cultural traditions. To fail to greet someone you know, or to greet them inappropriately, is to be 'rude'. This all gives meaning and purpose to the simple action of saying 'hello'.

The study of ritual, therefore, entails the search for these meanings, and particularly in actions which appear meaningless (either to observers, or to those performing ritual actions). Very often it is the latent meaningfulness of an action which leads us to describe it as 'ritualistic'. A basic definition could even be that rituals are actions carried out for more than their utilitarian purpose. That is, rituals are actions which have meanings beyond the actions themselves. Perhaps a simpler – indeed minimalistic – definition of ritual is 'meaningful action'. This definition is by no means watertight, and throws up more problems, since the 'utilitarian' purpose may well involve the meaning behind the ritual action itself. When most Hindus marry, the bride and groom walk together around a fire. This is not merely to keep themselves warm, or to stretch their legs after a lengthy period of sitting down, instead many Hindus interpret the action as representing the path they will be walking through life together as a new couple.

John Beattie describes this as a distinction between 'instrumental' and 'expressive' actions (Beattie 1964: 202–5). Instrumental acts are performed primarily for their practical value: to achieve some goal, to get something done. Thus a surgeon will cut open a patient's body and perform an operation to heal that patient. In contrast, expressive actions are performed for more than this obvious goal, they are done to express certain ideas, or maybe to act out in symbolic form (i.e. through abstract representations) ideas or wishes that cannot be achieved on an instrumental level. Thus ritual actions are defined as different from other forms of action because they are never solely instrumental, since the meanings attached to them make the actions expressive.

However, the distinction between the instrumental and the expressive is in practice quite ambiguous. For example, if I drive my car to work in the morning, then that could be described as a purely instrumental action: I need to travel the distance from my home to the office, otherwise I wouldn't be able to get there. However, as I drive my car I may be making some kind of expressive statement: the car may be big and flashy, showing I am wealthy enough to afford a 'good' car, or otherwise it may be more modest or run-down. In this way, many instrumental actions can have an expressive element, and many expressive actions can also be done instrumentally, and we must not forget the line between the two will be drawn differently by the people who are involved. For example, a wedding may be performed for the 'simple' sake of getting married, but also to show many other things as well: the love and commitment between the couple, the sanctity of the institution of marriage, and even the conspicuous wealth of the family who are hosting the event. Likewise, someone who attends a service of prayer for peace may take part literally (instrumentally) to bring about that peace, or otherwise to participate in the sentiments and hopes that are expressed through the ritual actions.

Rituals and symbolism

The search for meanings in rituals, and particularly Beattie's distinction between expressive and instrumental action, is founded on a *symbolist* approach to religion and ritual. That is, the importance and significance of rituals is that they 'work' through symbols. According to this view, therefore, ritual may be seen as 'symbolic action', and symbols are at the heart of rituals. Indeed the writer Victor Turner defined symbols as 'the lowest unit of ritual' (Turner 1967).

If symbols are so fundamental to the understanding of rituals, what do we mean by the term 'symbols'? Broadly speaking, symbols are things (material, and sometimes non-material items) that represent more than their material properties. They may often be visual objects, such as the Christian cross, or the Star of David, but this is not always the case. A special sound – such as a word, or a piece of music – may also be symbolic, in that it has a significance which goes beyond the sound itself. Symbols are thus items which have meanings and associations which are not intrinsic to their physical properties. There is nothing about a piece of wood shaped into a cross that intrinsically links it to notions of human redemption, resurrection, and the triumph of good over evil. The *associations* between the object and the ideas are arbitrary in the sense that they are *culturally determined*. Because of this arbitrariness, the meanings or significances behind symbols may not be immediately obvious.

For example, cow dung and *ghee* (clarified butter) have important symbolic values in certain Hindu rituals; blood trickling from an opened vein is of great symbolic importance in many Native Australian rituals; and the act of male circumcision is a symbol that is found in many cultures (although the meanings behind this symbol vary greatly). In each case the symbols are important because of their specific culturally determined meanings. A Christian may know why the eucharist or mass is important and the place within that ritual of bread and wine is symbolic of the 'body of Christ' – because they have some idea of the stories and ideas that lie behind it. Likewise a Hindu may take for granted the significance of *ghee* in sacrificial Vedic ritual. Looking at another's symbols, however, the substances may appear meaning*less* (and sometimes even repulsive), because we have no idea of their meanings.

In this approach, therefore, it is necessary to ask questions about the meanings and symbolism within actions: what are the associations between ideas or concepts and the symbols that are used to represent them? There are very few, if any, universal symbols, with meanings that are the same throughout all cultures. Several branches of psychoanalysis work on the assumption that there are such universal symbols. For example, Carl Jung's (1978) theory of the 'archetype' is based on the assumption that there are some fundamental symbols with meanings and associations shared by *all* humans. There is, however, little evidence to support this view: the presence of similar symbols in different contexts across the globe does not by any means imply that they all have the same meanings. Thus, for example, certain objects may make obvious symbols – such as the human body, or the by-products of the body such as faeces, blood, saliva, and semen. These 'natural symbols' (cf. Douglas 1973) appear again and again in the rituals and symbolic ideas of many people – in western cultures as much as in any others. But in each place they have specific culturally constructed meanings and references.

However, a thing-which-is-a-symbol does not have a single reference to be discovered, each symbol will have many *meanings*, some of which may be obvious, and others less so. For example, some symbols are considered to be specifically 'religious' – such as a Christian cross or a Jewish Star of David – since they are used primarily to represent ideas related to religious things. But the same symbol may also represent other ideas, some of which may not be specifically religious, or at least not in a narrow definition of religion as being concerned with spirits or gods.

For example, the Christian cross does not only represent the Christian message of salvation, but a host of other ideas as well. Thus a cross can also represent the authority of the church (for example, a Bishop's cross demonstrates his power as a Bishop), or the distinctiveness of Christianity *vis-à-vis* other religions (e.g. the cross as representing Christianity, in distinction to the crescent representing Islam, and the star representing Judaism). In some cases it can even be used to represent different Christian groups – such as when crosses and crucifixes are used to display the differences between Protestants and Catholics.

Each symbol, whether it is specifically religious or not, will have a host of such meanings associated with it, some of which may be more important than others, or more relevant to a particular context than others. The multiplicity of meanings that symbols can have is a vital element in the importance of symbols. When symbols are used in rituals, or in any other area of life, some meanings may be emphasised more than others, but the less obvious meanings or associations are still present, and may indeed be manipulated. This is well known to advertisers, who make careers and money out of the manipulation of symbols. A television commercial for a car uses a host of associations that a car symbolises: that is, a car is not merely a piece of metal used for transportation, it can also symbolise masculine virility (and sexuality), freedom, power, wealth and status, and many other things as well. When persuading us to buy a car, advertisers try to play upon these latent associations, manipulating them in subtle (or overt) ways.

In conclusion, no symbol can mean purely one thing. Instead it will have many different meanings, all of which are culturally determined, and can only be understood in the context of the specific cultural and local context. The analysis of the symbolic dimension of ritual action is not about discovering what a symbol or a ritual actually means, but how meanings are constructed and manipulated as people participate within certain contexts. Such a study of ritual as symbolic actions emphasises the sorts of transformations that are brought about by a ritual. But at another level, we can ask how a certain view of the world gets communicated to the participant by taking part in the ritual.

Rituals and communication

This brings us to the area of ritual and communication: rituals are often a means of communicating messages to participants. That is, through the performance of a ritual activity, those involved may come to be aware of some idea or concept or view-point. This can happen in subtle ways, for example through demonstrating the ideals of social life. Familiar rituals within western culture – such as marriages, funerals, and Thanksgiving, or Christmas – all involve a stress (in different ways) on the idea that the family group should be together. Through performing the ritual, that is, by visiting one's parents or other family for a festive dinner, the performers become aware of the importance of the ideal of 'family togetherness'. Even if the meal is a shambles, and everyone descends into bickering and arguments, the ritual process may well still communicate to those involved what the ideal should be, even if they don't live up to it.

Such messages may not necessarily be communicated clearly and unambiguously. It is quite possible to participate in a ritual (even a very significant one) without understanding it consciously. There is a common perception among western Christian traditions that this is hypocritical – that if the ritual is not understood (i.e. if the message is not communicated clearly and unambiguously) then it is meaningless, and even 'mumbo-jumbo'. Such a viewpoint, however, is rooted largely in the

Protestant Christian view of faith preceding action which I discussed in the previous chapter, that this is a theological perspective that might not work in other contexts.

So far I have assumed that rituals usually communicate in subtle ways, that they have hidden messages which are not straightforward despite their importance. But rituals may also communicate in very unsubtle ways, especially if they involve some verbal communication. When a Christian priest declares a couple 'husband and wife' at the end of a marriage service s/he is making an unambiguous statement about their relationship. When a preacher gives a talk, the message s/he communicates is often far from subtle. But even when there is this clarity of communication, it must also be remembered that the ritual may be communicating other messages *as well*, albeit more subtly.

The anthropologist Maurice Bloch (1989 [1974]) suggests another way to view the relationship between rituals and communication. Bloch argues that ritual is a type of language, albeit it is rather different since the basics of 'ritual language' are more formal and rigid: there are no words, and so rituals are harder to contradict. Thus, put simply 'you cannot argue with a song', or any other ritual performance, short of stopping the ritual itself. But the ways in which ritual languages work are quite distinct from verbal language, since they allow for far fewer variations in expression. Usually the form of a ritual is quite fixed: one does a certain action followed by another, a symbol may also be used in certain ways, etc. In contrast, an idea may be expressed through words in numerous ways. This, therefore, makes rituals quite distinct types of action, setting apart the experience from other aspects of life. At the same time, however, rituals are quite stable activities – since it is harder to innovate with a ritual, they are transferred through time in a form more unchanged than a spoken language.

Although there is much to be said in favour of Bloch's argument of ritual as a special type of language, it is in the end more of an analogy than an actual theory. The pseudo-linguistic element of ritual actions is interesting, highlighting how such actions are a form of non-verbal (as well as verbal) communication. But it is not the only way to understand the various practices that we call rituals, unless we wish to widen our understanding of the concept of language, and press the analogy harder than it probably needs to go. We should also keep open the idea that innovation in ritual is not only possible, but also happens regularly: the performative element of rituals makes each ritual action unique in its own way. In this sense, we could say that if ritual is a type of language it may be more similar to verbal language than Bloch's argument suggests.

Rituals and performance

As I have stressed already, rituals require action: they are a form of behaviour that is done. Ritual action won't happen simply by thinking about it, someone has to do something, people have to take part in it, and engage in it on a personal level. The performance may be fun to do, it may be a chore, or it is possible to perform a ritual without even thinking about it. Ritual action therefore is performative, involving people doing things (either consciously or unthinkingly), doing activities in a particular way.

To a certain degree ritual activity is often like theatrical performance. The script of a play may be read and understood, but it is not properly a play unless it is fleshed out with actors performing its various characters and their roles. In the same way that actors and audiences experience the themes and the important meanings of a play through its performance in a theatre, people will only understand the significance of rituals through engaging personally in a performative way.

The performance of ritual may involve special types of behaviour – a participant may be expected to assume a certain attitude, or to speak in a certain way, or to do certain actions. Much of this behaviour may be quite different from what is done in 'normal' life, it may even be the opposite of normal behaviour. In some cases there may be a particular 'script' or liturgy to follow – if one is attending a Christian marriage service, or a Jewish Passover Seder there are particular lines of speech that must be said, in order for the ritual to be completed. In the film *Four Weddings and a Funeral*, it is the protagonist's (played by Hugh Grant) refusal to follow the marriage service script and say the words 'I do' that marks his decision not to complete the wedding, and so remain unmarried. This prematurely completes the service unfinished, and results in him receiving a black eye, through being punched by his erstwhile bride-to-be. The script was clear and unambiguous – both for the fictive characters within the film, and for the audience – and the punishment for going 'off script' was severe (in the short term).

In most cases, however, there is no particular script, and instead participants are expected to improvise, but in doing so they must behave (and perform) appropriately. For example, at many funerals it is often hard to know exactly what to say, but everyone knows what type of behaviour is expected (calm, sympathetic, sombre) and what would be considered inappropriate behaviour (loud, jocular, outrageous). It is by taking on the particular role within a ritual context, and by becoming that role to a certain degree (by making that role part of one's own subjective experience), that the activity becomes meaningful. This personal element of performance means that no two ritual performances are ever quite the same. Even if the 'script' is fixed, the performers will always be different in some way (as may the location, the background of the ritual, or any other factors). The end result is that each ritual becomes specific to its circumstances.

Of course, rituals are not completely like theatre. Theatre is only a special form of ritual, which has strict rules of performance (for the audience as much as for the actors). All ritual actions involve a measure of performance, but it does not require a theatrical virtuoso to perform a ritual.

Rituals and society

A fundamental assumption of most twentieth-century studies of ritual has been that we cannot understand a ritual without relating it to the social context in which it is performed. Although there may be such things as personal rituals – actions that I do for myself in private – most rituals have a social dimension. They are done with reference to groups of people.

On one level this takes us back to the idea of studying the relationship between religion and culture. If ritual is a form of religious practice, this is not simply a matter of what an individual person does. It is instead bound up with a much wider network of relationships – other people, and the cultural values and practices of that wider group. What individuals do as rituals links them to the group in some way. As I will discuss below, this is expressed most obviously in studies of ritual as transformation, as individuals undergo rites of passage through which they do not simply change as individuals, but their group membership and identity also become transformed.

Lurking somewhere behind this link between rituals and society is the influence of Emile Durkheim, who I discussed briefly in Chapter 2. As I mentioned, for Durkheim (1964 [1915]) religion has a binding role for societies – religion brings people together and makes them feel part of a larger cohesive whole (society). And it is through ritual in particular that this happens, according to Durkheim. That is, ritual actions do not only involve people in relationships with each other, the performance of rituals actually creates those relationships. At its most simple level this argument suggests that regular attendance at a religious ritual (for example, going to the mosque each Friday) creates a sense of togetherness – through meeting others at the same place each week one enters into relationships that would not otherwise have existed.

Such an argument is so simple that it is both profound and trivial. It is true that some rituals may encourage this sense of solidarity (in some cases quite deliberately, as exemplified by large-scale events such as Hitler's Nuremburg rallies in the 1930s). But the argument also serves to trivialise the significance of the social dimensions of ritual activities. Not all rituals have a binding effect, ritual actions can also set up divisions and oppositions. The Ulster Protestant tradition of Orange Parades through Catholic neighbourhoods in Northern Ireland is perhaps a good example here. There are in fact many ways in which we can understand the connections between social relationships and ritual activities, particularly with relation to issues of power and control as I will discuss below.

Rituals and repetition

If there is one single element that is usually associated with the performance of rituals, it is repetition. That is, if any action is carried out time after time, then that often leads us to classify the action as a 'ritual', simply because it is repeated so often, and so mechanically. To this extent, we can often talk of the 'ritual' of going to a bar, or to a lecture, or the ritual of kissing our grandma goodbye. On this basis, we could say that any action, no matter how trivial it may be, is 'ritualistic' – for example, the act of cleaning one's teeth, or of catching a bus every morning.

The association between rituals and repetition works in another way, however, that is at the level of repetition within the ritual activity. Rituals often use repeated actions: such as visiting a building regularly, praying or meditating daily or weekly, or performing a stereotyped mode of greeting (like always saying 'hello'). At the same time, ritual actions often involve repetition within themselves: they may involve saying or doing the same action again and again. In Protestant church traditions the common order of service is structured hymn, prayer, hymn, prayer, and so on. It is, however, not only actions that may be repeated – the symbols used within a ritual are very often repeated and recycled.

Various theories have been used to 'explain' such repetition. Thus Edmund Leach (1976), argued that the repeating of ritual elements is a function of the way in which rituals are communicative. The more something is 'said' in the ritual, the more chance it will get through to the participants, in the same way a physical message sent more than once, say by email and text message, is more likely to reach its intended recipient. Others, most notably Claude Levi-Strauss (1968), have argued something more subtle. That is, the meaning of the ritual is transmitted through the relations between symbols and ideas in the ritual, and so the frequent repetition of symbols (often in a variety of different contexts) also means a repetition of the structural relationships between the symbols. Levi-Strauss' best example of this is the symbols we often find in rituals representing the concepts of nature and culture, non-human and human, raw and cooked, or whatever.

The repetitiveness of ritual also encouraged the great psychologist Sigmund Freud (1990b [1924]) to put forward his theory that ritual is akin to, and derived from, the actions of neurotics, who have fixed patterns of behaviour which they repeat again and again. This psychoanalytic theory of ritual assumes that ritual is merely a collective neurosis, demonstrating an unhealthy state of mind, as people (in groups and individually) find comfort from the pressures of the world in ritualistic/neurotic behaviour. One problem with this theory, however, is that it attempts to 'explain' social action in terms of individual psychological pressures – it is rather unhelpful to try to reduce the complexity of collective ritual actions primarily to an expression of sick minds. What is equally problematic about it is that there is far more to rituals than their repetitiveness.

Rituals and transformation

When talking about the symbolic dimensions of ritual actions I mentioned briefly that rituals can transform participants' perceptions of the world. It is this transformative element of ritual that has fascinated many writers on ritual, primarily because one of the most obvious and widespread elements of ritual action across the world has been to create changes – either in an obvious physical or social way, or at a more subtle level. Participating in a ritual *may* make the world actually change. Rituals of circumcision are obviously transformative: when a boy is circumcised he undergoes a lot of pain as his foreskin is cut off, which once done marks a very obvious and irreversible change to his penis. Circumcision rituals performed on women in certain parts of the world (most notably in some parts of north Africa) create even more severe physical changes: involving (in some cases) clitoridectomies and the removal of much of the soft tissue of the vulva.

On a (usually) less traumatic level, marriage services are also clearly transformative. The married couple are not obviously different after the ritual from how they were at the start. But by going through the ritual their views of themselves become transformed, as do other people's perceptions of them. The transformation is a conceptual transformation, the ritual brings about a change in people's conceptions of the world, and the social relations between those who live in that world. In fact, many rituals involve a change in a person's social status and their social group membership, and such rituals – which have become labelled 'rites of passage' or 'rituals of transition' – are often the primary focus of ritual studies.

'Rites of passage' can be any rituals which involve major transformations in some way or other. Such rituals most usually occur at important times within a person's life, and so in many cultures there are rites of passage associated with birth, childbearing, and/or the beginning of adult life. The change that occurs to an individual at his/her death is also often marked by a major rite of passage, demonstrating the transformation of that person from the world of the living to the world of the dead. In all such rituals, the main participants are transformed by the performance of the ritual itself into a new state, which most usually has associated with it a different type of lifestyle and identity, as well as membership of a new social group.

Two writers in particular are associated with the study of rites of passage in the last century: the Belgian anthropologist Arnold van Gennep, and the British anthropologist Victor Turner. In particular, van Gennep's work *Rites of Passage* (1960 [1908]) set out a theory which is still highly influential in the area of ritual studies. Whilst in a series of books in the 1960s and 1970s, Turner explored the ways in which key elements of van Gennep's scheme could be explored.

Van Gennep suggested that ritual actions often work in significant ways to transform people's concepts of time, space, and society. That is, rituals very often help to divide up time and create a sense not only of the passage of time, but also its measurement (into years, weeks, and so on), through the celebration of New Year feasts as well as personal temporal events such as birthdays and anniversaries. Likewise, physical boundaries are not only used through rituals, but are also created by rituals. Thus not only are certain rituals performed in special places (such as Christian services in churches), the performance of rituals also sets up boundaries and divides up the world. Thus an action as simple as removing one's shoes on entering a mosque, or covering one's head on entering a synagogue, sets up the significant boundary between outside and inside the building.

However, the most significant and well-discussed element of van Gennep's argument is his threefold (or tripartite) scheme, which he presented as being the basic structure of all rites of passage. That is, he argued that all rituals which involve transition have three important stages, these are: *separation*, *liminality*, and *incorporation*.

The first stage of rites of passage usually involves some *separation* between the participant and the world in which s/he normally lives. In this way the person is detached from the roles and obligations that have been associated with their lives up until that time. Such a separation may be portrayed in a very extreme form – with participants being regarded as 'dead' during this phase. The second stage of this ritual process was labelled *liminality* by van Gennep. This stage (like the other two) may last a long time, or it may be very short, but he argued it is a vital part of the transformation which rites of passage attempt to achieve. The word liminality has its origins in the Latin word '*limen*', which means a threshold. During this middle stage of the ritual the participants are expected to cross a threshold which marks the boundary between the world that they are leaving behind and the social world which the ritual is preparing them for. This threshold, which is betwixt and between two different worlds, is demonstrated in various ways in ritual. The threshold may be marked out physically, for participants to cross in some way – for example, by making them walk over a step or a line on the ground, to jump over a barrier, or to walk through a door.

It was this idea that rituals so often work on a concept of threshold that was enthusiastically pursued by Victor Turner (1967, 1969). For Turner, the threshold may also be marked in more abstract ways, by creating a sense of difference. This is often achieved by making use of behaviour and ideas which show a discontinuity with how things are normally meant to be.

Thus the liminal stage may entail an inversion of 'normal' life, marked by different forms of dress, a different place, and different kinds of behaviour. In fact, behaviour may even be the opposite of what is usually considered correct. If one is normally expected to be well behaved and respectful then the liminal phase may require participants to be disrespectful and badly behaved, as in the raucous behaviour of pre-wedding 'stag nights', or the wild exuberance of colour-throwing during the Hindu Holi festival. In many such rituals one may often find a fascination with the bizarre, with things that are turned upside-down. In a sense this liminal stage is about the expression of anti-structure, that is, expressing the opposite of the usual structures of life, and with the opposite of what is normal.

At the conclusion of a rite of passage, for van Gennep the third *incorporation* stage gives an indication of the new role that the participants are to take on. The participants are welcomed back from liminality, as new people who will be expected to behave differently. This incorporation will physically demonstrate a link between the individual who has been transformed, and the social group into which s/he is entering. They may be welcomed by their new peers, or be expected to stand amongst them, or they may be given a new title or name to indicate this change. The stage of incorporation demonstrates how the ritual has inwardly transformed and outwardly changed the participants, and it installs them into a new place in society.

For van Gennep and Turner there is no fixed limit on how long each stage should last: a stage may be very brief and hardly noticeable, and indeed two stages may merge together so the differences between them cannot easily be discerned. But the scheme gives some indication of how the transformations involved in a rite of passage are brought about. It is not all that useful to simply say that all rituals move from separation to liminality and then to incorporation, this merely gives us a framework upon which to build understandings of particular rituals. Indeed, various writers (for example Bynum 1996; Lincoln 1981) have critiqued the universality of the concept of 'liminality', and particularly its use as a dramatisation of 'anti-structure'. The models relied on by Turner (and van Gennep) depend quite heavily on specifically *male* initiation rituals (such as the Zambia Ndembu groups where Turner conducted his research), and so may not be as widely applicable as many assume (see Grimes 2000a). This notwithstanding, van Gennep's ideas have had a powerful influence on how several generations of scholars have perceived the wider processes by which a person can be changed through ritual action.

Rituals and power

So far my discussion has focused on what could be called traditional approaches to the study of ritual. For much of the second half of the twentieth century, there were ongoing debates about why and how rituals could best be described as symbolic, communicative, and performative. There has also been intense debate about which rituals are transformative, and how and why liminality has been such a prominent feature of rites of passage.

However, in the 1990s a debate has emerged within ritual studies about the viability of the field itself. This focuses on the question of whether or not there are such things as rituals – that is, whether or not the term describes a universal category of action that can be applied cross-culturally. In a very similar way to the debates over the category of religion, it is argued, particularly by writers such as Catherine Bell (1992, 1997) and Talal Asad (1993), that the term ritual is used as an explanation, not a description. That is, when we call something a 'ritual' we then begin to think we understand what it is, since it brings to mind the analytic concepts that I discussed earlier. That is, if we label something as a ritual, then it will, we assume, also be symbolic, and transformative, etc. Instead, it is argued that each action should be understood within a broader totality of context. How does a particular action fit into a wider picture, of the person's (or people's) lives and cultures, their social and physical environment, the relationships that they have with each other, and the ways in which they themselves perceive those relations? Such questions are not answered by labelling the action as 'ritual', and indeed by imposing the label we are shutting down some of those questions rather than opening them up.

What much of this new debate focuses on is the relationship between those actions that we call ritual (for want of a better term) and the network of social and power relations in which each person lives. All ritual actions are about expressing power, about making people subordinate, or challenging such subordinacy. This can be seen most obviously in large-scale state rituals, such as the inauguration of a president, or in Britain the coronation or funeral of a monarch. One function of such rituals is not merely to make the necessary transformation – to invest the presidency or monarchy on to a person – but also to make this transformation clear to the wider social group. In particular, the rituals are performed to involve this wider group, to make it seem that they are part of the social, symbolic, and political order that is being presented through the ritual actions. By taking part in such a state ritual – whether through being actually present, or being virtually present by watching the event on television – each participant is helping to legitimise the authority and power of not only the individual at the centre of the ritual (the new president or monarch), but also the wider system of power and control.

However, we need to be careful that we do not assume that a ritual will impose such power simply because it is a ritual. Here again the distinction between ritual and ritual action is important, it is the activities of those involved which create and channel the power relations. For example, in a historical analysis of royal rituals in Madagascar, the anthropologist Maurice Bloch (1986) shows how the same rituals have, over the process of 150 years, been used in a variety of ways by different political regimes. The rituals have themselves remained fairly constant in structure, but their meanings and the ways in which participants have related to them have been adapted to changing political circumstances. In a similar way, it could be argued, the rituals of royalty of the British state are notable for their 'tradition' and constancy. For example, the funeral of the Queen Mother Elizabeth in spring 2002 was modelled on the funeral of her husband, King George, who had died fifty years before. Despite the similarities of the rituals (such as public processions of the coffin, and public 'lying-in-state'), it is clear that British society and culture has changed considerably during that half-century, as indeed has the role of the constitutional monarchy within that society.

But the analysis of power and ritual can be applied to *any* ritualised or ritualistic action. According to Catherine Bell, the process of setting some behaviour off as ritualised – the creation of that sense of ritualisation – is itself a way of expressing power relations. And so all ritual activity is bound up with the ways in which the participants relate to each other, and possibly to some other, non-human being. She uses as an example an act of ritual subordination: a woman going down on her knees in supplication to a deity, in the presence of male priests who remain standing (Bell 1992: 100). At one level, this action clearly expresses the hierarchical relations of power between the men and the subordinate woman. However, what are also at stake are the ways in which that woman experiences and acts out the relations of power. The ritual does not simply set up the relationship of power, it can give her a format for making meaning from it, and perhaps to challenge such relationships. Each ritual action is, therefore, special and particular – what is going on is not predetermined by it being a ritual, nor by the cultural system of meaning and symbols which lies behind it. Its meanings are dependent on the specific context, who is involved, how they perform the actions, and what meanings they choose to impose.

In conclusion, there are certainly elements of ritual activities that can be understood through looking at meanings and symbols. Rituals do involve elements of performance, communication, and repetition, and the obvious purpose of many rituals is to create transformations. But, as Bell argues, what we mean by the term ritual is most usually a 'strategic way of acting', performed by individuals and groups, through which the participants engage with and also construct particular types of meaning and value. So not only do rituals express authority, the process of performing rituals – or doing things with that sense of ritualisation – is a means by which people construct relationships of authority and submission (Bell 1997: 82).

Summary

- Although not all rituals are specifically religious, the study of religion and ritual highlights the viewpoint that religion is a matter of practice, and not just belief.
- The term ritual is ambiguous, since rituals are not things that exist in themselves, but are ways of acting and behaving. Ritual is better described as 'ritual action' or, in Catherine Bell's phrase, as 'ritualisation'. Ritual is a way of thinking in action, working on creating a 'sense of ritualisation'.
- Classical studies of ritual have analysed ritual with respect to meanings, symbols, communications, performance, society, repetition, and transformation. Each of these approaches give us certain perspectives on some of the ways in which people perform rituals, but none explains 'what rituals are about'.
- As with all other forms of action, ritual actions express and create relations of power between people.

Suggestions for further reading

For some useful introductions to the field of ritual studies, see Ronald Grimes, *Beginnings in Ritual Studies* (1982; revised edn. 1995); and on transformations see his *Deeply into the Bone* (2000b). He has also written an article on 'Ritual' (2000a). Catherine Bell's two main works are as given at the end of the previous chapter, that is: *Ritual Theory, Ritual Practice* (1992); and *Ritual: Perspectives and Dimensions* (1997). Her essay on 'Performance' (1998) is more accessible than her books, and is a good starting point. A good recent introduction to anthropological studies of ritual and religion is Fiona Bowie's 'Ritual Theory, Rites of Passage, and Ritual Violence', in her *Anthropology of Religion* (2000).

For further discussion of the concept of ritual and its problems, see Talal Asad, 'Towards a Genealogy of the Concept of

Ritual', in *Genealogies of Religion* (1993). See also Jonathan Z. Smith, *To Take Place: Toward Theory in Ritual* (1987); Maurice Bloch, *Prey into Hunter* (1992); and Felicia Hughes-Freeland, *Ritual, Performance, and Media* (1998).

Chapter 7

Texts

The nineteenth-century German writer Max Müller (1972 [1870]) argued that scholars of religion should make sacred texts their primary focus of study. After all, for him such documents contain the authentic 'doctrine of the [religion's] founders and their immediate disciples'. He went on to add that these ancient sources stand in contrast to the actual practices of the present, which are merely 'the corruptions of later ages' (Müller 1972 [1870]: 20). Following this line of thinking, the people that we encounter today – people practising, talking about, and living their religions and cultures – are getting in the way of our understanding of their religion.

For much of the twentieth century scholars of religion have seemed to follow this advice, largely focusing on the study of texts: of books written and read within religious contexts. Generations of scholars have assumed that the primary way of learning about a religious tradition is to look in detail at the texts that are used: whether that be the Bible for Christians, the Qur'an for Muslims, the

Vedas for Hindus, the Adi Granth for Sikhs, and so on. In such texts there has been the expectation that the scholar will find the 'essential' basics of the particular religion, which through careful study can be made accessible.

Such a view of texts as the basis of the study of religion is very similar to the idea of the study of culture as 'high' (or elitist) culture, which I discussed in Chapter 2. Religious texts, as particular cultural products, are distinguished both by those who use them (religious practitioners within specific religious traditions), and many of the scholars who study religions. Both tend to collude in the view that such texts reflect the apogee of the religion, and that any study that goes beyond the text risks straying into murky waters (as Müller suggests). Indeed, there is a similarity here with the discipline of English literary studies, which has tended to concentrate on (high cultural) classics of dead white western writers, at the expense of popular fiction, such as romances, non-western English, or post-colonial litera-ture. In a similar way, religious studies has tended to be focused primarily on written texts of the 'great' or 'world' religions, in classical written form.

In fact, the study of religion, culture, and texts is *not* only the study of such 'great' texts. There are in most cases a large number of quite different texts that can be studied which form the basis of particular religious cultures. That is, the idea of texts can be widened to a number of other textual (or text-based, or text-like) formats. In this chapter, I will be looking at the idea of religion in (and as) culture, with reference to the idea of 'culture' as a specific area of cultural products – in Raymond Williams' terms, of culture in the ideal and documentary sense. Although not all of such culture is textual (there is also music, art, and so on), the strong emphasis by scholars of religion on culture-as-texts has largely defined this field of study.

When looking at texts there are a number of aspects of textu-ality that can be examined. Thus Jonathan Culler (1997) suggests the distinction between poetics, hermeneutics, and responses. That is, any text can be analysed in terms of its poetics – its form, style, and rhetoric, looking in particular at the way it is presented, how it presents 'itself' as a form of communication (and perhaps as a work of art). The hermeneutics of a text works on a different level, since it is concerned not so much with how the text works, but instead with what the text is saying. Hermeneutics is about recovering and understanding the meanings of texts – sometimes this may be quite easy and literal, but it may also be a subtle process, uncovering meanings that perhaps even the author did not intend or was not aware of. However, texts are not simply about poetry and meaning, they are also about being read – a point that is easy to miss within the study of any text, including religious texts. A large part of the analysis of texts is not only what can be understood from the text itself, but also from how it is interacted with in a social and cultural context.

What is a text?

So which texts should a student of religion be looking at? Is it enough to read the Bible, Qur'an, or Vedas? To what extent are other texts *also* important, such as novels, fiction, literature, poetry, film, and indeed the diverse range of texts that can now be found on the internet?

There are, of course, some texts in the study of religion that appear familiar and 'straightforward' – largely because they are easily identified as the 'high culture' of particular religious traditions (for example the Bible for Christians). Other religious texts may appear less familiar, particularly if we are unfamiliar with the religious tradition (we may or may not be aware of the Book of Mormon for the Church of the Latter Day Saints). That is, the study of Christianity, or any other religious traditions, in the contemporary world should also take account of other texts (and other media) through which religious ideas and assumptions are expressed.

Alongside the 'great works', however, there are also many books, and films, with religious references. Any text that is circulated on a popular basis is relevant in this sense. Indeed, many of the key cultural texts may not be conventional texts at all. In many contemporary cultures it is not only written texts that convey issues, but other media such as film. That is, the study of texts and religion goes beyond simply looking at books. It is instead a study that encourages us to *widen* our sense of 'text' beyond the specifically written, to include other cultural products that can be 'read' as texts – such as television, music, art, and architecture. This is easiest to see, perhaps, with respect to films where there is an underlying text (the film script) – although a reading of a film requires more than simply an analysis of its dialogue.

Such an approach of looking at films, and other cultural products, as texts to be read derives in a large part from the cultural studies tradition associated with Roland Barthes. In what is probably his most famous work, *Mythologies* (1972), Barthes examined a range of aspects of his contemporary culture to decode what he saw as the underlying political and social messages communicated. Thus he explored car design (the new Citroën), wrestling and boxing, representations of women authors in magazines, soap powder, and so on. We do not necessarily need to agree with his conclusions on how to 'read' the signs and significances of the various examples that he took. But his point was well taken – it is largely in the fabric of the everyday life around us (whoever the 'we' may be), that we can understand important issues of culture, and by extension of religion. To understand how people in a particular context relate to religious ideas, traditions, and practices it is not enough to read important canonical texts – we must also learn to read how those texts are reproduced and woven into other cultural outlets.

Textual forms of the Bible

To take one example, the Bible in contemporary Christian culture, we can find a number of such connections. Rather than understanding this as a simple two-cornered fight between high and low culture, or between the Bible and popular culture, we need to acknowledge that 'great' works such as the Bible often have a prominent place within popular culture. That is, the great textual works frequently appear in numerous different formats and genres, not all of which would be considered 'high' art or literature.

For example, most people have some idea of what 'the Bible' is (usually a single volume book, printed in a traditional font and binding). But in practice, the Bible exists in many different ways: not only through private reading of this book, but also through public performances (at church services), as well as through other media. In the USA and Britain the majority of people are most familiar with Biblical stories through films, TV programmes, and popular literature. For example, there have been numerous portrayals of specifically Christian narratives in Hollywood films over the past half-century (see Telford 1997; Pearson and Moyise 2002), ranging from now classical films such as *King of Kings* (1961) and *Gospel according to St Mark* (1966), to *Jesus Christ Superstar* (1973), and *Jesus of Nazareth* (1977).

In a similar way, there have been attempts by Hollywood directors to make filmic versions of the texts of other religious traditions. For example in 1993, the Italian producer Bernardo Bertolucci attempted a sympathetic exploration of Buddhist traditions in his *Little Buddha*, casting Keanu Reeves as Gautama Buddha. However, the *Little Buddha* was a film made by a religious and cultural outsider. His treatment of both the life of the Buddha and the Tibetan Buddhist traditions that form the main storyline of the film are largely respectful and unquestioning, providing a fairly basic and unreflexive view of ways of seeing Buddhism from a western perspective (see Mullen 1998 for a critique of his rather rosy picture of Tibetan Buddhism).

In contrast to this, the American Catholic Martin Scorsese's *The Last Temptation of Christ* in 1988 – based on the novel by Nikos Kazantzakis (1975) – portrayed an insiders' reading of the Christian Gospels which proved to be highly controversial. Through an ambiguous narrative device – having a sequence portraying Christ dreaming on the cross – the film suggested an 'alternative' Jesus story in which he foresook martyrdom and instead married Mary Magdalene and had children. Despite the widespread protests that were made against Scorsese and the film on its release, there are in fact many ways to read this film. The film, as a reading of a text (Kazantzakis' novel), which was itself a reading of the Gospel texts, is primarily concerned with a 'traditional' exploration of Jesus' life. That is, the film concentrates on the narrative dichotomy between Jesus as human and Jesus as divine person, which is most clearly portrayed through the choice on the cross – to come down and live a 'normal' life, or to die as the saviour. In fact, the resolution of this dilemma was not as controversial as the critics assumed. The film ends with the dream terminating, and Jesus accepting his death, in line with conventional Biblical narratives.

The Last Temptation was indeed quite a traditional textual elaboration of Catholic Christian themes. The controversy it generated had, perhaps, more to do with the presentation of these ideas within the context of the contemporary medium of film, in which – like many similar movies of its time – Scorsese interwove the traditional Biblical narratives with screen representations of explicit heterosexuality and fairly realistic violence. In many ways, a much finer line was trod by the Monty Python team in their earlier film *Life of Brian* (1978), which told an alternative narrative which clearly touched on the Christian story, but also explicitly challenged (through humour) many aspects of what they saw as the foibles of messianic martyrdom. The conclusion of *Life of Brian*, with the eponymous hero being crucified (almost by accident) to the tune of 'Always look on the bright side of life', was clearly engaging with a profound element of Christian imagery. (Davies (1998) gives an interesting reading of the Biblical themes that can be read in this film.)

Similarly, it is possible to find Biblical and Christian themes on a wider level in literary and filmic works that are not specifically 'about' Jesus or the Bible. One recent example is Kevin Smith's film *Dogma* (1999), which engages quite specifically with a number of Christian (specifically Catholic) religious themes in a fairly controversial way. A more traditional example is the English writer C.S. Lewis' *Narnia Chronicles*, written in the 1950s as a deliberate attempt to transmit the Gospels to a new audience of children. More contemporaneously, although the *Harry Potter* series is about a magical world of witches and wizards, its themes and underlying philosophy are based largely on a Christian perspective on the triumph of good over evil.

Text, context, and the world

The overall focus on texts within the study of religion, and particularly on major texts such as the Bible, is in fact no accident. In Britain and the USA, there has been an immense influence on the study of religion from Protestant Christian traditions. As I suggested with the study of belief, the emphasis on texts is a product of that particular form of Christianity. After all, the central religious authority for most Protestants is one particular book, that is the Bible. In the early development of the study of religion, when most scholars were themselves practising (Protestant) Christians, it seemed only 'natural' to assume that if their own religious tradition was focused on the Bible, then other religions would likewise be focused on particular texts. The fact that there are other religious traditions and cultures where texts play a very significant role (such as among Jewish, Muslim, and Sikh traditions) does seem to add weight to this view.

It must be recognised, however, that although texts (in many forms) are often important, the uses of religious texts are always part of a larger field of cultural activities. An important question is how texts are used within particular religious locations: not only what they are saying, and what their authors intended them to say, but how they are being read and understood by particular religious practitioners. This requires us to develop ways of effectively reading religious texts (often in other languages, written in a culture and time very different from our own), and also to learn ways of understanding other people's own readings of their texts. In this sense, the study of religious texts becomes the study of texts and contexts.

Jacques Derrida, the French philosopher and post-structuralist, has offered a particularly challenging starting point for the study of texts. He famously made the comment in his book *Of Grammatology* that 'il n'y a pas de hors-texte' (Derrida 1976: 163), which has most often been interpreted as saying 'there is nothing outside the text'. This in itself indicates something to us of the perils faced in the translation of texts from other languages (in this case French) into English. The phrase as quoted here seems to imply an idea of literary reductionism – that everything is textual, and there is nothing that exists beyond texts. As such it suggests that the only sources for the study of culture (and perhaps religion) are texts – whether they be literary and/or religious texts – since there is no real reality beyond such texts. In a way it appears to echo Müller's comments on the need to study texts and not people.

However, Derrida's point is more complex than this and presents us with not so much a theory of texts, but a way of analysing the relationships between language (as expressed in written form in texts) and culture. Thus a number of writers (see, for example, Culler 1997: 12; Bennett and Royle 1999: 31) have suggested an alternative translation from the French as 'there is no outside-of-text'. Such a phrase is more subtle, and relies on a closer reading of Derrida's idea of language and reality. It is language, not texts, which is everything – if there is such a thing as reality beyond words, then it is not possible for us to know such reality without the use of words. The words that we use – to speak, to describe, to communicate, to evoke, and so on – are not only the key to experiencing the world, they are the world in themselves.

Further to this, however, he argues that the links between language and reality are not reliable, the meanings that are given to words are unstable, coming out of the interplay of differences between words as they are used. Thus words do not have fixed meanings: not only do they change, they also shift in subtle ways through the juxtapositions of words when spoken or written. Words, and more generally language, do not offer us a 'window onto the world', or a means of accessing reality – it is our misplaced faith that they do so that Derrida describes as *logocentrism*.

So to return to his argument that 'there is no outside-of-text', Derrida appears to be making two important points. First, human experience is mediated through language, or as Bennett and Royle describe it 'there is no perception or experience which is not bound up with effects of text or language' (1999: 31). And so it is not the case that everything can be reduced to texts, but rather the other way around: texts are the world in which we live, we all live in worlds that are shaped and formed by texts.

So, to return to the example of western culture, one particular text has profoundly shaped the worlds in which most people live. As Hugh Pyper points out, the Bible has exerted more influence on western culture than any other book. 'In art, literature, politics and religion, biblical thought, forms, narratives and quotations are all-pervasive' (Pyper 1998: 70; a similar point is also made by Carroll 1998). This refers not only to the obvious elements of the Biblical texts – such as the stories and teachings of Jesus and other figures. Rather, the worldview and discourses of the Bible are so 'all-pervasive' in western cultures it is hard to imagine what the western world would be like if there was no Bible.

We can, therefore, use Derrida's idea to explore the social and cultural dimensions of texts, not only to see where a text is coming from but also how it is used. I will return to this point when I explore readings of texts later in the chapter. His critique of logocentrism also leads to the conclusion that if there is no fixed point of reference between text and reality – that is if texts are fluid in their meanings – then there can be no single and definitive reading of any text. All texts can be read in a multitude of different ways, as each text is a play of words and meanings both within and between texts.

This indicates an approach to the study of religious texts that is almost completely at odds with Müller's view. Even if we follow his advice and read the great/high works of a religious tradition, in so doing we are adding our own interpretations to all the other interpretations that exist on those particular texts. Such a reading is simply a starting point, it cannot be taken as the primary basis for 'knowing' or 'understanding' the religious tradition.

The context and uses of texts

So even if we put aside Müller's optimism, texts are still of great significance to the study of religions and cultures, not because they embody the religion, but because we (as well as other people) cannot help reading the culture through such texts, and texts through culture. Even so, with the plethora of meanings that texts produce, we are left with the profound problem of how we can find a way of making a sympathetic reading of someone else's books. How can we know how to read them, unless we know something about who wrote them, and how they should be read?

To understand a religious text requires more than just a reading of it. We also need to have an idea of where it comes from, perhaps who wrote it, and more importantly how it is (or was) meant to be read. In contemporary literature this is known at a general level as *genre*: we know that we should read a 'detective novel' in a different way to a 'romance', or a 'serious/literary' novel. Part of how we know this is in the way we are told how to read it, what it is. This is very often communicated in obvious ways to us, in the packaging and presentation of the book (through its cover, where it is in the bookstore, as well as the way in which it is written). If we follow this idea of genre further, we know that something is a 'religious text' because that is where we can find it in a bookstore: in the religion section. We do not expect to find a sacred text among the fiction, or with cookery books, or gardening, or sex manuals.

In some cases, the text might be marked out and special – in a way that we can recognise – so that it is only used in special ways and at special times. For example, in Sikh traditions the main religious book is the Adi Granth – a large collection of religious songs and devotional hymns, which was put together by the founding Sikh religious leaders in India in the sixteenth and seventeenth centuries. The Adi Granth has a fundamentally important status, it is considered to be an embodiment of the spiritual basis of the religious tradition: it has the status of Guru (often it is called the Guru Granth), and it is at the centre of Sikh religious buildings (*gurdwaras*). Worship in a gurdwara is usually focused directly at a copy of the Adi Granth, which is placed on an elevated stand at the front of the building, and every morning and evening the book is retrieved from and returned to a side room, where it is left to rest at night.

Within the Adi Granth there are no clear indications that this is how the book should be used. Instead there are many different religious verses which describe (in diverse ways) human reflections and devotions towards a particular image of god. The actual use of the book is something which exists outside of the text itself. The text can be examined, read, and scrutinised in detail, either in English translation, or in the original languages: various Panjabi and Hindi dialects of 300–400 years ago. And in so doing we can develop a very rich understanding of the ways in which Sikhs describe and imagine concepts of god and humanity. However, the book itself must also be understood in terms of the way it is used, or *practised* – what is done with it, not only how it is read, but how it is treated in other ways. The two are connected, and most importantly we should not assume that the primary purpose of reading the text is to get knowledge simply of what it says about 'religious belief'.

Reading and translating texts

So far I have glossed over an issue which is so simple, it is very easy to forget the complexities that arise from it: that is the issue of translation. If, as Derrida suggests, the text and the world exist together in the complexities of language, then in what ways can one address differences across languages? Is the textual world of another culture accessible through translation?

The following verse is a very short snippet from an important Hindu book called the *Bhagavad Gita* (or the Gita) which is used in many important religious and cultural ways. Thus, for example, the nationalist leader Mahatma Gandhi considered the Gita to be the Hindu equivalent of the New Testament. Like the New Testament, the Gita is a part of a larger, epic book – called the *Mahabharat* – which is made up of many different texts. The quote is:

> It is better to practise your own inherent duty deficiently than another's duty well. It is better to die conforming your own duty; the duty of others invites danger.
> (*Bhagavat Gita*, chapter 3 verse 35, quoted in Johnson 1994)

So what does this actually mean, and what sort of insight does it give us into Hinduism? Of course, on its own, there is not a lot we can learn. To learn about Hindu religious traditions, we need to read a lot more extensively than this. The verse contains important issues that are understood in different ways within the diverse cultural and religious traditions that are called Hinduism. In a sense it does encapsulate some central issues for most Hindus, in a similar (but also very different) manner to the following phrase from Gospel of John, in the Christian New Testament:

> I am the way, and the truth, and the life; no one comes to the Father but by me.
>
> (John 14.6, RSV)

To start with, how do the phrases fit in with the narrative, or story, as they are told within the text? In the quote from John's Gospel, the narrator is St John, who is giving his account of a particular historical figure called Jesus, a man born in Bethlehem and who had become a religious leader. Much of John's Gospel is made up of reported quotes from Jesus' religious teachings, and the passage selected is one such quote.

The passage from the Gita is from a speech by a man called Krishna, holding a discourse on a chariot with a prince called Arjun, at a moment just prior to a vast and devastating battle. Krishna is considered to be a human incarnation (*avatar*) of the god Vishnu, and is discussing important philosophical and religious principles. Indeed, most of the Gita recounts this speech by Krishna to Arjun. In knowing this context, we can see that as the phrase is attributed to a deity-in-human-form, the reader is expected to take the text and its meanings seriously.

However, between us and the writer of the Gita is, of course, the issue of language and translation. The quote I gave was an English language translation from Sanskrit, an ancient language of India. In Sanskrit the quote reads:

shreyaan svadharmo vigunah
paradharmaat svanushthitaat

sva-dharme nidhanam shreyah
parodharmo bhayaavahah

So, how reliable are the translation and the translator? Well, the translation I quoted was not my own – I cannot read or speak Sanskrit, so I am myself having to rely on someone else. In this case it is the scholar William Johnson, whose translation of the Gita into English is a recognised classic. However, consider the following alternative translations of the same verses:

It is far better to discharge one's prescribed duties, even though faultily, than another's duties perfectly. Destruction in the course of performing one's own duty is better than engaging in another's duties, for to follow another's path is dangerous.

(Prabhupada 1983 [1971])

Better is one's own law though imperfectly carried out than the law of another carried out perfectly. Better is death in the (fulfilment of) one's own law for to follow another's law is perilous.

(Radhakrishnan 1948)

Better to do one's own duty (*dharma*) [to perform], though void of merit, than to do another's well. Better to die within [the sphere of] one's own duty. Perilous is the duty of other men.

(Zaehner 1966)

And do thy duty, even if it be humble, rather than another's, even if it be great. To die in one's duty is life: to live another's is death.

(Mascaró 1962)

Each translator has intended to convey what they thought the passage meant. But whose version do we accept as most authoritative? Which one is actually closest to the real meaning of the Gita? These are not easy questions to answer and depend largely on the translator's own interests. Bhaktivedanta Swami Prabhupada was a religious leader, who received an extensive Hindu devotional education, and went on to inspire many religious followers in the service of Krishna. Radhakrishnan, however, was an academic scholar who also became the first president of the Indian Republic.

One thing we also see here is the problem with translating the word *dharma*, as I noted in Chapter 1. Although the word is often translated as 'religion', in this case it is more specifically meant to refer to the idea of 'duty': of one's role in life. Even so, Radhakrishnan translates the word as 'law' rather than 'duty'. None of these translations are necessarily correct or incorrect, since all three words (religion, duty, law) give us some of the sense of what the term is usually held to mean in Sanskrit.

So whose translation is closest to the original text? The answer may be to not trust any translation but one's own, and so to read the text in its original language (in this case Sanskrit). For in-depth study of a particular religious tradition and culture this is essential – it is not enough to rely on any person's translation, the student is expected to learn the language(s) of the original. However, a translation is a useful starting point, as a sort of 'here's-one-I-prepared-earlier' – so long as we remain aware we are reading it as a translation.

This point is also relevant for John's Gospel (and the other gospels and books in the Christian Bible), which was also not written in English. The quote I gave was from a particular translation of the Gospel (Revised Standard Version), a translation made from a text originally written in a particular form of Greek called *koiné*, or 'New Testament Greek'. Most of the New Testament was written in this language, although parts of it were themselves translated into it from the local Palestinian language of Aramaic. In the centuries of Christian history the matter became even more complex. The Greek was translated into Latin, which became the dominant version of the Bible in western Europe, and this in turn was translated into English – most notably in the 'Authorised Version' of the Bible, produced in England in the seventeenth century (the 'King James Version').

As English itself has changed over the centuries, there are now a plethora of contemporary translations, all of which attempt to accurately convey the message of the original gospels. On top of this, though, most readers of the Bible consider the text as an English text – many people read it as though the English version is the 'original' version. Going back to the original source may give a more 'accurate' way of reading the text, and discussing the author's intentions, but in most cases in the west the biblical textual world is an English-speaking one.

Authorship

We expect that a good translation should bring us closer to the intentions of the author of the text. On one level, we assume that texts can 'speak for themselves', but at the same time we cannot help assuming that behind each text is a person (often a man), who is using the text to communicate directly with us. In this respect, it is not the text that has life, it is merely a 'dead object' which acts as a medium between two people (author and reader).

Of course, the situation is more complicated than this. Texts might not have lives, but they are treated as though they do. As you read this book, you may be aware of my authorial voice (me speaking to you), but you are interacting with the book and not necessarily me as a person. On the other hand, I cannot know who 'you' (the reader) are, or where or when you are reading 'my' words. This seems quite a one-sided conversation: I am speaking without giving you any chance to talk back to me (or at least not immediately). In this way, every text has an author – a person who is attributed with the production of the discourse of the text (who produced the words that are on the page). This may not necessarily be the person who wrote the words.

For example, in the Gita we have a complex hierarchy of authors: the main part of the text, as I mentioned above, is made up of Krishna speaking. But his words come to us through the medium of Sanjay, an adviser to the king Dhritarashtra (who is himself on the 'wrong' or 'bad' side of the great battle of the epic Mahabharat). Sanjay is speaking of events which he cannot physically see, since his conversation with Dhritarasthra is happening in a room in the king's palace, well away from the scene of the battlefield (in another way, Sanjay 'sees' for his king who is also physically blind). Furthermore, it is not Sanjay himself who is said to be writing the words, the overall author-ship of the Gita, as well as the Mahabharat, is attributed to the great Hindu *rishi* (or sage) Vyasa.

Such multiple layers of authorship are not particularly unusual, especially with texts that have been around for a long time. After all, the Bible is a single book with a number of different authors. The New Testament in particular is attributed to five particular writers: the four gospel writers, Matthew, Mark, John, and Luke, the latter who also wrote the account of early Christian missionary activities after the death of Jesus (in Acts). The fifth main author is Paul, whose letters are included together with those of a few other early Christians. But other authors are implied within the writing of the book, particularly the gospels. The three 'synoptic' gospels of Matthew, Mark, and Luke are so-called because of strong similarities between them, suggesting that all three drew on a single earlier text, whose authorship is unknown (s/he may have been one of the gospel writers, or another unacknowledged author).

In contrast, for Muslims the Qur'an is a single-authored volume which is the direct word of god, that is Allah. This divine revelation was spoken through the Prophet Muhammad in the seventh century CE, and written down as the Qur'an shortly after his death. The verses of the Qur'an are therefore consid-ered to be the 'words of god', quite literally. Indeed, it was the suggestion by the lapsed Muslim Salman Rushdie, in his book *The Satanic Verses* (1988) (a piece of magico-real fiction), that Muhammad had made up the Qur'an for his own ends that caused so much upset for many Muslims in the late 1980s. In this respect, for many Muslims the issue of authorship is uncontestable, the Qur'an is a text (indeed *the* text) in which Allah speaks to the world.

The Rushdie case indicates an important point about authorship: the attribution of authorship, saying who created a text, is not necessarily a neutral activity. It is, in fact, highly political. A great deal rests on who a text is seen as coming from: authority comes from authorship. It is because of this that it is hard to imagine a text which has no author, or at least in which the issue of authorship is unimportant. Even a text which is anonymous (where the authorship is unattributed, or is unknown) has a particular 'authored' status, in a sense, by coming to us from tradition.

Against this, it sounds strange to consider accounts that talk of 'the death of the author'. This in particular refers to the work of Roland Barthes (1968), whose paper with that title explored some critical questions in the link between author and authority. Barthes returns us to the issue of the dialogue between 'author' and 'reader' – the 'me' and 'you' that I spoke of above (of course, as you read this, the 'me' is the reader, and the 'you' is the author). Although the process of reading appears to be more of a one-way monologue than a dialogue, there is an exchange going on. In an important sense, the authority of the author, and authorship itself, is not so much claimed by the author, but given by the reader. The reader ('you') assumes that these words are coming from an author (and not generated haphazardly by a computer), and as you read you attempt to understand what I am meaning as the author.

Authorship implies intentionality, an author wants his or her text to be read in a particular way. Thus the author of the Qur'an is Allah, and Muslims are expected to read the text implying an intention of meaning by Allah. That is, Allah wants Muslims to behave according to the precepts that are set out in the text. This issue vexes the translator in particular, since one hopes that the process of translation conveys the sense and intention of the original authorship, and does not replace the original author's voice with that of the translator. Indeed, this very problem with translation is integral for Muslims with regard to the Qur'an. The Qur'an as a text can only be properly known and read in the original Arabic, any other version (such as in English) is not a translation but an interpretation, mediating Allah's words through the vehicle of the translation, and thus diffusing the authorship.

What Barthes argues against here is the idea that texts have fixed meanings, that there can be (or is) an authoritative reading to be made of a text, which depends on the author's own intentions. It is true that an author may wish us to read a text in a particular way. So when the book called *The Divine Principle* talks of a 'Lord of the Second Coming', who will be born in an eastern country (such as Korea) in the early twentieth century, the intended meaning for the reader is to identify a particular person – Sun Myung Moon – as that messianic figure. Such a reading is made mostly by certain readers, those who belong to the Unification Church (otherwise known as the 'Moonies'). Other readers may see that intention but reject the conclusion, and indeed some may even raise other intentions behind the text. For example, some Christians have denounced the text as proclaiming a 'false messiah', whose intention is to exploit his followers, not to lead them to salvation.

Whatever resolution we may choose to make of these interpretations of the text – whether or not we agree or disagree with the linkage between the idea of a second messianic coming and the ministry of Reverend Moon – does not depend on a simple recourse to the author. For one thing, *The Divine Principle* has no formal author – it was revealed to Moon over a number of years, but Moon himself does not claim authorship. And because of Moon's controversiality, many are tempted to disregard his authority as spurious and false. In this case, at least, we see a 'death' of the author (figuratively, not literally), as s/he is sidelined in our attempt to analyse the text.

In practice, however, the death of the author, in terms of Barthes, is not so easily achieved. Salman Rushdie faced the deadly paradox of applying such a critical perspective to late twentieth-century Muslim readings of the Qur'an. He did not proclaim so much the death of god (or Allah), but (through fictional devices) the separation of the text (the Qur'an) from the imputed author (Allah) for the sake of what he hoped would be a richer textual and historical analysis of that most influential book. In turn, Rushdie himself provoked a reaction that centred on the issue of his own intentionality (did Rushdie as author intend to provoke and upset Muslims in his text?), and of course the bitter irony of being under threat of his own (all too literal) death, by assassination.

For Rushdie, as with 'the author' in general, it is possible perhaps to concur with Mark Twain's remark that 'rumours of my death are greatly exaggerated'. In fact, Michel Foucault's response to Barthes' paper, 'What is an author', points out the ways in which authors are created within a context of social power relations and deriving from a particular set of historical circumstances. What we see as an author is what we as readers impute them to be, to allow us to give sense and meaning to a text. That is, for Foucault the author is 'the ideological figure by which one marks the manner in which we fear the proliferation of meaning' (Foucault 1979 [1970]: 159).

This returns us again to the point made by Derrida, and on which both Foucault and Barthes concur. Whatever the role of the author (and regardless of the existence of an author), texts often work in paradoxical ways. On the one hand, every text is rooted within the strictures of language, which seem to presume authoritative and fixed logocentric meanings, but which do in fact produce a surplus of meanings because of the fluidity and ambivalence of words. The idea of authorship does not resolve this ambivalence. Instead it is a means of fixing meaning, albeit perhaps temporarily, and in so doing it produces and sustains certain relations of power – as well as aiding the reader to make an ordered and coherent reading of the text.

Authorship also helps us to generate other meanings, in particular those behind the meanings of a text. Indeed, such meanings exist in an ever-increasing cycle of meaning, in the sense of Derrida's idea of nothing being outside-text. Texts decipher the meanings of texts, which themselves help frame our decoding of texts. This issue has been important in particular for feminist readings of Christian Biblical texts. In Chapter 4 I spoke of Elisabeth Schüssler Fiorenza's 'hermeneutics of suspicion' (1984), which is based on an obvious and seemingly unresolvable issue. That is, any reading of the Christian Bible cannot avoid the deep veins of misogyny, patriarchy, and in several places extreme violence by men against women that are found within the text. For feminist (and other) scholars of Christianity who are also Christians, the problem is one of how the putative goodness of Christianity can be reconciled with a negative and abusive treatment of women. Is there a decent 'core' of Christianity that has struggled to break free from the constraints of male oppressiveness? There are very obvious theological answers to these questions – indeed the questions themselves are premised on a theological idea that there is a spiritual or moral core to Christianity that exists beyond the many cultural and historical differences between Christian cultures.

This theological core is usually defined by Christians as the Bible, and this requires some interpretation of what the many authors of the Bible intended in their writings. Thus Schüssler Fiorenza's hermeneutics of suspicion gives an alternative way of reading against the androcentrism of the biblical authors, as well as the androcentrism of the many historical and contemporary Christian commentators on the Bible. That is, by recognising that most Biblical texts were written at a time when gender political relations were very different to those of the present day, then the sense and meaning of such texts can be explored with reference to the assumptions and cultural locations of the texts' authors.

If the authors were sexist, misogynist, or (at best) gender blind, then contemporary readings can be made which challenge such assumptions. After all, we are working within a surplus of meanings, and the authors' original intentions for reading a particular text (if they can even be discerned) are not necessarily the same as those of a reader in a completely different time and culture. Thus, a questioning of the intentions of the author, as rooted within a particular patriarchal culture and milieu, can 'allow' and encourage alternative readings of these texts.

In this case, the author does not necessarily 'die' or become lost: Luke and Paul, and the other Christian evangelists, do not disappear from the analysis. Instead, their roles as authors – as creators of texts which have subsequently developed into highly significant documents – become an important part of the analysis. At the same time, however, the intention is not necessarily to find a fixed interpretation of what the authors 'really' meant. Instead, the focus is more on the possible range of interpretations that can be made of a particular text, often against the grain of the author's discerned intentions. This can be explored through the multiple readings that have been made over time. Just where the authority in the interpretation of the texts is held to lie is ambiguous, but there is an important shift away from vesting that authority primarily in terms of the authors' intentions, and with those who have traditionally claimed the authority to restate such intentions. For a number of feminist scholars, including Schüssler Fiorenza, the authority in fact should lie primarily with the reader, to interpret Biblical texts in alternative ways.

Readers and reading

The above discussion leads to one of the key areas of textual studies in recent decades. This goes broadly by the label of 'reader-response theory', which has generally been applied to the study of literary texts, but which has very important implications for the study of any texts, including those used in specifically religious contexts. This theory is based on an examination of what Wolfgang Iser (1980) calls 'the interaction between text and reader'. The focus is not only on the reader (rather than the author), but on how the relationship between the two is mediated. It is not quite as simple as Barthes suggests, when he says 'the birth of the reader must be at the cost of the death of the Author' (Barthes 1968). The study of texts requires we pay close attention to both author *and* reader, and how they exist together in a relationship through the text.

On one level this produces a simple set of questions – in particular, where does the meaning of a text come from, or who gives such meaning? In the case of Schüssler Fiorenza, the argument is obviously that meaning is given not by the author, but by a reading that goes against the grain of the text and the author's intentions. However, the structure, content, and poetics of a text are still important. Even though a reading of Derrida may suggest that there are infinite possibilities of meaning for a text, how particular readers respond to particular texts is itself determined by how the text is presented. It would seem bizarre, perhaps, to 'read' (and interpret) the traditional 'Three Little Pigs' fairy-tale as a slasher-horror story, or the Gospel of John as a detective novel. Thus Wolfgang Iser (1980) suggests that texts produce readings: narrative structures, and other poetic/structural devices make the reader interpret the text in certain ways. The gap of experience between the author and reader needs to be bridged, since the reader is coming to the text with a different set of experiences from the author. In order to do this, a text will have both guidance for the reader on how to read the text, and gaps within narration – which Iser calls 'blanks' – in which the reader can supply meaning and interpretation for her/himself.

This needs to be tempered, however, with placing such analysis within a wider social and cultural context. Texts may give a reader space to bring her/his projections into the 'blanks', but the projections, interpretations, and meanings that come from them are not solely a matter of personal or individual taste. The way that I might read the Gita is going to be very different from others' readings – for example, a Gujarati British Hindu living in London will probably read and interact with the text in a very different way. This is what Stanley Fish (1980) describes as 'interpretative communities', how one reads a text and gives it meaning comes from one's particular cultural location.

Someone who was brought up as a Muslim reads the Qur'an very differently to someone who was not, and Muslims from different countries, traditions, or cultures all read the Qur'an in particular ways. On the other hand, Salman Rushdie's *Satanic Verses* (1988) was read very differently by white liberals in Britain to how it was read by Muslims in India, Iran, or Britain. Although it was the same text that was read, the text became meaningful to its various readers in quite distinct ways. Rushdie himself might wish to argue that the irate Muslims who read his work were reading it 'wrong' (as he did in an article in 1990, see Rushdie 1992). But it could equally be argued that Rushdie's critics were making just as legitimate a reading of the book as any other potential reading, and that Rushdie had himself 'got it wrong' by writing a book that could generate such an aggravated (and potentially deadly) response.

This point raises the issue of the politics of reading. Reading is not necessarily a neutral activity, but happens within a sphere of political relations. How a person responds to a text may, or may not, matter considerably. At one point in European history it was possible to be executed simply for translating the Bible from Latin into the local vernacular language (for example, John Wycliffe died in 1384 for making an English version). Today this might be less likely to happen, but battles do still occur over how that particular book should be read. A state school in Durham, in northern England, received public condemnation in April 2002 because its teachers were presenting a reading of the book of Genesis which took the text as a 'literal' rather than 'mythical' account of creation. The incompatibility between this Creationist viewpoint (based very clearly on an interpretive community's reading of Genesis) and other readings is also clear to see in many parts of the USA. For example, the state of Kansas has legislated to protect the Creationist reading from (what they consider) the infringements and dangers of evolutionary science.

It should also come as no surprise to consider issues of gender in the politics of reading. At one level, it seems almost too obvious to suggest that women and men may read texts differently. Certain texts may be read more by women than men, and vice versa. And how a person reads a text may well be determined by their gender, as well as other cultural factors of difference, such as their ethnicity, age, class, and culture. Thus Judith Fetterley (1978) argues that what is taken as 'classic' literature often consists of masculine texts, written by and for men. This literary sexual politics is equally important with respect to specifically religious texts. The ways in which women read and give significance to key religious texts (such as the Qur'an, or the Bible) may well be quite different to the more authorised, and academically reported, readings done by men. Thus Julia Leslie (1989) shows how certain Hindu Dharmashastras (or religious law guidelines) portray a set of ideal (men's) expectations for the behaviour of Hindu women, which are interpreted quite differently by actual women.

What this leads to, however, is a tricky methodological question. If a text is being read in different ways by diverse groups and individuals, how can we find the reading being made in any particular circumstances? Our own reading of the text will not give us any answer to this, since we are engaging with it in ways specific to ourselves. One particular response has been to combine textual studies with more socially based, or ethnographic studies – that is, to bring together an analysis based on reading texts with interviewing of readers. Janice Radway (1987), for example, pursued this strategy in her work *Reading the Romance*, where she sought to examine how and why women engage with the popular genre of romance books, through conducting a series of interviews with women readers.

This ethnographic approach to texts and reading has been regularly used in other areas of the study of culture, particularly in social and cultural anthropology, and also in recent decades in the study of television, music, and film. There are now classic studies made by David Morley (1986) on viewer reception of television news programmes, Ien Ang (1985, 1991) on the US soap *Dallas*, John Fiske (1989a) on Madonna fans, and Valerie Walkerdine (1997) on young girls' viewings of the film *Annie*. In the contemporary study of films it is audiences that are now as important as the films themselves – with the emphasis being placed on how films are 'read' and experienced (Morley 1997; Jensen and Pauly 1997; Moores 1990). There have been some similar studies made within the context of readings of religion in the USA, most notably by Stewart Hoover and Knut Lundby (1997) in Colorado.

None of these authors, however, place the focus *solely* on the reader or the viewer. The importance of reader-response theory and audience studies is not only on how the text is received, but how it is produced. As I highlighted in Chapter 2, texts, films, and other cultural products are *sold* to consumers, and so are part of a wider economic and political sphere. An effective understanding of a text on all these levels – in terms of author, reader, reception, and production – requires a multifaceted analysis that combines a number of different approaches including ethnography, a detailed examination of the text, how the text was produced, and the political economics of its distribution or marketing.

The study of religious texts may appear more detached from such a perspective – for example, it may seem unusual to think about the economics of the Bible, the Qur'an, Gita, or any other such text. Robert Carroll (1998), however, points out that the Bible is a number one all-time best-seller, and a similar level of commercial importance can be found with other texts including the Qur'an and the Gita. Studying these texts requires an approach that examines all these layers of production and reception, and authorship. So far, most of the analysis in the study of religion has been primarily focused on the much narrower issue of textual hermeneutics – finding a definitive and authorised meaning for such texts.

Not only do texts express important ideas within particular religious traditions, they also act as places in which ideas are examined, re-evaluated, and in many cases put into practice. Texts are read, as well as being lived and performed, and the examination of any particular text cannot do any more than produce another text that seeks to elaborate on its many fluid meanings.

To return to Max Müller's comments, religious practitioners do not get in the way of the study of religions (and religious texts), it is only through them that it is possible to make any analysis of such texts. It reminds me of a classic quote from the Walt Disney film *Winnie the Pooh*. When Pooh Bear becomes stuck in Rabbit's front door-hole, the Gopher (in trying to fix the problem) says: 'first thing t' be done is get rid of that bear, he's gummin' up the whole project'. To this an exasperated Owl replies, 'dash it all, he *is* the project!'

Summary

- The study of religious texts involves both major religious works, and more 'minor' or popular texts, including other cultural products such as films.

- Religious texts are always part of a larger field of cultural activities, through being read, spoken, and performed. The study of religious texts requires that we examine more than the content of such texts, but also their context and use.
- Texts create cultural worlds and are the world in which we live. That is, they are often the means by which we think about and experience the world.
- The idea of the 'death of the author' does not suggest the end of authored texts, but rather that authorship gives authority and particular meanings to a text.
- Understanding of texts also requires us to look at how readers create meanings, either as individuals or as members of 'interpretative communities'. That is, texts come to have particular meanings through being read, not only through being written.
- The study of religious texts requires a study of human activity, not simply written words.

Suggestions for further reading

Two good starting points for contemporary textual theory are Jonathan Culler's *Literary Theory: A Very Short Introduction* (1997), and Andrew Bennett and Nicholas Royle's *Introduction to Literature, Criticism and Theory* (1999, particularly the chapters on 'The World', and 'The Author'). See also Hans Bertens, *Literary Theory: The Basics* (2001).

For the particular arguments about the death of the author, see Roland Barthes, 'The death of the author' (1968), and Michel Foucault, 'What is an author?' (1979 [1970]). For a good introductory reader on reader-response theory, see the collection of essays put together by Andrew Bennett called *Readers and Reading* (1995).

There are a number of good resources on the Rushdie affair, some of which discuss in particular the textual issues of

Rushdie's uses of the Qur'an (and Muslim responses to this). See, for example, James McGuigan, 'Dilemmas of culture and politics: author killing', in *Cultural Populism* (1992); Sara Suleri, 'Salman Rushdie: embodiments of blasphemy, censorship of shame', in *The Rhetoric of English India* (1992); Chetan Bhatt, 'The Rushdie affair and the deceptive critique of imperialism', in *Liberation and Purity* (1997); and Richard Webster, *A Brief History of Blasphemy* (1990).

Chapter 8

Contemporary religions, contemporary cultures

Conventional wisdom assumes that religion is on the decline in western societies – that the forces of modernisation and particularly secularisation are simply too strong, and so the once dominant force of religion in public life has now been radically curtailed. Despite this, it is very hard to understand the modern world without understanding the major religious traditions and influences that cut across global boundaries and feed into and shape global politics.

The most obvious example of the way in which the twenty-first century world is being shaped by religion was the attacks in New York and Washington in September 2001 and the ensuing 'war on terrorism'. On one level, the motivation behind the atrocity was strongly religious. Osama bin Laden and the Al-Qa'eda network are organised by their interpretations of Islamic traditions, and have carried out their actions in the name of their religious values. There were, of course, other factors involved such as political, economic, and military issues, but the religious issues are entwined

with these other forces – they are not distinct from them. Religious practices are shaped by and also shape the global political landscape. In this final chapter I will explore some of the ways in which religions are very much part of the processes of modernity, and need to be analysed within these frameworks.

Post-colonialism and globalisation

There are many ways in which one can describe and account for the structure of global politics and economics at the beginning of the twenty-first century. In Europe and North America the past decades have generally been peaceful, despite relatively small-scale conflicts such as in Afghanistan, Serbia, and Iraq. There are high standards of living in the west, and stable governmental systems. Since the collapse of the Soviet Union around 1991, and the end of the Cold War, the USA is now the single world super-power, which attempts to maintain and enforce order across the globe. Western prosperity and general interests are also strongly defended through economic tariffs, sanctions, and political actions in other nations as and when necessary.

Prior to the middle of the twentieth century, global politics were shaped rather differently. For over a century, until roughly 1950, Britain was a major global power which directly controlled large areas through colonisation. At its height, at the end of the nineteenth century, the British Empire included much of Africa, the Indian subcontinent, and many other territories. The passage from that colonial era to the present day post-colonial world happened with almost breathtaking speed, with severe repercussions that are still being worked out. Areas of substantial European settlement, such as north America and Australia, are now principal global powers. In contrast, the areas where colonial rule relied on economic exploitation rather than settlement, such as Africa and India, are now considered as the 'Third' or 'Developing' World. Such countries at the beginning of the twenty-first century are no longer subject to direct colonial rule, but the global economic order still makes them strongly indebted to the 'First World', to the extent that some argue the post-colonial world of independent nations is a continuation of the colonial era (see Sardar and Davies 2002).

Present-day global structures were clearly produced by recent colonial history, and most aspects of contemporary life – including contemporary religions – can only be understood with reference to that history. The term *globalisation*, refers to the complexities of this new world order, of which there are a number of facets: such as economics (for example, high volumes of trade and other money flows), high-speed communications (internet, email, telephone, and fax), and travel, along with sophisticated technologies (genetic engineering, cloning, and industrial by-products). Together, these all make national boundaries extremely porous and hard to define.

With globalisation it is not only things, but people also who move about the globe, either physically or virtually (through communications technology). An obvious example of this glob-alised world were the men born in Middle Eastern countries (such as Egypt), educated in Europe, and then resident in the USA, who received milita.y training in Afghanistan, and went on to kill others from scores of different countries in New York on 11 September 2001. Of course, many of the people who move about the globe do so for quite different, and far less violent, reasons than Muhammad Atta and his fellow 9/11 hijackers. It was not globalisation that caused the tragedy, but rather that the tragedy could only have happened within the context of the forces of globalisation that so powerfully shape the contemporary world.

It is quite clear that bin Laden is not an isolated madman acting purely on a personal vendetta or crusade. He is a product of many of the forces that he has sought to challenge, not least because of his vast financial resources, which came to him through his position in a prominent and wealthy Saudi Arabian family. But the conflict he is fighting, as well as the conflict fought by those belonging to his Al-Qa'eda network, has been largely framed within the context of the political imbalance of post-colonialism. Or to put this another way, they are trying to challenge the current political structures of globalisation. This cannot simply be reduced to an Islam v. west distinction, since bin Laden is primarily at odds with the ruling elite in Saudi Arabia over the control and custody of the Muslim holy cities of Mecca and Medina (see Esposito 2002; Ruthven 2002).

There are, however, many differences between Islamic traditions in this globalised and post-colonial perspective. For example, between bin Laden's Sunni Islam, and the dominance of Shi'ite Islam in post-revolutionary Iran. There was also the further difference between bin Laden's radical Islamism and Saddam Hussein's more socialist and nationalist forms of Sunni Islam in Iraq. From a western perspective, perhaps, these are all seen as being alike, but they all frame in different ways a reaction against the political and economic dominance of the western global powers (on contemporary Islamic politics, see Esposito 1998), and each are embedded within the processes of globalisation. For example, the religious founder of revolutionary Iran, Ayatollah Khomeini, lived in France for many years in exile before he returned in 1979.

The forces of globalisation and post-colonialism impact on and shape all contemporary religious traditions, not only Islam. To take just a few examples, the ideas and politics of religious differences in present day India – between Sikh, Hindu, and Muslim communities – are derived from colonial legacies in a post-colonial age. In turn, these groups have changed and developed through international migrations of people to western countries, and the creation of Hindu, Sikh, and Muslim diasporas within predominantly secular Christian cultures such as the USA and the UK. Through the two-way flows of people and traditions from India to the west, and across multiple global networks, new ideas, practices, and traditions are created.

Nationalism and localisation

Globalisation is not simply about the creation of a 'global village', and the breakdown of distance and boundaries through technology and travel will not inevitably produce a single common global culture. The case of bin Laden shows that globalisation does not produce homogeneity (making everyone and everything the same), it can bring out substantial differences.

The flip-side of globalisation is localisation, the processes by which a sense of the local and the distinct is produced – not always as an opposite of globalisation, but sometimes as a process of globalisation itself. The close relation between the two has been given a specific name: *glocalisation* (Robertson 1995), reflecting the idea that one produces the other.

Such localisation is often expressed through the idea of nationalism. Following the breakdown of the colonial powers, power was transferred primarily through the construction of political nation-states. In the years since, changes to the global political structures have been based around this concept of nationality. For example, with the creation of new nations such as East Timor (from part of Indonesia) and Eritrea (from Ethiopia), and the disintegration of the former nation of Yugoslavia in the 1990s into separate nations such as Croatia, Slovenia and Bosnia.

Looked at from above, a particular nation represents a distinct local entity, similar to other nations, but different in terms of its culture(s), language(s), outlook, and symbols (such as its flag, national anthem, etc.). Looked at from below, the nation is held to encompass various local differences into a manageable political unit that includes all (or most) of its citizens, either through consensus or coercion. This idea of nationality and nationalism provides a framework for local identity, for thinking about who a group of people are. As Benedict Anderson (1983) has famously suggested, the populations of nations work hard at the cultural and ideological level to create themselves as cohesive 'imagined communities'. In some cases this can overlap, or conflict, with other identities such as ethnicities, as I will discuss below.

Religious organisations and identities are often an important part of such nationalism. For example, the USA is a distinctively religious nation, despite the constitutional separation between the state and churches. This religious dimension of US nationalism is primarily understood in broadly liberal Protestant Christian terms, but also more inclusively in terms of a general and inclusive American religious identity. Likewise, most European countries combine an explicit or implicit identification between nationality and, usually Christian, religiosity. Such a crossover between religion and nationalism is not usually intended to be deterministic – so in the UK, despite the presence of the established Church of England, there is no legal or social requirement that all English people should belong to that particular church. However, ideas of nationality (i.e. what it generally 'means' to be English) are usually thought of with some reference to such religion.

In many cases, however, the relationship between religion and nationality is a source of controversy and sometimes conflict. To remain within the UK, in the province of Northern Ireland (or Ulster), there are two very different ideas of nationalism and religion. That is, the predominantly Protestant perspective that the province is part of the United Kingdom (including England, Scotland, Wales, *and* Northern Ireland), which together make up a political and national entity which is largely Protestant. In contrast, there is a predominantly Catholic view that the province is part of a quite different entity: the island of Ireland, which is the nation of the people of Eire, who are broadly Catholic. These conflicting perspectives have been a basis for other divisions, particularly economic differences, which in turn have been expressed through several periods of political and social violence – most recently between the late 1960s and the 1990s ('The Troubles'). It would be simplistic to say that religion has been the cause of the violence in Northern Ireland. Rather, religious identities and differences have been part of other aspects of social life, such as national traditions and identities and socio-economic differences.

The various nations that emerged from colonialism in the Indian subcontinent likewise show some of these issues. The large area of 'India' – which is as large as Europe, with a similar scale of cultural diversity – gradually came under British colonial rule in the eighteenth and nineteenth centuries. In 1947, however, the British withdrew from direct political control, resulting in the construction of independent nation-states. The initial proposal from Indian nationalists to create a single independent nation called India later developed into an idea for two nations based on what were seen as fundamental differences between the Indian peoples. That is, into the states of India, covering areas with a predominantly Hindu population, and Pakistan, for regions with a majority Muslim population and in which Hindus were a minority.

This 'partition' of India had profound consequences, not least the violence and terror that resulted between local communities when people found themselves on the 'wrong' side of the new border. Large populations of Hindus (and Sikhs) in what became Pakistan, and Muslims in what became India, were 'ethnically cleansed' and forced to move. A tragic irony was that such conflict erupted between groups of people who shared strong cultural and linguistic similarities, and who were primarily divided by their religious identities. That is, communities that had prior to independence been fairly homogeneous, because of the identification of nationalism with religion separated into divided communities in which religious identity became the most important aspect of difference.

The complications of this did not end with the establishment of the states of India and Pakistan. One problem built into this settlement was the fact that Pakistan was made up of two regions – West and East Pakistan – which were at two different ends of India, separated by a thousand miles. The economies, languages, and cultural traditions of these two regions were quite different, and so although they were united in having Islam as their national religion, the differences (not least the distance) between them began to create tensions. In 1973 Pakistan was divided into two separate Muslim nations: West Pakistan became, simply, Pakistan, whilst East Pakistan became Bangladesh (the Muslim country of the Bengali people).

India itself has also been subject to a number of internal conflicts based around this uneasy equation of nationalism and religious identities. Despite the large Hindu majority in the country, the dominant national ideology of India has been from its foundation to encourage a distinction between nationalism and Hinduism. To achieve this, there has been an emphasis on the idea of *secularism* within state politics, resisting the political dominance of religious (i.e. Hindu) values and identities (see Bhargava 1998). In practice, this secularism has lived uneasily with communal tensions between the Hindu majority and various minorities, in particular Sikhs and Muslims.

In the 1970s and 1980s Sikhs in the state of Panjab, in north-western India, found themselves in a violent conflict with the Indian state, as certain Sikh leaders fought to establish an independent Sikh nation-state called Khalistan, that would be the homeland of this distinct religious national group. The campaign did not succeed, but it led many Sikhs and other Indians to re-examine the complex relationship between Indian-ness and non-Hindu identities, such as Sikhism. Similarly, there has been almost continual conflict between Muslims and Hindus in various parts of India since 1948, emerging from resentment and stigmatisation from both communities against each other. In particular, the Indian state of Kashmir has been the source of a number of wars between India and Pakistan, largely because of its Muslim majority, as well as an ongoing campaign by Kashmiris for independence. There is also the unresolved question of a disputed mosque and temple site in the town of Ayodhya, as well as sporadic communal violence against Muslims, such as pogroms in Ahmedabad, Gujarat in 2002.

The main political party in India has been the Congress Party, which is associated with figures such as Jawaharlal Nehru (the first Indian prime minister), his daughter Indira Gandhi, and her son Rajiv. The Congress Party has continually promoted a secularist ideology, and so has claimed to represent *all* Indians, including Muslims and Sikhs, as well as Hindus. Against this, some commentators have argued that the Congress Party have hidden a strong Hindu nationalism behind this secular ideology.

However, in the 1990s a strong surge of popular support developed for a new and more explicit form of Hindu nationalism, based on the idea of India as a nation, culture, and place that is defined historically by its Hindu-ness. According to this idea India is, in a sense, a 'sacred entity' and all who live in the place are Hindu. Thus Indian Muslims are Muslim through conversion – that is, people whose ancestors converted centuries ago from Hinduism to Islam. Such an idea of religious nationalism is certainly much less pluralistic and accommodating than the more mainstream Congress form, and is associated with various organisations including the Vishwa Hindu Parishad (the World Hindu Council), and the Bharatiya Janata Party (or BJP, a Hindu nationalistic political party). The BJP have been in government in India since 1999, although their policies in power have tended to be less extremely anti-Muslim/pro-Hindu than their rhetoric has led observers to expect.

Ethnicity

Contemporary globalisation is also framed by idea of ethnicity. This refers to the sense of shared culture and identity, bonded by such things as a shared language, way of life, a body of cultural products, and a sense of common connection or relatedness. There is some ambiguity about how ethnicity and nationalism differ, although nationalism usually has a more explicit and tangible connection to political entities (i.e. nation-states). However, many nations are premised on the idea of a shared ethnicity – for example, Scotland is the nation of the Scottish people, England likewise of the English people, etc. But ethnicity and nationality are not always the same, indeed most nation-states are made up of more than one ethnic group. The USA is not ethnically homogeneous – there are many different cultures and ethnicities in the American nation. India likewise has many *regional* ethnic groups within its nation (including Panjabis, Bengalis, Gujaratis, Tamils, Telegus, Maharashtrians, and many others). Even within a small nation such as England there is a diversity of cultural groups (between the north, the west, and the southeast). Furthermore nationalism in England often relates to British nationalism, which condenses various nationalities into a single nation-state of England, Scotland, and Wales.

One could say that ethnicity is a more localised form of nationalism, relating to a particular (and usually smaller) area of land. The concept of ethnicity usually brings together an idea of a people, a culture, a place, and the unity of blood ties: a group of people who are descended from common ancestors, who own and belong to a particular area. This is often also linked to a concept of biological (or genetic) homogeneity – in a sense, a racial conceptualisation of ethnicity. If an ethnic group is bound together by shared blood ties (as well as their culture), then it is thought they must be all alike in a physical sense. Thus, there is a popular image of red-headed Scots, or 'stiff upper lip' English.

In this regard it is hard to make a clear distinction between ethnicity and race. For many, the term ethnicity is often used euphemistically, to politely avoid using the term race. As a scientific concept, race has itself been largely discredited as a way of describing and accounting for differences between humans – in terms of genetics, there is no real way of differentiating a Scot from a German, nor indeed differences that are usually marked out in terms of skin colour. Instead, the *idea* of race was a concept developed by scientists in the colonial era to give ideological justification for the political and social idea of differentiating the powerful 'white' Europeans from the exploited 'black' Africans and Asians (see, for example, Young 1995).

Some argue that the concept of ethnicity does something similar, using social scientific rather than biological ideas of difference (Caglar 1997). In particular, the term 'ethnic' is most often used in relation to people and groups perceived as 'different' from the mainstream. So culturally distinct groups, such as Arabs and Indians, may be labelled as 'ethnic minorities' in the UK, whilst there is little recognition of the fact that Scots and other *majority* groups are similarly ethnic. In that sense, the term refers primarily to a sense of distinction and difference, based on a concept of skin colour differentiation. That is, from a 'white' ethnic perspective in a country such as the UK, 'ethnic' people are those of a different skin colour from the majority, as perceived by that majority.

Given the ambiguities of this term ethnicity, what uses does it have in understanding religious differences within the contemporary world? Some religious groups are primarily organised around a concept of shared ethnicity, where indeed it is nearly impossible to say which is more important. The sharing of Jewish-ness by Jewish people highlights this most clearly: to be Jewish is not only about belonging to a religious community, following the religious practices coming from the Torah, from

Abraham, Moses, and the prophets, but also to a distinctive (and biologically determined) cultural group with their own traditions and history. For many Jews in the contemporary world, one or other of these elements is more important. Secular Jews may emphasise the ethnic/cultural identity, orthodox Jews may emphasise the religiosity, but many agree that it is a matter of both.

Even so, although many would label Judaism as an 'ethnic religion', there is considerable ethnic diversity within the Jewish people. There are profound cultural differences between the Sephardic Jews, who have lived for centuries in Arab countries and so are largely Arabic (or Middle-Eastern) Jews, and the Azkhinazian Jews, who are descended from the Jewish communities of mainly central Europe. At one level, what unites them is a common religion and ethnicity: that is, a common religious heritage of Judaism, and a sense of descent from common ancestors, the ancient Jews of Judea and Israel. And, furthermore, the issue of nationalism helps to bring this ethnically diverse ethnic group together into a political unit, in the state of Israel. To complicate this even more, Israel itself is not an explicitly religious state, and it also includes other non-Jewish ethnic groups (such as Israeli Arabs), and religions (Arab Muslims and Christians).

Multiculturalism, transnationalism, and diasporas

The German anthropologist Gerd Baumann (1999) has argued that we should understand these various aspects of the contemporary world as making up an interactive framework with profound social and cultural consequences. Together, nationalism, ethnicity, and religion comprise what he calls the 'multicultural riddle', a matrix of complex ideas which can only be understood if we rethink the terms of the questions we ask. All three reflect each other, none are fixed categories, but come out of and blend with the others, and vary according to other factors (both historical and sociological).

In saying this, Baumann is highlighting one of the most challenging political and social debates at the beginning of the twenty-first century: that is, what is multiculturalism, and how can it be made to work? As his argument shows, the study of religion forms an important part of this debate, since diversity and cultural differences are often bound up with religious differences – in ways that are sometimes not acknowledged even by those who study and implement political policies of multicultural society.

But what does it mean to talk of multiculturalism? Globalisation and post-colonialism help give some answers to this question, since these particular forces have led to multiculturalism in many contemporary countries. In western Europe there are now very significant minority groups with cultural and ancestral links to places outside of Europe. In Britain, up to 5 per cent (i.e. 3 million) of the total population is 'minority ethnic' (mostly descended from African Caribbeans and South Asians, see Modood *et al.* 1997). In France there is a sizeable population (approximately 2.8 million) of north Africans (mainly Muslims), whilst in Germany the population of Turks who migrated to the country as 'guest workers' now numbers around 1.8 million (Shadid and van Koningsveld 1991).

Such minority populations have emerged because of the prior histories of colonial rule. Thus it is no accident that Britain has Caribbean and South Asian minority groups – I have already mentioned the significance of British colonial rule in South Asia, whilst in eighteenth-century Caribbean countries Britain became extremely wealthy through the businesses of slave labour and sugar plantations. France's north African minorities (from Algiers and Tunisia) likewise reflect their own colonial interests in those same countries. Such minority groups, formed through migration, explain their presence by saying 'we are over here [in Europe] because you [Europeans] were over there'.

This movement of people across the globe, for permanent settlement and for temporary travel, is described in general terms as transnationalism. That is, we can talk of 'transnational' movements of people (across nations), and even of 'transnational communities' – groups of people who are linked across national boundaries by a common culture and a common sense of belonging. Thus people from India have travelled across the world. In the colonial era there were large transnational movements from India to East Africa (what are now Uganda and Kenya), South Africa, Fiji, and the Caribbean (particularly Trinidad, Guyana, and Surinam). In the post-colonial era, particularly in the 1960s and 1970s, other Indians migrated to the UK, whilst since 1965 there has been fairly constant migration of Indians to work and settle in the USA.

These transnational Indians came from different areas of India, migrated for different reasons, have different religions and cultures, and experience quite different social and economic conditions where they have settled. Together they make up a 'transnational Indian community', brought together by a sense of having their common ancestral roots in the Indian nation – albeit rather distant historically and geographically for many. The term *diaspora* is often used to describe this: thus there are for example Indian, Hindu, Sikh, Pakistani and Panjabi diasporas. Diaspora refers to the cultural dispersion of people across the globe, creating a diffuse network of people who are separated from each other, but who perceive themselves as united by transnational and cultural connections. These diasporas may exist primarily in the people's imaginations, or may have some tangible reality – such as communication links (through new technologies such as the internet) or physical travel.

The development of diasporas through transnational migration and settlement creates a range of culturally complex situations. Within the broad 'Hindu diaspora', there are now people of Indian ancestry settled in new contexts across the globe. In each context, their cultures and religions are involved in processes of transplantation and adaptation, as individuals and groups seek to accommodate their own expectations and ways of life to the local circumstances. The experience of 'being a Hindu' is different in England from the USA, or Fiji, or South Africa. And in particular, the children and later descendants of migrants will make further adaptations and recontexualisations of their traditions.

Likewise, in Britain there are now around 1.6 million Muslim people, mostly children and grandchildren of people who left rural Pakistan in the 1960s. The majority of these 'second generation' British Muslims are not 'immigrants', they are people born in the UK, who are as familiar with the native British cultures as with the religion and culture of their parents. In such cases their practices of Islam are shaped not only by their communities' teaching and expectations, but their own sense of how to make Islam relevant to their particular lives.

The processes of transnational migration and the development of diasporas create many different cases of *hybridity*. That is, a British Muslim is *both* Muslim *and* British: s/he is not one or the other, nor caught in the middle between the two, but is creatively trying to find ways in which that new combination can be brought into being and practised. This is most usually talked about in terms of cultural hybridity (such as being British Pakistani), and most examples of hybridity refer to cultural fusions (see Modood and Werbner 1997). For example, there are numerous instances of new cultural forms arising out of the interplay between Asian and British cultures (from the growth of 'Indian restaurants', to bhangra music). However, it is less easy perhaps to see the connections between such hybridity and religious groups and identities in such a multicultural context. As I noted in Chapter 2, the idea of 'religious hybridity' somehow brings to mind an idea of 'syncretic' and 'inauthentic' fusions of religions.

Although there are some examples of consciously syncretic and hybrid religions, most syncretism usually occurs discretely, creating changes in groups that consider themselves to be 'traditional' (see Shaw and Stewart 1994). For example, the International Society for Krishna Consciousness (ISKCON, or the 'Hare Krishnas'), is a traditional form of Hinduism from eastern India which became prominent in the west in the late 1960s and 1970s, when it attracted significant numbers of converts to its rigorous way of life. In many senses the content of the religion is not hybridising and it is not syncretic. Converts to ISKCON follow a strict Hindu way of life, including an intense ritual-devotional routine, and strictly vegetarian and non-violent practice. But the idiom of ISKCON is to make a particular form of Hindu tradition accessible within a western context, and so demonstrates the hybridising process of a religious culture changing through transplantation. Further to this, in the past twenty years or so, ISKCON in Britain and the USA has also become an important place for Hindus of Indian descent, particularly those who have been raised within a western context. Because of ISKCON's adaptation to western cultural forms (such as its use of English, and a wide-ranging literature and set of teaching methods that are designed to communicate the tradition within a western context), the group are reaching second-generation British and American Hindus.

Thus hybridity creates traditional religious cultures that are simultaneously new and innovative. This can also be applied to many developments of Islam within western contexts. Muslims of Pakistani descent in Britain are now beginning to ask how much the Islam that they practise should be Pakistani, or whether it should relate more specifically to their British and transnational context. The relationship between Islam and ethnicity is complex. Muslims think of Islam as transcending particular national, cultural, or ethnic boundaries – because of the central religious idea of the *ummah*, or community of Islam, which unites all its followers. At the same time, however, the history and literature of Muslim traditions identifies much of Islam with specifically Arabic cultures. However, Islam is a clearly transnational religion, in which there are many different forms of Muslim ethnicity, with their own cultural or local forms of Islam: Pakistani, Malay, Indonesian, sub-Saharan African, and now British and American, etc. Therefore Muslims in Pakistan (whether they are living in Pakistan itself or elsewhere) practise a form of Islam which is orthodox to Islamic traditions, but is also particular to the local ethnic and national cultures.

So among young British Muslims whose families originated from Pakistan, questions are now being asked about whether they should practise a less ethnically Pakistani form of Islam. Or whether there is a more pure, de-ethnicised, or more global set of practices that could be re-oriented to the particular local circumstances of Britain. In most cases, this leads to various groups interpreting Islamic basics (as set out mostly in traditional texts such as the Qur'an and the Hadith) with reference to predominantly Arab-derived social organisations, whilst accepting that the English language is a dominant form of social communication.

Events in recent years, such as the Muslim outrage in the UK against the publication of Salman Rushdie's book *The Satanic Verses* (in 1988), and the 2001–3 military campaigns by the USA and the UK against the Taliban and Al-Qa'eda in Afghanistan, and Saddam Hussein in Iraq, have prompted a range of responses to how Muslim values should be adapted to new cultural circumstances. The media dwelt on how a small minority of British Muslims reacted fiercely in an anti-western way, with them arguing that Islam transcends nationalities, and so their Britishness is far less important than following Islam. In a very few cases, some Muslim men travelled to Afghanistan to fight on the side of the Taliban against the US and UK forces. However, by far the larger majority of Muslims in this context responded in a quite different way, considering Al-Qa'eda's violence as an affront against Muslim values, and so reaffirming their own nationality and religion (as British or American Muslims) as not contradictory, but as integrated.

More generally, however, the issue of multiculturalism in western countries is not only about the relatively small pockets of religious and cultural diasporic groups who are marked out as obviously 'different' from the mainstream, such as British Muslims, American Hindus, etc. Multiculturalism also concerns the wider society, and the study of multiculturalism and religious diversity in the contemporary western world is about how whole societies and cultures are being transformed by such globalisation and transnationalism.

In Europe this has come to the fore very recently in a number of ways. In Holland in May 2002, a charismatic political leader called Pim Fortuyn was brutally assassinated shortly before a national election, bringing to prominence an already evident rise of anti-immigration and anti-multiculturalist sentiment in many European nations. Fortuyn was a popular figure, and his death put his political party briefly into a prominent role in the Dutch parliament. His primary message was one that proclaimed the tolerance of Dutch culture, whilst it simultaneously complained very intolerantly of what he saw as the 'threat' of immigration and the minority cultural, ethnic, and religious groups who had already settled in the Netherlands. Fortuyn's polemic was not only against 'immigrants' and outsiders, but also against Muslims and Islam in particular. In short, he argued that the Dutch (i.e. non-Muslim Dutch people) should not tolerate what he described as the intolerance of Muslim people. On a number of occasions Fortuyn described Islam and Muslims as 'backward', compared with the liberal progressiveness of Dutch culture.

Similar linkages between anti-multiculturalist agendas and specific anti-religious intolerance can be found in other contexts, usually directed at Islam in particular. For example, the British National Party, a right-wing extremist organisation – much more obviously fascistic than Fortuyn – have likewise managed to get a measure of political support in parts of England where they have argued vociferously against the 'Islamic threat'. Indeed, much public discussion on multiculturalism in the west relies increasingly on issues of not only cultural, but also religious diversity. In general, certain religious and cultural minority groups (such as Hindus, Sikhs and Jews) are seen as 'acceptable' and generally well respected by the majority population, whilst other minorities (particular Muslims and black Africans) are largely defined as problematic and a 'threat'. The discrimination and also violence that this has produced in recent years has come to be known as 'Islamophobia', which some argue is as insidious a social problem as anti-semitism was at the beginning of the twentieth century (Runnymede Trust 1997).

Fundamentalism and violence

Behind many of these perceptions of Islam as 'backward' and intolerant is the lingering association of the concept of *fundamentalism* with Muslims. There is now a long history of events and images in which Muslims have been seen, by westerners, as 'fundamentalist' extremists at odds with (what is seen as) the tolerant liberalism of the west. From the creation of the Islamic state of Iran in 1979, through events such as the *Satanic Verses* affair, to the Gulf War, to 9/11, and beyond, there has been no shortage of occasions for westerners to build up stereotypes of Muslims as intolerant fundamentalists. The simplicity of this perspective is rarely considered, nor the diversity of Muslim ideas, nor indeed the ways in which the image of the one-dimensional threatening Arab Muslim is largely a media (particularly Hollywood) fiction (see Said 1985).

The term fundamentalism is not only used about Muslims, although it has come to be defined primarily in terms of Muslims. In fact, the term is derived from self-descriptions of particular American Christian groups in the early twentieth century, who wished to orient their religious practice to the fundamentals (as they saw them) of particular Biblical Christian teaching. Beyond that the term has been extended to other religious groups – many Sikhs in the 1980s were labelled as 'fundamentalists' because of their campaign for Khalistan. In the 1990s extremist Hindu nationalists became labelled as 'Hindu fundamentalists'. There are also 'Jewish fundamentalists', referring to those who see the eradication of the Palestinian presence in 'Greater Israel' as a divine imperative, and 'Buddhist fundamentalists' who are engaged in a civil war in Sri Lanka with Tamil Hindus.

These cases share a common theme of religious values and identities helping to create and justify violent political conflicts. The term 'fundamentalist' also often highlights a very strict code of living and unequal power relations between women and men. But this does not necessarily give justification to the very widespread use of the general term 'fundamentalist', which tends to act as a broad and simplistic explanation for complex situations. Most Muslims are not fundamentalist in any real sense of the term, and it is particularly unhelpful to perceive all Muslims as 'vicious and violent extremist' fundamentalists simply because they are Muslims. On the other hand, many religious people are fundamentalist in the sense that they live by and try to practise a set of fundamental assumptions about the world. On that level, indeed, one can also talk about fundamentalist humanists, liberals, or whatever.

Because of these problems and ambiguities with the term 'fundamentalist' it is more useful to find other ways of talking about the various religious contexts that the term tries to describe. In recent decades there has been a revival of *political Islam* in the Muslim world, led by a number of prominent political and religious leaders, largely reacting against colonial and post-colonial policies. This political and revivalist Islam is often described as Islamism, and its practitioners as Islamists, but it must be noted that the majority of such Islamists are not advocates of the brutal political violence that is normally associated with the crude stereotype of the 'Muslim fundamentalist'. Organised political violence, such as practised by Hamas suicide bombers in Israel, is no more representative of Islamism than sectarian Loyalist violence in Northern Ireland is representative of Protestant Christianity.

On a more general level, however, this connection between religion and violence raises questions about whether religion is 'naturally' disposed to violence or otherwise whether certain religions promote or encourage violence more than others. In response to the first question, many assume that there is a connection – there is, for example, the commonly repeated phrase that 'religion is the cause of most wars'. My argument so far in this book, however, has been that there is nothing 'inherent' about the 'nature' of religion, and that religious aspects of culture are integral to and inseparable from the wider cultural picture.

People may go to war about their religious identities, and the politics of religious interests and differences may be bound up with other political differences, such as nationalisms and ethnicities. Religious values can give very clear ideological justifications and rationalisations for warfare and violence, particularly because religious ideologies, like other ideologies, can be presented as involving strong certainties. But this does not necessarily 'explain' the connections between conflicts and religions. It simply points out that conflicts can arise from those elements of cultural life that we generally call religious – as they do from other related and intertwined elements of cultural life, such as politics, economics, ethnicity, nationalism, and so on.

Instead of looking for such generalisations, it is therefore more useful to focus on the specifics of particular conflicts which involve religious differences. Factors such as globalisation, localisation, ethnicity, nationalism, transnationalism and diasporas all create a complex web of explanations behind all conflicts in the contemporary world. However, it is also necessary to understand the historical development of such conflicts, and how global and local forces of economics, ethnicity and individual human agency have brought about particular situations. In these respects, there are no simple explanations.

Secularisation in the west

Returning to comments I made at the beginning of this chapter, the study of religions in the contemporary world also needs to consider the general question of whether religion is on the decline, indeed perhaps dying out. This view is most prevalent in western societies, where the simple equation is that modern industrial and economic progress ('modernity') is antagonistic to religion, and that the progress of modernity will mean the inevitable decline of religion. What is quite blatantly ignored about this idea is that it refers in particular to certain traditions of religion in western culture: that is the Christian churches. So when most writers talk about secularisation, they are actually referring specifically to the 'decline of Christianity' rather than the more general decline of religion.

But even so, what is the term referring to? In what ways is secularisation occurring, or more particularly what aspects of mainstream religion are being affected by the processes of secularisation? It must be stressed that the term itself is usually intended to refer in a neutral way to the processes of the decline of religion. Secularisation is about saying that there is a decline that can be observed and perhaps accounted for (see Wilson 1991). It is not the same as claiming that the process is 'good' or 'bad', or indeed what the inevitable consequences of the process will be. And furthermore, to say that there is a general secularisation process does not mean that religion has disappeared. There are still a lot of people practising Christian and other traditions, regardless of whether secularisation is taking place.

There are, in fact, many ways of interpreting the social processes that the term secularisation refers to, and indeed there is a distinct lack of agreement between sociologists of religion as to whether and to what extent it is possible to say that there is such a thing. The 'common-sense' view seems to suggest that religion (primarily Christianity) is on the decline (e.g. Bruce 1996). In Britain, there is a lot less going on that we can call religious than was the case 100 years ago – although the same cannot be said quite so clearly for the USA. If we look primarily at church attendance and membership figures, then Christianity does seem to be on the decline. In most churches in Britain, and other European countries, fewer people go to church on Sundays, and fewer people actually belong to churches.

But the secularisation argument is a little more subtle than this. For Bryan Wilson (1982, 1991), the numbers are not the only thing of importance, the processes of secularisation refer more importantly to the role of religion within contemporary society. That is, for Wilson religion (and again I must stress he means Christianity in particular) has lost the social significance that it once had. He says secularisation is 'the process by which religious institutions, actions, and consciousness lose their social significance'. This explains why there might still be a lot of religious practice going on. People have not necessarily stopped being religious, it is simply that the way people are religious, and the way that religion works in the social (or public) domain have been transformed by social changes.

Wilson refers to this as a 'privatisation' of religion. That is, there is a general tendency for religion to be practised as an individual or private pursuit, rather than in a more communal or social network. It is up to each person, within such a secularised society, to practise her or his own private religion, for her or his own sake. Traditional aspects of Christian practice in western culture, such as status and community, have become much less important. However, whilst this may be a useful description of the way in which religion is generally perceived in Britain at the beginning of the twenty-first century, it fails to take into account the fact that the sum of all the private religions is in itself a strong social force. The idea of a 'privatised religion' brings to mind the line from the Monty Python film *Life of Brian*, when the eponymous anti-hero tells a crowd of his would-be disciples that they are 'all individuals', to which they respond in unison, *en masse*, by saying 'yes, we are all individuals'.

The historian Callum Brown (2001) presents a rather different perspective on the secularisation argument. Rejecting the idea that secularisation can be proven or disproven by the use of statistics, he looks instead at the overall ways in which Christianity has worked as a discourse in Britain. The idea of discourse here derives from Foucault, and overlaps to an extent with the concept of culture. That is, Brown looks at the ways in which Christian discourse and culture have changed in Britain in particular over the past century. Rather than seeing a gradual decline in religion, Brown argues that the immediate post-Second World War era (the 1950s) was a time of intense religious practice, in which Christian values played a prominent role in many aspects of cultural life. But this collapsed during a period of wide-ranging cultural change in the 1960s and after, at the same time as the rise of the counter-culture of the 'hippy' era.

Brown explains this transformation in terms of the changing roles of women in British society during this period. Previously women had been seen as predominantly home-makers in the domestic sphere, and ideology given religious justification with woman as the 'angel in the house'. So in 1950s Britain, the weight of maintaining Christian religious practice largely came down on women. In spite of the leadership of the main churches being exclusively male, it was women (particularly in the domestic sphere, and in supporting roles in church organisations) that kept the churches, and Christianity in general, as a prominent part of cultural life. So the rise of feminism in the 1960s and 1970s, along with economic and educational changes that gave women more opportunities to work beyond the home, left the churches without a crucial part of their power base. If the churches no longer had women playing this supportive role of maintaining the Christian discourse at the local level, then it was no wonder that their influence had collapsed. This is what Brown sees as having happened – leading to a process that he predicts (rather controversially) will lead eventually to 'the death of Christian Britain'.

Again, however, we must pick out from this the distinction between talking of the decline of Christianity in Britain and the decline of religion in general. All of these theories highlight in particular transformations in the ways in which religions are practised in Britain. This refers either to the decline of a particular discourse or tradition (i.e. Christianity), or otherwise to the ways in which religion is understood to have significance (e.g. moving, as Wilson says, from the social to the private sphere). Secularisation could, therefore, be seen as predominantly a way of talking about religious transformations – that is, changes to the religious culture of particular countries.

Such an idea of transformation may then be related to the wider context of changes within the contemporary world. Each country has its own mix of social changes, in which the changes of secularisation or transformation are occurring according to the specific contexts. In many, but not all, of the European nations where Christianity has traditionally been culturally dominant, there has been a decline in the way Christianity is viewed and practised. Alongside this, and indeed alongside the growth of transnational communities and multiculturalism, there has also been a process of religious pluralisation: of cultures and people interacting on a popular level with a number of different religious traditions.

Pluralism, alternatives, and de-/re-traditionalisation

Arguments on secularisation are rather diffident about the issue of religious pluralism, or diversity. Most writers tend to dismiss the presence of minority religious groups, such as Hindus or Muslims, on the basis that they are statistically irrelevant to the wider social picture. Some writers do, however, address another area of religious diversity, that is, the development of many different alternative religious traditions alongside (or in place of) the seeming decline of Christian churches.

The sociologists Stark and Bainbridge, however, point to the rise of alternatives as a proof of their own theory of secularisation. For them, secularisation is the 'erosion of belief in the supernatural' (1985), which they do not consider to be happening on the scale most observers assume. Instead, although people are losing interest in Christian practice, religiosity is still present in the many different alternative sources of religious practice. In most cases the attention has focused on the rise of particular religious groups: organisations with clear structures and teachings, which have been given the general label of 'new religious movements' (or NRMs).

I tend not to like the term NRMs, for various reasons. In its favour, it was coined by scholars of religion in reaction to the more popularly used term 'cults'. The word cult is inadequate, and is indeed pejorative. It is often used unthinkingly to describe an extremely diverse set of religious groups, which share nothing in common with each other except that they are new, or at least seem new to the context of western culture. 'Cults' also brings to mind problems and violence, and draws on a stereotypical image, based on a very small number of cases, of groups in which tragedies have occurred. There is no denying that there have been some religious groups where violence has been committed, the most famous being in the People's Temple, Jonestown in 1978, when 900 adults and children died through suicide and murder. But the term 'cult' generalises from such extreme and very rare cases to a wide range of other groups. So as a means of avoiding this loaded word, scholars of religion decided to replace it with the term 'new religious movement', which was felt to be more neutral.

My sense, however, is that NRM tends to be used quite euphemistically – as a polite way of talking about 'cults' (in the way that the term 'ethnic' is often a way of saying 'race'). Much of the debate over NRMs has tended to repeat many of the assumptions of the term 'cult', whilst trying to go beyond them. Thus NRM scholars usually discuss together such disparate groups as Pagans, Hare Krishnas, the Unification Church, New Agers, Scientologists, and many others. Despite attempts to distinguish these groups into types (such as by Roy Wallis (1984) into 'world-affirming', 'world-accommodating', and 'world-rejecting'), the tendency has been to homogenise them. If

NRMs are not necessarily 'cults' they are still seen as being in a class of their own, to be explained by certain theories such as the redirection of religion in response to secularisation, or as a form of social protest.

The diversity of the various groups that are called NRMs is probably far more important than their similarities, and so it is unhelpful to lump 'them' all together under the single term. The term also glosses over other significant elements of a number of the groups so labelled. In particular, if we take a few 'typical' NRMs – for example, the Unification Church, the Hare Krishnas, and Soka Gakkai – we find that one thing they have in common is not their newness, but the roots they have in globalisation and transnationalism. The Unification Church (or the Moonies) was founded by the Korean minister Sun Myung Moon in the 1950s, and spread to the USA and other western countries in the 1970s. The Hare Krishnas were formed in the west by an Indian called Prabhupada in 1966, whilst Soka Gakkai is a Japanese Buddhist group (a breakaway from Nicheren Soshu), which spread to the west in the 1970s and 1980s.

All of these movements are products of globalisation – they are transnational movements that have taken root through conversion in western contexts, and in all three cases have sizeable followers of not only western converts, but also western (American and British) Koreans, Indians, and Japanese. That is not to ignore the specific contexts in which they are found, or their seeming 'newness' in these new contexts. But the term NRM simplifies these complexities. Again we can return to the concept of hybridity – like most religions in the contemporary world, they are traditional religions that are practised in the context of hybridity, by people within the globalised contexts of multicultural and transnational communities.

Furthermore, not all new or alternative forms of religion are quite so organised as the term 'new religious movements' seems to suggest. Many people do still belong to specific religious groups with clear structures, such as churches, but others take part in what can be described as 'disorganised religion'. This fits in, to an extent, with Bryan Wilson's idea of 'privatised' religion, and is commonly referred to as the advent of a 'spiritual supermarket' in which the 'believer' (or religious practitioner) can 'pick and mix' their religion.

These terms reflect a general sense of anxiety about this development, that religion 'should be' more structured than this. Of course, such an assumption is itself premised on the idea that religion 'should be' something like Christianity (that is, organised), and so religious practices that do not conform to this expectation are 'not right'. In some ways, the advent of disorganised religion is a reaction against what are seen as the constraints of Christian traditions, and so it is not surprising that in some respects certain elements of Christian practice are being rejected.

The word commonly used to describe this disorganised religiosity is 'spirituality'. Many people now say that they are 'not religious' (often taken to be associated with Christian practices), but they do have a 'spirituality' (which is unfocused, eclectic and personal). There are many ways in which such a spirituality may be practised: often through reading certain types of books (such those found in the prolific 'Mind-Body-Spirit' sections of most bookshops), through certain practices such as meditation and chanting, and through leading an ethical lifestyle (see Sutcliffe and Bowman 2000). In most cases such spirituality is no more formal than this, and is influenced by many different religious and cultural traditions. One common characteristic is not so much its actual content (in terms of particular beliefs, or things that are done), but rather a common orientation to 'finding something more' – seekership. The end results of this seekership can be quite diverse – some people's paths of seekership lead them to some form of 'traditional' Christianity, whilst for others it may be a form of Native American shamanism. Others may take various traditions (e.g. Japanese Reiki, Tantra, Sufism), either separately or together, in a blend that they feel makes sense to them. Again such diversity cannot be understood without reference to globalisation. The global international currency of such 'foreign imports' gives them additional status in comparison with what are seen as the constraints of the 'home-grown' product.

In these respects, the growth of alternatives is a result of processes of de-traditionalisation, which relates to the idea that modernity is about moving on from the conventions of the past to new, less traditional forms of culture and practice. However, such de-traditionalisation is not always so straightforward. Few of the new or alternative forms of religion or spirituality are completely non-traditional, they just seem less traditional than traditional Christian cultures. Moreover, very often the quest of 'seekership' can produce new forms of tradition – whether that involves immersing oneself in traditional Indian Hindu culture and religion (for example, within ISKCON), or some other more organised group. In such cases, the 'new' traditions can be more rigid and conservative than the ones being rejected. However, in other cases, the tradition turned to is seen as more liberating and less constricting, perhaps because of its antiquity.

One significant example of this is the rapid growth of Paganism in the 1980s and 1990s, in the USA, Britain, and various other parts of the world. Paganism relates to the set of religious traditions that existed in various parts of Europe and beyond prior to the rise of Christianity, such as ancient Greece, Scandinavia, Celtic Britain, and Egypt. The Pagan revival, sometimes called Neo-Paganism, in the contemporary era relates these ancient traditions (as much as they can be reconstructed from historical and archaeological records) to the conditions of the early twenty-first century. Pagan ideology stresses gender equality, at the level of social practice and in terms of theistic ideas (with a goddess and god), and also is strongly oriented to an ecological awareness (seeing 'nature' and 'the earth' as a living deity and life-force). Much of this places Paganism within the general trends of contemporary culture, as does its emphasis on small fluid social organisations and personal autonomy – what one believes and practices as a Pagan is up to the individual.

The development of Paganism also comes from an interesting mixture of newness and innovation. Much of Pagan practice was brought together self-consciously in the twentieth century from cultural currents such as Druidry, esotericism, magic beliefs and ideas, as well as spiritual traditions (on gender and nature) that have also developed within Christian churches. But one significant area of Pagan practice is the idea of the antiquity of the movement – because of its pre-Christian heritage, Pagans tend to describe Christianity as the 'new religion' (being a 'mere' two millennia old). Pagans tend to look towards rediscovering a 'new' sense of traditionalism – or a re-traditionalisation – that extends the sense of history of culture and place far beyond the modern era. Thus, within Celtic Paganism, the religious practice is related to connecting with the ancient Celtic cultures and religions of Scotland, Wales, and Ireland, which in themselves involve a refound sense of ethnicity and nationalism.

In conclusion, what can be said about the future of religion in the twenty-first century? Of course, the main response is *which* religions? It is likely that some religions may decline – such as Christian churches in Britain and other parts of Europe. Even so, Christianity in other parts of the world (such as in Africa, Asia and South America) is thriving and is likely to continue to do so. There can be no single explanation to account for possible changes – secularisation may tell us something about certain social processes, but only if related to a much wider global picture. Other trends, such as fundamentalism (or revivalism) seem to oppose the secularisation process, but are themselves produced by a recent history of colonialism and post-colonial inequalities and western political domination. The transformation of most European nations into multicultural societies has thrown up certain challenges which are only now beginning to be realised and addressed. One such challenge is how countries that are predominantly Christian in culture can accept diversity, and how transnational religious cultures – such as the various Muslim traditions – can be accommodated for and recognised as part of the western cultural sphere.

The seeming decline of Christianity within western cultures is by no means absolute, and it is probably still too early to predict its 'death' in Britain or anywhere else. But recent decades have produced substantial transformations of religious practices and identities, which are still in the process of development. Whether this is described as 'religion' or 'spirituality', the study of religion is a means by which these significant aspects of human activity can be related to the cultural forces of which they are a part.

Summary

- Contemporary religious traditions are embedded within the processes of modernity. All religions are shaped by forces such as post-colonialism, globalisation, nationalism, ethnicity, and transnationalism.

- To study any particular religion we must look at both the local and the global level, to see how particular processes in a region or country may be affected by global issues such as the movement of people and international communications and travel. Post-colonial economic and political inequality may also produce both global and local responses.

- Multiculturalism can be understood not only in terms of nationality and ethnicity, but also with regard to religion. All three parts of this 'multicultural triangle' can change and influence each other.

- The discussion of a decline in religion in western countries has largely been concerned with changes in traditional Christian churches. Secularisation can be seen as a transformation in religious practice, producing responses of privatisation, pluralisation, innovation, and de/re-traditionalisation.

- For many people in the west, 'religion' has become 'spirituality' – that is, de-institutionalised and more individualist religion.

Suggestions for further reading

For some useful introductions to globalisation, see: Roland Robertson, *Globalization* (1992); and Ulf Hannerz, *Transnational Connections* (1996). See also David Lehmann,

'Religion and Globalization' (2002); Peter Beyer, *Religion and Globalisation* (1994); and Arjun Appardurai, *Modernity at Large* (1996). See also Linda Woodhead and Paul Heelas, *Religion in Modern Times* (2000).

On multiculturalism see Gerd Baumann's *The Multicultural Riddle* (1999); and C.W. Watson's *Multiculturalism* (2000). On ethnicity, see Thomas Hylland Eriksen's *Ethnicity and Nationalism* (1993). On issues of cultural and religious diversity in Britain, see Roger Ballard's collection *Desh Pardesh: The South Asian Presence in Britain* (1994); and Gerald Parson's *The Growth of Religious Diversity* (1993). On more theoretical issues of hybridity see Tariq Modood and Pnina Werbner's *Debating Cultural Hybridity* (1997); and Rosalind Shaw and Charles Stewart's 'Introduction: problematizing syncretism' (1994).

On political Islam and Islamic see John Esposito, *Islam and Politics* (1991); and R. Hrair Dekmejian, *Islam in Revolution* (1995). On the issues arising from the study of Islam and 11 September 2001, see John Esposito, *Unholy War: Terror in the Name of Islam* (2002); and Malise Ruthven, *A Fury For God* (2002).

Bryan Wilson's argument on secularisation can be found in his essay 'Secularization' (1991). Some good introductory chapters on the secularisation debates are in Alan Aldridge's *Religion in the Contemporary World* (2000), chapters 4 and 5; and in Malcolm Hamilton's *The Sociology of Religion* (1995), chapter 15. See also Peter Berger's 'Secularization and de-secularization' (2002).

There are numerous introductory books on 'new religious movements' of which the best are probably: George Chryssides, *Exploring New Religions* (1999); Bryan Wilson and Jamie Cresswell, *New Religious Movements* (1999); Eileen Barker and Margit Warburg, *New Religions and New Religiosity* (1998); and Eileen Barker, *New Religious Movements: A Practical Introduction* (1995).

On 'New Age' and alternative spirituality see Steven Sutcliffe and Marion Bowman's collection *Beyond New Age: Exploring Alternative Spirituality* (2000); Steven Sutcliffe's *Children of the New Age* (2002); and Paul Heelas' *The New Age Movement* (1996).

Appendix

The study of religion and culture

Below are listed some of the key assumptions behind this book, and which I consider to be essential elements of the study of religion and culture. They are not necessarily meant to be definitive, nor to sum up all of the key issues in this book – for these, you are advised to make use of the summaries at the end of each chapter. Instead, the points listed below are intended to give a general summary of the purpose and shape of the area of study which I have outlined in the book.

- Religion is studied as a human activity. In short, religion is a part of culture. The term refers to a wide range of activities which are part of, not separate from, the practice of culture and everyday life.
- The study of such 'religion' is concerned with what humans do, the texts and other cultural products they produce, and the statements and assumptions they make. In this sense it is something that is done, not something

that does – religious activity ('religioning'), rather than religion.

- 'Religion' is a not a *sui generis* category that exists in itself – that is, there is no essence of 'religion'. Instead it is a term with a multitude of meanings and references, to be understood with reference to other human activities.

- The study of religion and culture is based on methodological pluralism and interdisciplinarity. That is, it encompasses different methodological and disciplinary approaches. This includes both social science-based studies such as anthropology, psychology, and sociology, and humanities-based studies such as history, language and literature, cultural and media studies, politics and philosophy.

- There is a strong emphasis on studies with an empirical basis. Although there are many abstract and philosophical issues raised in the study of religion and culture, there needs to be some attempt to ground such issues in cultural practices in either contemporary or historical contexts. This requires a particular methodological approach, such as fieldwork, interviewing, surveying, archival research or textual analysis, or a combination of several of these.

- The study of religion and culture requires a measure of theoretical and methodological relativism. Although it is, perhaps, unavoidable, the student should avoid asserting one set of truth claims over any other – whether they are claims of metaphysical or cultural truth or superiority.

- As religion is a human activity, the analysis of religion and culture is the analysis of gender, ethnicity and other social relations and categories. Such gender, ethnic, sexual, and religious differences (and experiences) are in turn a product of (and also produce) power relations.

- The study of religion and culture is cross-cultural, multicultural, and post-colonial. The discipline is located in a global context of profound cross-cultural differences, which themselves are part of wider issues of power and inequality. Such studies are located within a particular context of historical and political circumstances, in which cultural (and religious) differences are largely framed by colonial and post-colonial processes.

- The use of the concept (or category) of religion is culture-bound – it is itself a product of these histories and political processes. It is not an objective or 'free-floating' term, but one that carries powerful political meanings on a range of different levels. It is put to use as a way of describing (and classifying) our conceptualisations of a range of experiences and practices.
- The study of religion and culture is highly relevant to our understanding of the contemporary world. Religion is a key element of many cultural issues, as well as a significant factor in the historical development of the worlds and contexts in which we live.

Bibliography

Adorno, Theodor and Max Horkheimer. 1972 [1947]. 'The culture industry: enlighten-ment as mass deception', in *Dialectic as Enlightenment*, trans. John Cumming. New York: Seabury Press. [Reprinted in Simon During, 1999, *The Cultural Studies Reader*, 2nd edition. London: Routledge.]

Ahmed, Leila. 1992. *Women and Gender in Islam*. New Haven: Yale University Press.

Aldridge, Alan. 2000. *Religion in the Contemporary World: A Sociological Introduction*. Cambridge: Polity.

Althusser, Louis. 1971. 'Ideology and ideological state apparatuses', in *Lenin and Philos-ophy*. New York: Monthly Review Press. [Reprinted in John Storey, 1994, *Cultural Theory and Popular Culture: A Reader*. London: Harvester Wheatsheaf. (Quotations taken from this reprint.)]

Anderson, Benedict. 1983. *Imagined Communities*. London: Verso.

Ang, Ien. 1985. *Watching Dallas: Soap Opera and the Melodramatic Imagination*. London: Methuen.

—— 1991. *Watching Television*. London: Routledge.

Anzaldúa, Gloria. 1999 [1987]. *Borderlands/La Frontera: The New Mestiza*, 2nd edition. San Francisco: Aunt Lute Books.

Appardurai, Arjun. 1996. *Modernity at Large: Cultural Dimensions of Globalization*. Minneapolis: University of Minnesota Press.

Arnal, William. 2000. 'Definition', in *Guide to the Study of Religion*, ed. W. Braun and R. McCutcheon. London: Cassell.

Asad, T. 1993. *Genealogies of Religion: Discipline and Reasons of Power in Christianity and Islam*. London: Johns Hopkins Press.

—— 2000. 'Agency and pain: an exploration', in *Culture and Religion* 1(1): 29–60.

Ballard, Roger. 1994. *Desh Pardesh: The South Asian Presence in Britain*. London: Hurst.

Barker, Eileen. 1995. *New Religious Movements: A Practical Introduction*. London: HMSO.

Barker, Eileen and Margit Warburg. 1998. *New Religions and New Religiosity*. Aarhus: University of Aarhus Press.

Barthes, Roland. 1968. 'The death of the author', in *Image, Music, Text*. London: Fontana.

—— 1972. *Mythologies*. London: Jonathan Cape.

Baumann, Gerd. 1999. *The Multicultural Riddle: Rethinking National, Ethnic, and Religious Identities*. New York: Routledge.

Beattie, John. 1964. *Other Cultures: Aims, Methods, and Achievements in Social Anthropology*. London: Routledge and Kegan Paul.

Beckerlegge, Gwilym. 2002. 'Hindu sacred images for the mass market', in *From Sacred Text to Internet*, ed. Gwilym Beckerlegge. Aldershot/Milton Keynes: Ashgate/Open University Press.

Bell, Catherine. 1992. *Ritual Theory, Ritual Practice*. Oxford: Oxford University Press.

—— 1997. *Ritual: Perspectives and Dimensions*. Oxford: Oxford University Press.

—— 1998 'Performance', in *Critical Terms for Religious Studies*, ed. Mark C. Taylor, Chicago: University of Chicago Press.

Bennett, Andrew (ed.). 1995. *Readers and Reading*. London: Longman.

Bennett, Andrew and Nicholas Royle. 1999. *Introduction to Literature, Criticism and Theory*, 2nd edition. Harlow: Prentice Hall.

Berger, Peter. 2002. 'Secularization and de-secularization', in *Religions in the Modern World*, ed. Linda Woodhead, Paul Fletcher, Hiroko Kawanami, and David Smith. London: Routledge.

Bertens, Hans. 2001. *Literary Theory: The Basics*. London: Routledge.

Beyer, Peter. 1994. *Religion and Globalisation*. London: Sage.

Bhabha, Homi. 1994. *The Location of Culture*. London: Routledge.

Bhargava, R. (ed.). 1998. *Secularism and Its Critics*. New Delhi: Oxford University Press.

Bhatt, Chetan. 1997. *Liberation and Purity: Race, New Religious Movements, and the Ethics of Postmodernity*. London: UCL Press.

Blackwood, Evelyn and Saskia E. Wieringa. 1999. 'Sapphic shadows: challenging the silence in the study of sexuality', in *Female Desires: Same Sex Desires and Transgender Practices across Cultures*. New York: Columbia University Press. [Reprinted in Darlene Juschka (ed.), 2001, *Feminism in the Study of Religion: A Reader*, London: Continuum.]

Bloch, Maurice. 1985. 'Religion and ritual', in *Encyclopaedia of Social Science*. London: Routledge and Kegan Paul.

—— 1986. *From Blessing to Violence: History and Ideology in the Circumcision Ritual of the Merina of Madagascar*. Cambridge: Cambridge University Press.

—— 1989 [1974]. 'Symbols, song, dance and features of articulation', in *Ritual, History and Power: Selected Papers in Anthropology*. London: Athlone Press.

—— 1992. *Prey into Hunter: The Politics of Religious Experience*. Cambridge: Cambridge University Press.

Bocock, Robert and Kenneth Thompson (eds). 1985. *Religion and Ideology: A Reader*. Manchester: Manchester University Press.

Bourdieu, Pierre. 1977. *Outline of a Theory of Practice*, trans. Richard Nice. Cambridge: Cambridge University Press.

—— 1984. *Distinction: A Social Critique of the Judgement of Taste*, trans. Richard Nice. London: Routledge.

—— 1992. *The Logic of Practice*, trans. Richard Nice. Cambridge: Polity Press.

Bowen, John. 1998. *Religions in Practice*. Boston: Allyn and Bacon.

Bowie, Fiona. 2000. *Anthropology of Religion*. Oxford: Blackwell.

Boyarin, Daniel. 1998. 'Gender', in *Critical Terms for Religious Studies*, ed. Mark C. Taylor. Chicago: University of Chicago Press.

Braun, Willi. 2000. 'Religion', in *Guide to the Study of Religion*, ed. W. Braun and R. McCutcheon. London: Cassell.

Brown, Callum. 2001. *The Death of Christian Britain: Understanding Secularization*, London: Routledge.

Bruce, Steve. 1996. *Religion in the Modern World: From Cathedrals to Cults*. Oxford: Oxford University Press.

Butler, Judith. 1990. *Gender Trouble: Feminism and the Subversion of Identity*. London: Routledge.

Bynum, Caroline Walker. 1996. 'Women's stories, women's symbols: a critique of Victor Turner's theory of liminality', in *Readings in Ritual Studies*, ed. R.L. Grimes. Upper Saddle River, NJ: Prentice Hall.

Caglar, Ayse. 1997. 'Hyphenated identities and the limits of "culture"', in *The Politics of Multiculturalism in the New Europe: Racism, Identity and Community*, ed. T. Modood and P. Werbner. London: Zed Books.

Carrette, Jeremy (ed.). 1999. *Religion and Culture by Michel Foucault*. Manchester: Manchester University Press.

—— 2000. *Foucault and Religion: Spiritual Corporality and Political Spirituality*. London and New York: Routledge.

Carroll, Robert. 1998. 'Lower case bibles: commodity culture and the Bible', in *Biblical Studies/Cultural Studies*, ed. Cheryl Exum and Stephen D. Moore. Sheffield: Sheffield Academic Press.

Casanova, José. *Public Religions in the Modern World*. Chicago: University of Chicago Press.

Chidester, David. 1996. *Savage Systems: Colonialism and Comparative Religion in Southern Africa*. Charlottesville: University Press of Virginia.

—— 2000. 'Colonialism', in *Guide to the Study of Religion*, ed. W. Braun and R. McCutcheon. London: Cassell.

Chryssides, George. 1999. *Exploring New Religions*. London: Continuum.

Clarke, J., S. Hall, T. Jefferson, and B. Roberts. 1976. 'Subcultures, cultures, and class', in *Resistance through Rituals*, ed. T. Jefferson. London: Hutchinson.

Clarke, Peter B. and Peter Byrne. 1993. *Religion Defined and Explained*. Basingstoke: Macmillan (Palgrave).

Comstock, Gary David and Susan E. Henking (eds). 1997. *Que(e)rying Religion: A Critical Anthology*. New York: Continuum.

Cooper, Gary. 1988. 'North American traditional religion', in *The World's Religions*, ed. Stewart Sutherland, Leslie Houlden, Peter Clarke and Hardy Friedman. London: Routledge.

Culler, Jonathan. 1997 *Literary Theory: A Very Short Introduction*. Oxford: Oxford University Press.

Daly, Mary. 1973. *Beyond God the Father*. Boston: Beacon Press.

Davies, Philip R. 1998. 'Life of Brian research', in *Biblical Studies/Cultural Studies*, ed. Cheryl Exum and Stephen D. Moore. Sheffield: Sheffield Academic Press.

Dekmejian, R. Hrair. 1995. *Islam in Revolution: Fundamentalism in the Arab World*. New York: Syracuse University Press.

Delphy, Christine. 1993. 'Rethinking sex and gender', *Women's Studies International Forum* 16: 1–9. [Reprinted in Darlene Juschka (ed.), 2001, *Feminism in the Study of Religion: A Reader*, London: Continuum.]

Derrida, Jacques. 1976. *Of Grammatology*, trans. Gayatri Spivak. Baltimore: Johns Hopkins Press.

Donaldson, Laura E. and Kwok Pui-Lan. 2002. *Postcolonialism, Feminism, and Religious Discourse*. New York: Routledge.

Douglas, Mary. 1973. *Natural Symbols: Explorations in Cosmology*. Harmondsworth: Penguin

During, Simon. 1999. *The Cultural Studies Reader*, 2nd edition. London: Routledge.

Durkheim, Emile. 1964 [1915]. *The Elementary Forms of the Religious Life*. London: Allen and Unwin.

Eliade, Mircea. 1963. *Patterns in Comparative Religion*, trans. Rosemary Sheed. New York: Meridian Books.

Eriksen, Thomas Hylland. 1993. *Ethnicity and Nationalism*. Cambridge: Polity.

Erndl, Kathleen M. 1993. *Victory to the Mother: The Hindu Goddess of Northwest India in Myth, Ritual, and Symbol*. New York: Oxford University Press.

Esposito, John L. 1991. *Islam and Politics*. Sycracuse: Syracuse University Press.

—— 1998. *Islam and the World*, 4th edition. Sycracuse: Syracuse University Press.

—— 2002. *Unholy War: Terror in the Name of Islam*. New York: Oxford University Press.

Fetterley, Judith. 1978. *The Resisting Reader: A Feminist Approach to American Fiction*. Bloomington: Indiana University Press.

Feuerbach, Ludwig. 1974 [1841]. *The Essence of Christianity*, trans. Marion Evan (George Eliot). New York: Harper Torchbooks.

Fish, Stanley. 1980. *Is there a Text in this Class? The Authority of Interpretive Communities*. Cambridge, MA: Harvard University Press.

Fiske, John. 1989a. *Reading the Popular*. Boston: Unwin Hyman.

—— 1989b. *Understanding Popular Culture*. London: Routledge.

—— 1995. 'Popular culture', in *Critical Terms for Literary Studies*, 2nd edition. Chicago: University of Chicago Press.

Fitzgerald, Timothy. 1990. 'Hinduism and the world religion fallacy', *Religion* 20: 101–18.

—— 1995. 'Religious studies as cultural studies: a philosophical and anthropological critique of the concept of religion', *Diskus: a disembodied journal of religion* 3(1): 35–47, at http://www.uni-marburg.de/religionswissenschaft/journal/diskus

—— 1999. *The Ideology of Religious Studies*. New York: Oxford University Press.

Forbes, Bruce David and Jeffrey H. Mahan (eds). 2000. *Religion and Popular Culture in America*. Berkeley: University of California Press.

Foucault, Michel. 1979 [1970]. 'What is an author?', in *Textual Strategies: Perspectives in Post-structuralist Criticism*, ed. Josué V. Harari. London: Methuen.

—— 1977. *Discipline and Punish: The Birth of the Prison*, trans. Alan Sheridan. London: Allen Lane.

—— 1981. 'Method', in *The History of Sexuality*, volume 1. Harmondsworth: Penguin. [Reprinted in John Storey, 1994, *Cultural Theory and Popular Culture: A Reader*. London: Harvester Wheatsheaf.]

—— 1990 [1984]. *The Care of the Self. History of Sexuality, Volume 3*, trans Robert Hurley. London: Penguin.

—— 1992 [1984]. *Uses of Pleasure. History of Sexuality, Volume 2*, trans. Robert Hurley. London: Penguin.

Franks, Myfanwy. 2001. *Women and Revivalism: Choosing 'Fundamentalism' in a Liberal Democracy*. Basingstoke: Palgrave (formerly Macmillan).

Freud, Sigmund. 1990a [1918]. 'Totem and taboo', in *The Origins of Religion. The Penguin Freud Library, Volume 13*. London: Penguin.

—— 1990b [1924]. 'Obsessive acts and religious practices', in *The Origins of Religion. The Penguin Freud Library, Volume 13*. London: Penguin.

Geertz, Clifford. 1973. *The Interpretation of Culture*. London: Fontana.

Gill, Sam. 1998. *Storytracking: Texts, Stories, and Histories in Central Australia*. Oxford: Oxford University Press.

Gombrich, Richard. 1971. *Precept and Practice: Traditional Buddhism in the Rural Highlands of Ceylon*. Oxford: Clarendon Press.

Gramsci, Antonio. 1971. *Selection from Prison Notebooks*, trans. Quintin Hoare and Geoffrey Nowell-Smith). London: Lawrence and Wishart. [Extracts reprinted in John Storey, 1994, *Cultural Theory and Popular Culture: A Reader*. London: Harvester Wheatsheaf.]

Grimes, Ronald L. 1982. *Beginnings in Ritual Studies*. Washington, DC: University Press of America. [Revised edition, 1995, Columbia: University of Southern Carolina Press.]

—— 2000a. 'Ritual', in *Guide to the Study of Religion*, ed. W. Braun and R. McCutcheon. London: Cassell.

—— 2000b. *Deeply into the Bone: Re-inventing Rites of Passage*. Berkeley: University of California Press.

Gross, Rita. 1977. *Beyond Androcentricism: New Essays on Women and Religion*. Missoula, MT: Scholars Press.

—— 1993. *Buddhism after Patriarchy: A Feminist History, Analysis, and Reconstruction of Buddhism*. Albany, NY: SUNY Press.

Hall, Stuart. 1981. 'Notes on deconstructing "the Popular"', in *People's History and Socialist Theory*, ed. R. Samuel. London: Routledge and Kegan Paul. [Reprinted in John Storey, 1994, *Cultural Theory and Popular Culture: A Reader*. London: Harvester Wheatsheaf.]

Hamilton, Malcolm. 1995. *The Sociology of Religion: Theoretical and Comparative Perspectives*. London: Routledge.

Hannerz, Ulf. 1996. *Transnational Connections: Culture, People, Places*. London/New York: Routledge.

Harlan, Lindsay. 1992. *Religion and Rajput Women*. Berkeley: University of California Press.

Harvey, Graham. 1997. *Listening People, Speaking Earth: Contemporary Paganism*. London: Hurst.

Hawley, John Stratton. 1994. *Sati, the Blessing and the Curse: The Burning of Wives in India*. New York: Oxford University Press.

Haynes, Jeffrey. 2002. 'Religion and politics', in *Religions in the Modern World*, ed. Linda Woodhead, Paul Fletcher, Hiroko Kawanami, and David Smith. London: Routledge.

Hebdige, Dick. 1979. *Subculture: The Meaning of Style*. London: Methuen.

Heelas, P. 1996. *The New Age Movement*. Oxford: Blackwell.

Hick, John. 1989. *An Interpretation of Religion: Human Responses to the Transcendent*. Basingstoke: Macmillan (Palgrave).

Hinnells, John (ed.). 1997. *The New Penguin Handbook of Living Religions*, 2nd edition. Harmondsworth: Penguin.

hooks, bell. 1982. *Ain't I A Woman*. London: Pluto.

Hoover, Stewart M. and Knut Lundby (eds). 1997. *Rethinking Media, Religion, and Culture*. Thousand Oaks, CA: Sage.

Hughes-Freeland, F. (ed.). 1998. *Ritual, Performance, and Media*. London: Routledge.

Hulsether, Mark. 2000. 'Like a sermon: popular religion in Madonna videos', in *Religion and Popular Culture in America*, ed. Bruce David Forbes and Jeffrey H. Mahan. Berkeley: University of California Press.

—— forthcoming 2003. 'New approaches to the study of religion and culture', in *New Approaches to the Study of Religion*, ed. P. Antes, A. Geertz, and R. Warne. Berlin: Verlag de Gruyter.

Idinopolous, Thomas A. and Edward A. Yonan. 1994. *Religion and Reductionism: Essays on Eliade, Segal, and the Challenge of the Social Sciences for the Study of Religion*. Leiden: E.J. Brill.

Irigaray, Luce. 1985a [1974]. *Speculum of the Other Woman*, trans. Gillian C. Gill. Ithaca: Cornell University Press.

—— 1985b [1977]. *The Sex which is not One*, trans. Catherine Porter. Ithaca: Cornell University Press.

—— 1987. 'Divine Women', in *Sexes and Genealogies*, trans. Gillian C. Gill. New York: Columbia University Press.

Iser, Wolfgang. 1980. 'Interaction between text and reader', in *The Reader in the Text: Essays on Audience and Interpretation*. New Jersey: Princeton University Press. [Reprinted in Andrew Bennett (ed.), 1995, *Readers and Reading*. London: Longman].

Jantzen, Grace. 1998. *Becoming Divine: Towards a Feminist Philosophy of Religion*. Manchester: Manchester University Press.

Jenkins, Richard. 1991. *Pierre Bourdieu*. London: Routledge.

Jensen, Joli and John J. Pauly. 1997. 'Imagining the audience: losses and gains in cultural studies', in *Cultural Studies in Question*, ed. Marjorie Ferguson and Peter Golding. London: Sage.

Johnson, W.J. 1994. *The Bhagavad Gita* (translated with notes). Oxford: Oxford University Press.

Jung, Carl. 1978. *Man and his Symbols*. London: Pan.

Jurgensmeyer, Mark. 2001. *Terror in the Mind of God. The Global Rise of Religious Violence*. Berkeley: University of California Press

Juschka, Darlene (ed). 2001. *Feminism in the Study of Religion: A Reader*, London: Continuum.

Kaufman, Debra Renee. 1991. *Rachel's Daughters: Newly Orthodox Jewish Women*. New Brunswick: Rutgers University Press.

Kazantzakis, Nikos. 1975. *The Last Temptation*, trans. P.A. Bien. London: Faber.

Keesing, Roger. 1994. 'Theories of culture revisited', in *Assessing Cultural Anthropology*, ed. Robert Borofsky. New York: McGraw-Hill, pp. 301–12.

Keller, Mary. 2002. *The Hammer and the Flute: Women, Power, and Spirit Possession*. Baltimore. Johns Hopkins University Press.

King, Ursula (ed.). 1995. *Religion and Gender*. Oxford: Blackwell.

Klass, Morton. 1995. *Ordered Universes: Approaches to the Anthropology of Religion*, Boulder: Westview Press.

Lane, Jeremy F. 2000. *Pierre Bourdieu: A Critical Introduction*. London: Pluto Press.

Leach, Edmund. 1969. 'Virgin birth', in *Genesis as Myth and other essays*. London: Jonathan Cape.

—— 1976. *Culture and Communication*. Cambridge: Cambridge University Press.

Lease, Gary. 2000. 'Ideology', in *Guide to the Study of Religion*, ed. W. Braun and R. McCutcheon. London: Cassell.

Lehmann, David, 2002. 'Religion and globalization', in *Religions in the Modern World*, ed. Linda Woodhead, Paul Fletcher, Hiroko Kawanami and David Smith. London: Routledge.

Leslie, Julia. 1989. *The Perfect Wife*. New Delhi: Oxford University Press.

—— (ed.). 1991. *Roles and Rituals for Hindu Women*. London: Pinter.

Levi-Strauss, Claude. 1968. *Structural Anthropology*. London: Penguin.

Lewis, J. and Melton, J.G. 1992. *Perspectives on the New Age*, New York: SUNY Press.

Lincoln, Bruce. 1981. *Emerging from the Chrysalis: Studies in Rituals of Women's Initiations*. Cambridge, MA: Harvard University Press.

—— 1998. 'Conflict', in *Critical Terms for Religious Studies*, ed. Mark C. Taylor. Chicago: University of Chicago Press.

—— 2000. 'Culture', in *Guide to the Study of Religion*, ed. W. Braun and R. McCutcheon. London: Cassell.

McCutcheon, Russell T. 1997. *Manufacturing Religion: The Discourse on Sui Generis Religion and the Politics of Nostalgia*. New York: Oxford University Press.

McGuigan, James. 1992. *Cultural Populism*. London: Routledge.

Magee, Penelope Margaret. 1995. 'Disputing the sacred: some theoretical approaches to gender and religion', in *Religion and Gender*, ed. Ursula King. Oxford: Blackwell.

Malinowski, Bronislaw. 1932. *The sexual life of savages in North-Western Melanesia: an ethnographic account of courtship, marriage, and family life among the natives of the Trobriand Islands, British New Guinea*. London: Routledge and Kegan Paul.

Marx, K. 1986 [1888]. *Theses on Feuerbach*, reproduced in *Karl Marx: a Reader*. Cambridge: Cambridge University Press.

Marx, K. and F. Engels. 1957. *On Religion*. Moscow: Progress Publishers.

—— 1986 [1888]. *Manifesto of the Communist Party*, reproduced in *Karl Marx: a Reader*. Cambridge: Cambridge University Press.

Mascaró, J. 1962. *The Bhagavad Gita* (translated from the Sanskrit with an introduction). London: Penguin.

Masuzawa, Tomoko. 1998. 'Culture', in *Critical Terms for Religious Studies*, ed. Mark C. Taylor. Chicago: University of Chicago Press.

Maynard, Mary. 1994. ' "Race", gender, and the concept of "difference" in feminist thought', in *The Dynamics of 'Race' and Gender: Some Feminist Interventions*, ed. H. Afshar and M. Maynard. London: Taylor and Francis. [Reprinted in Darlene Juschka (ed.), 2001, *Feminism in the Study of Religion: A Reader*, London: Continuum.]

Modood, Tariq and Pnina Werbner. 1997. *Debating Cultural Hybridity: Multi-Cultural Identities and the Politics of Anti-Racism*. London: Zed Books.

Modood, Tariq, R. Berthould, J. Lackey, J. Nazoo, P. Smith, S. Virdee, S. Beishon *et al.* 1997. *Britain's Ethnic Minorities: Diversity and Disadvantage*. London: Policy Studies Institute.

Moore, Henrietta. 1999. 'Whatever happened to women and men? Gender and other crises in anthropology', in *Anthropological Theory Today*, ed. H. Moore. Cambridge: Polity.

Moores, Shaun. 1990. 'Texts, readers, and contexts of reading: developments in the study of media audiences', *Media, Culture, and Society* 12: 9–29.

Morley, David. 1986. *Family Television: Cultural Power and Domestic Leisure*. London: Comedia.

—— 1997. 'Theoretical orthodoxies: textualism, constructionsim, and the "new ethnography" in cultural studies', in *Cultural Studies in Question*, ed. Marjorie Ferguson and Peter Golding. London: Sage.

Morley, David and Kuan-Hsing Chen (eds). 1996. *Stuart Hall: Critical Dialogues in Cultural Studies*. London: Routledge.

Mullen, Eve. 1998. 'Orientalist commercializations: Tibetan Buddhists in American popular film', *Journal of Religion and Film*, at http://www.unomaha.edu/~wwwjrf/OrientalMullen.htm

Müller, F.M. 1972 [1870]. *Introduction to the Science of Religion: Four Lectures Delivered at the Royal Institution in February and May, 1870*. Varanasi: Bharata Manisha.

Needham, Rodney. 1972. *Belief, Language, and Experience*. Chicago: University of Chicago Press.

Nye, Malory. 2000. 'Religion, post-religionism, and religioning: religious studies and contemporary cultural debates', *Method and Theory in the Study of Religion* 12(3): 447–76.

—— 2001. *Multiculturalism and Minority religions in Britain: Krishna Consciousness, Religious Freedom, and the Politics of Location*. London: RoutledgeCurzon.

Paden, William. 1988. *Religious Worlds: The Comparative Study of Religion*. Boston: Beacon Press.

Palmer, Susan J. 1994. *Moon Sisters, Krishna Mothers, Rajneesh Lovers: Women's Roles in New Religions*. Syracuse: Syracuse University Press.

Pals, Daniel. 1996. *Seven Theories of Religion*. New York: Oxford University Press.

Parkin, Frank. 1982. *Max Weber*. London: Routledge.

Parsons, Gerald. 1993. *The Growth of Religious Diversity*, volume 1. London: Routledge.

Pearson, Joanne and Steve Moyise. 2002. 'Jesus in film', in *From Sacred Text to Internet*, ed. G. Becklerlegge. Aldershot/Milton Keynes: Ashgate/Open University Press.

Prabhupada, A.C. Bhaktivedanta Swami. 1983 [1971]. *Bhagavad-Gita As It Is*. Watford: Bhaktivedanta Book Trust.

Puttick, Elizabeth. 1997. *Women in New Religions: Gender, Power and Sexuality and Spiritual Power*. Basingstoke: Macmillan.

Pyper, Hugh. 1998. 'The selfish text: the Bible and memetics', in *Biblical Studies/Cultural Studies*, ed. Cheryl Exum and Stephen D. Moore. Sheffield: Sheffield Academic Press.

Radhakrishnan, S. 1948. *The Bhagavadgita*. London: George Allen and Unwin.

Radway, Janice. 1987. *Reading the Romance*. London: Verso.

Redfield, James. 1994. *The Celestine Prophecy*. London: Bantam.

Roald, Anne-Sophie. 2001. *Women in Islam*. London: Routledge.

Robertson, R. 1992. *Globalization: Social Theory and Global Culture*. London: Transaction.

—— 1995. 'Glocalization: time–space and homogeneity–heterogeneity', in *Global Modernities*, ed. M. Featherstone, Scott Lash, and Roland Robertson. London: Sage.

Ruel, Malcolm. 1982. 'Christians as believers', in *Religious Organizations and Religious Experience*, ed. J. Davis. London: Academic Press. [Reprinted in M. Lambek (ed.), 2002, *A Reader in the Anthropology of Religion*. Oxford: Blackwell. (Quotations taken from this reprint.)]

Runnymede Trust. 1997. *Islamophobia: A Challenge for us all: Report of the Runnymede Trust Commission on British Muslims and Islamophobia*. London: The Runnymede Trust.

Rushdie, Salman. 1988. *The Satanic Verses*. London: Viking.

—— 1992. 'In good faith', in *Imaginary Homelands: Essays and Criticism, 1981–1991*. London: Granta (in association with Penguin).

Ruthven, Malise. 2002. *A Fury for God: The Islamist Attack on America*. London/New York: Granta.

Said, Edward W. 1985. *Covering Islam: How the Media and the Experts Determine How We See the Rest of the World*. London: Routledge and Kegan Paul.

Salomonsen, Jane. 2001. *Enchanted Feminism*. New York: Routledge.

Sardar, Ziauddin and Merryl Wyn Davies. 2002. *Why do People Hate America?* Cambridge: Icon Books.

Schüssler Fiorenza, Elisabeth. 1984. *Bread not Stone: The Challenge of Feminist Biblical Interpretation*. Boston: Beacon Press.

Scott, Joan. 1986. 'Gender: a useful category of historical analysis', *American Historical Revew* 91(5): 1053-75.

Sered, Susan Starr. 1994. *Priestess, Mother, Sacred Sister: Religions Dominated by Women*. New York: Oxford University Press.

Shadid, W.A.R. and P.S. van Koninsgveld. 1991. 'Blaming the system or blaming the victim? Structural barriers facing Muslims in Western Europe', in *The Integration of Islam and Hinduism in Western Europe*, ed. W.A.R. Shadid and P.S. Koningveld. Kampen: Kok Pharos.

Shaw, Rosalind and Charles Stewart. 1994. 'Introduction: problematizing syncretism', in *Syncretism/Anti-Syncretism: The Politics of Religious Synthesis*, ed. C. Stewart and R. Shaw. London: Routledge.

Shaw, Rosalind. 1995. 'Feminist anthropology and the gendering of religious studies', in *Religion and Gender*, ed. Ursula King. Oxford: Blackwell.

Shukrallah, Hala. 1994. 'The impact of the Islamic movement in Egypt', *Feminist Review* 46: 15–32. [Reprinted in Darlene Juschka (ed.), 2001, *Feminism in the Study of Religion: A Reader*, London: Continuum. (Quotations taken from this reprint.)]

Smart, Ninian. 1989. *The World's Religions: Old Traditions and Modern Transformations*. Cambridge: Cambridge University Press.

Smith, Jonathan Z. 1982. *Imagining Religion: From Babylon to Jonestown*. Chicago: University of Chicago Press.

—— 1987. *To Take Place: Toward Theory in Ritual*. Chicago: University of Chicago Press.

—— 1998. 'Religion, religions, religious', in *Critical Terms for Religious Studies*, ed. Mark C. Taylor. University of Chicago Press.

Smith, W.C. 1978. *The Meaning and End of Religion*. London. SPCK.

Spivak, Gayatri. 1993. 'Can the subaltern speak?', in *Colonial Discourse and Post-colonial Theory: A Reader*, ed. P. Williams and L. Chrisman. New York: Harvester Wheatsheaf.

—— 1996. *The Spivak Reader: Selected Works of Gayatri Chakravorty Spivak*, ed. D. Landry and G. MacLean. London: Routledge.

—— 1999. *A Critique of Postcolonial Reason: Towards a History of the Vanishing Present*. Cambridge, MA. Harvard University Press.

Stark, R. and W.S. Bainbridge. 1985. *The Future of Religion: Secularization, Revival, and Cult Formation*. Berkeley: University of California Press.

Stewart, Charles. 1994. 'Syncretism as a dimension of nationalist discourse in Modern Greece', in *Syncretism/Anti-Syncretism: The Politics of Religious Synthesis*, ed. C. Stewart and R. Shaw. London: Routledge.

Storey, John. 1994. *Cultural Theory and Popular Culture: A Reader*. London: Harvester Wheatsheaf.

—— 1996. *What is Cultural Studies*. New York: Arnold.

—— 1997. *Cultural Theory and Popular Culture: A Reader*, 2nd edition. London: Harvester Wheatsheaf.

—— 2000. *Introduction to Cultural Theory and Popular Culture*, 3rd edition. London: Prentice Hall.

Strinati, Dominic. 2000. *An Introduction to Studying Popular Culture*. London: Routledge.

Suleri, Sara. 1992. *The Rhetoric of English India*. Chicago: University of Chicago Press.

Sutcliffe, Steven. 2002. *Children of the New Age*. London: Routledge.

Sutcliffe, Steven and Marion Bowman (eds). 2000. *Beyond New Age: Exploring Alternative Spirituality*. Edinburgh: Edinburgh University Press.

Swain, Tony and Garry Trompf. 1995. *The Religions of Oceania*. London: Routledge.

Telford, William. 1997. 'Jesus Christ movie star: the depiction of Jesus in the cinema', in *Explorations in Theology and Film: Movies and Meaning*, ed. C. Marsh and G. Ortiz. Oxford: Blackwell. [Reprinted in G. Becklerlegge (ed.), 2002, *From Sacred Text to Internet*. Aldershot/Milton Keynes: Ashgate/Open University Press, 2002.]

Tonkinson, Robert. 1978. 'Semen versus spirit-child in a Western Desert culture', in *Australian Aboriginal Concepts*, ed. L. Hiatt. Canberra: Australian Institute of Aboriginal Studies.

Tooker, Deborah. 1992. 'Identity systems of highland Burma: "belief", Akha *zan*, and a critique of interiorised notions of ethno-religious identity', *Man (Journal of the Royal Anthropological Institute)* (n.s.) 27(4): 799–819.

Turner, Bryan S. 1992. *Max Weber: From History to Modernity*. London: Routledge.

Turner, Stephen (ed.). 2000. *Cambridge Companion to Weber*. Cambridge: Cambridge University Press.

Turner, Victor. 1967. *The Forest of Symbols*. Ithaca: Cornell University Press

—— 1969. *The Ritual Process*. Ithaca: Cornell University Press.

—— 1982. *From Ritual to Theater and Back: The Human Seriousness of Play*. New York: PAJ.

Tylor, Edward B. 1871. *Primitive Culture: Researches into the Development of Mythology, Philosophy, Religion, Language, Art and Customs*. London: Murray.

van der Veer, Peter. 1994. *Religious Nationalism: Hindus and Muslims in India*. Berkeley: University of California Press.

van Gennep, Arnold. 1960 [1908]. *The Rites of Passage*. London: Routledge and Kegan Paul.

Walker, Alice. 1983. *In Search of Our Mothers' Gardens*. New York: Harcourt, Brace, Jovanovich.

Walkerdine, Valerie. 1997. *Daddy's Girl: Young Girls and Popular Culture*. Basingstoke: Macmillan.

Wallis, Roy. 1984. *The Elementary Forms of the New Religious Life*. London: Routledge and Kegan Paul.

Warne, Randi R. 2000. 'Gender', in *Guide to the Study of Religion*, ed. W. Braun and R. McCutcheon. London: Cassell.

Watson, C.W. 2000. *Multiculturalism*. Buckingham: Open University Press.

Weber, Max. 1930. *The Protestant Ethic and the Spirit of Capitalism*, trans. Talcott Parsons. London: Allen and Unwin.

Webster, Richard. 1990. *A Brief History of Blasphemy*. Southwold: Orwell Press.

Wiebe, Donald. 1981. *Religion and Truth*. The Hague: Mouton.

—— 1999. *The Politics of Religious Studies: The Continuing Conflict with Theology in the Academy*. Basingstoke: Macmillan

Williams, Raymond. 1961. 'The analysis of culture', in *The Long Revolution*. London: Chatto and Windus. [Reprinted in John Storey, 1994, *Cultural Theory and Popular Culture: A Reader*. London: Harvester Wheatsheaf.]

—— 1976. *Keywords: A Vocabulary of Culture and Society*. London: Fontana.

—— 1977. *Marxism and Literature*. Oxford: Oxford University Press.

Wilson, Bryan. 1982. *Religion in Sociological Perspective*. Oxford: Oxford University Press.

—— 1991. 'Secularization', in *The Study of Religion, Traditional and New Religions*, ed. P.B. Clarke and S. Sutherland. London: Routledge.

Wilson, Bryan and Jamie Cresswell. 1999. *New Religious Movements: Challenge and Response*. London: Routledge.

Woodhead, Linda. 2002. 'Women and religion', in *Religions in the Modern World*, ed. Linda Woodhead, Paul Fletcher, Hiroko Kawanami and David Smith. London: Routledge.

Woodhead, Linda and Paul Heelas. 2000. *Religion in Modern Times: An Interpretive Anthology*. Oxford: Blackwell.

Woodhead, Linda, Paul Fletcher, Hiroko Kawanami and David Smith (eds). 2002. *Religions in the Modern World*. London: Routledge.

Young, Robert. 1995. *Colonial Desire: Hybridity in Theory, Culture, and Race*. London: Routledge.

Zaehner, R.C. 1966. 'Bhagavad Gita', in *Hindu Scriptures* (translated and edited). London: J.M. Dent and Sons.

Index

Adi Granth 9, 149, 158–9
Adorno and Horkheimer 30–1
Afghanistan 58–9, 69, 90, 178, 179, 191
Africa 10, 110, 178, 189, 204
African Americans 35, 43, 44
African Traditional Religions 10–11
agency 86–9, 120
Ahmed, Leila 90–1, 199
Akha 112–14
Allah 8,9, 10, 102, 106, 111–12, 164–6
Althusser, Louis 50, 57–62, 64, 67, 69–70,
    84, 119
American Christianity 2, 5–6, 12, 27, 45,
    56–7, 121, 181, 194
Anderson, Benedict 181
androcentrism 74, 80, 84, 85, 91, 95
Anglican Christianity 6, 7, 49, 55–6, 83,
    182
anthropologists 4, 39–40, 43, 45, 112–16,
    208
Anzalduá, Gloria 44
Arrernte 11, 42, 107
Asad, Talal 68, 71, 87–8, 103, 116, 122,
    144, 147
Atta, Muhammad 179
Australia 11, 110, 114–17, 178
authorship 163–9, 174
Ayodhya 184

Bangladesh 183
Barthes, Roland 152, 165–7, 169
Baumann, Gerd 187–8, 206
Beatles 23, 30

Bell, Catherine 119–21, 123, 126–9, 144,
    146, 147
Bhabha, Homi 44
Bhagavad Gita 159–62, 163–4, 170, 173
Bible 8, 9, 23, 24, 47, 49, 82–3, 95, 149,
    151, 152–4, 155, 160, 162–4, 167–9,
    171, 173
Big Brother 65–6.
bin Laden, Osama 1, 18, 177, 179–80
Birmingham Centre for Cultural Studies
    43
Bloch, Maurice 126, 135–6, 145, 148
Bollywood 26–7, 36
Book of Mormon 151
Bosnia 181
Bourdieu, Pierre 33, 37, 61, 119–21, 123
Britain 6, 44, 55–6, 58, 59, 79, 93–4, 96,
    104, 145–6, 153, 155, 170, 178, 180,
    185–6, 188–90, 197–99
Brown, Callum 96, 198–9
Buddhism 2, 8–11, 45, 103, 153
Buddhists 11, 194, 201
burqa 90
Bush, George W. 87, 88
Butler, Judith 77–8, 99

Capercaillie 29
capitalism 50–2, 62, 73
Catholic Christianity 5, 10, 27, 35, 38, 55,
    58, 60, 62, 66–7, 83, 88, 96, 102, 103,
    121, 138, 153–4, 181
Celestine Prophecy 28
Chidester, David 110, 122
China 2, 8

Christianity 2, 5–14, 24, 25, 32, 43–45, 49, 54, 55, 59, 65, 75, 78–80, 82–6, 88, 89, 101–2, 128, 133, 152–4, 196–9, 202; creed 101; and Freud 4; and Marx 51, 52; see also American Christianity, Anglican Christianity, Catholic Christianity, Orthodox Christianity, Pentecostalism, Protestant Christianity
Church of the Latter Day Saints 151
cinema 14, 26–7, 30, 31, 35, 152–4, 193
circumcision: male 140; female (genital mutilation) 75, 140
civil religion 14
Clinton, Chelsea 87
colonialism 15, 42, 54–5, 89, 90–1, 109–11, 178–9, 182, 188, 204; see also postcolonialism
common-sense 115–17
confession 66–7
counter-hegemony 55–7, 60, 90; see also Gramsci, hegemony
Creationism 171
cultural hybridity 44–6, 47, 190–1, 201
cultural studies 21–2, 24, 25, 43, 208
culture 2–3, 4–6, 17, 18–19, 21–48: and society 36–9; as religion 14; as a 'way of life' 39–42, 47; types of 22–5; see also cultural hybridity, elite culture, mass culture; popular culture, sub-culture

Daly, Mary 75, 79–80, 82, 85–6
'Death of the Author' 165–7, 169, 174
Derrida, Jacques 155–7, 159, 167, 169
de-traditionalisation 203, 205
dharma 15, 17, 18, 160–2
diaspora 180, 189–90, 196
Dickens, Charles 22
din 18
discourse 67–70, 77, 198
Divine Principle 166
Dogma 35, 154
Durkheim, Emile 37–9, 138

Egypt 90–3, 179, 203
Eire 182
Eliade, Mircea 105–9, 122
elite culture 22–3, 24–5, 35, 47, 54, 57, 149, 151; see also culture
Eminem 26, 28, 35, 44

England 6, 55, 171, 182, 185
ethnicity 96–7, 185–7, 196, 205, 208

Father Ted 35
feminist hermeneutics of suspicion 76, 167–9
Fetterley, Judith 171
Feuerbach, Ludwig 61, 104–5
Fish, Stanley 170
Fiske, John 30–2, 172
Fitzgerald, Timothy 12, 15, 108, 122
Foucault, Michel 50, 63–70, 77, 79, 87, 94, 167, 198
Four Weddings and a Funeral 136–7
France 59, 180, 188
Franks, Myfanwy 93–4
Freud, Sigmund 4–5, 80–1, 104, 140
fundamentalism 46, 193–6, 204

Gandhi, Mahatma 159
Geertz, Clifford 37, 39–43, 115–16
genre 158
Germany 188
Gita see Bhagavad Gita
globalisation 178–80, 181, 183, 196, 201, 202, 205
glocalisation 181
Gramsci, Antonio 34, 43, 50, 53–7, 60, 63, 64, 67, 70, 84
Grimes, Ronald 127, 129, 144, 147
gurdwaras 158
Guru Nanak 10

habitus 61, 119–21, 122
Hall, Stuart 25–36, 42
Harry Potter 29, 154
Hebdige, Dick 42–3
hegemony 53–7, 60, 63, 70, 84; see also counter-hegemony, Gramsci
Hemingway, Ernest 33
heterosexuality 78
Hick, John 105–9, 122
hijab 90–4
Hinduism 7, 9, 10, 12, 13, 45, 75, 86, 110, 159–62, 171–2
Hindus 10–12, 15, 18, 29–30, 36, 75, 86, 89, 102, 110, 112, 132, 170, 172, 180, 183–5, 189–91, 203; in the West 29–30, 170, 180, 189–91
Holland 188, 192–3
homosexuality 78

Hoover, Stewart 172
Hussein, Saddam 180, 191

ideological state apparatus 58–9, 67; see also Althusser
ideology (and religion) 50–63, 66–7, 69–70, 71, 73, 79–80, 82–5, 87, 118–19
India 1, 8, 9, 12, 26–7, 36, 45, 54, 110, 170, 178, 180, 182–5, 188–9
indigenous religions 11, 13
Indonesia 2, 10, 181, 191
interpellation 59–60, 70, 84
interpretative communities 170, 174
Iran 170, 180, 193
Iraq 178, 180, 191
Irigaray, Luce 80–2, 85–6, 118
Iser, Wolfgang 169–70
ISKCON (Hare Krishna) 29–30, 32, 190–1, 200, 201, 203
Islam 2, 7, 8, 9, 10, 11, 13, 14, 18, 44, 45, 55, 58–9, 74, 75, 86, 90, 94, 98, 103, 177, 179–80, 190–3: Shi'a 10, 180; Sunni 10, 180; see also Muslims
Islamism (political Islam) 195
Islamophobia 193
Israel 2, 9, 187

Jainism 8, 10
Jantzen, Grace 80–2
Japan 8, 201, 202
Jesus Christ Superstar 153
Jesus of Nazareth 153
Jigalong 116–7
Judaism 9–10, 86, 88, 102, 103, 155, 186–7; and Freud 4; and Marx 51, 52
Jewish people 86, 88, 102, 186–7, 194
Jung, Carl 132
Juschka, Darlene 73–4, 97, 98

Kashmir 184
Kazantzakis, Nikos 153
Keesing, Roger 43
Keller, Mary 114, 123
Khalistan 184, 194
Khomeni, Ayatollah 180
King, Stephen 23, 33–4
Kiriwinans (Trobriand Islanders) 114–15, 118
Klass, Morton 7, 19
Krishna 160

Lacan, Jacques 80–1, 84
Last Temptation of Christ 153–4
Leach, Edmund 114–17, 139
Lewis, C.S. 154
Life of Brian 154, 198
liminality 142–3
Little Buddha 153
localisation 181, 196
logocentrism 156–7, 167
Lopez, Jennifer 26

Madonna 23–5, 32–33, 41, 172
magic 110
Mahabharat 36, 159, 164
Malinowski, Bronislaw 114–15
Marx, Karl 49, 50–3, 54, 57, 59, 61–2, 63, 64, 67, 70, 80, 82, 104
mass culture 26–32, 47; see also culture
Mayflower 56
McCutcheon, Russell 19, 108, 122
Mecca and Medina 180
Melville, Herman 22
Middle East 1, 55, 179, 187
Milton, John 22, 28
modernity 1, 177, 196
Monty Python 154, 198
Moon, Sun Myung 166, 201
Moore, Henrietta 78, 98
morality 3
Morley, David 172
Mozart, W.A. 22, 23–4, 32, 41
Muhammad 9, 164
Müller, Max 149, 150, 156, 157, 173
multiculturalism 187–93, 204, 204–5, 208
Muslims 1, 10, 18, 55, 69, 75, 78, 89, 90–4, 96, 106, 111–12, 149, 155, 164–5, 170, 175, 179–80, 183–5, 188, 189–94, 204; British 93–4, 170, 189–92; women 90–4; see also Islam

Narnia Chronicles 154
Nation of Islam 43
Nationalism 180–85, 187, 196, 205; as religion 14
Native Americans 5, 11, 15, 31, 202
Native Australians 11, 37, 42, 107, 110, 114–17, 132
Navajo 11, 15
Needham, Rodney 103
New Age/Alternative Spirituality 28, 200, 202

'new religious movements' (NRMs) 99,
   200–2
New York 1, 41, 177, 179
niqab 90
Northern Ireland 1, 38, 138, 182, 195

Orthodox Christianity 10

Pagans 86, 200, 203–4
Pakistan 183, 189, 190, 191
Palestine 2, 9, 194, 195
panopticon 65–6
Paradise Lost 22, 28
Pentecostalism 35
Peoples Temple, Jonestown 200
phallocentrism 80, 84
phenomenology 107–8, 121
Pilgrim Fathers 56
Pilgrims Progress 28
popular culture 25–36, 47, 152; *see also*
   culture
postcolonialism 178–80, 188, 204, 205,
   208; *see also* colonialism
Prabhupada, Swami Bhaktivedanta
   161–2, 201–2
privatisation (of religion) 197, 201
Protestant Christianity 7, 10, 38, 55–7,
   62–3, 67, 83, 102–4, 108–110, 112,
   121, 138, 155, 181; and the rise of
   capitalism 62–3; and the development
   of the study of religion 102–4,
   108–110, 112, 121, 155
psychoanalytic theory 80–2; *see also*
   Freud, Lacan
Pyper, Hugh 157

Al-Qa'eda 1, 2, 177, 179, 191
queer theory 78
Qur'an 8, 9, 149, 151, 164–6, 170–1, 173,
   175, 191

Radhakrishnan 161–2
Radway, Janice 172
Ramayana 36
readers and reading (of texts) 165,
   169–73, 174
Real, the *see* John Hick
reductionism 104–9, 121
Reeves, Keanu 153
Reiki 202
Roald, Anne-Sofie 90, 99

Rowling, J.K. 29
Ruel, Malcolm 103, 111–12, 122
Rushdie, Salman 164–7, 170–1, 174–5,
   192

sacred, the *see* Eliade
salvation 3, 62
Satanic Verses 164–5, 170–1, 191, 193
Saudi Arabia 2, 9, 10, 90, 179–80
Schüssler Fiorenza, Elisabeth 76, 167–9
Scorsese, Martin 153
Scotland 2, 46, 182, 185, 204
Scott, Joan 74, 96
secularisation 177, 196–99, 200, 205
secularism 183–4
seekership 202–3
September 11th 2001 (9/11) 1, 2, 177, 179,
   193
Sered, Susan Starr 95
sexuality 77–8, 96–7
Shakespeare, William 22, 23, 32, 47
shamanism 107, 202
Shintoism 8, 10
Shona 11
Shukrallah, Hala 92 3
Sikhism 9–10, 150, 155, 158–9
Sikhs 158–9, 180, 183–84, 194
Smith, Jonathan Z. 12, 16–17, 19, 148
Soka Gakkai 201
South Africa 11, 49, 110
Southern Baptists 5–6, 56
Spears, Britney 26, 28, 29, 32–33
spirituality 202–4, 205
Spivak, Gayatri 64, 89
Stigmata 35
subaltern 54, 89
sub-culture 42–3; *see also* culture
subjectivity 80–2, 119
surveillance 65–6, 94
Sutcliffe, Steven 202–3, 206
symbols 40–1, 128, 131–4
syncretism 44–6, 190–1; *see also* cultural
   hybridity

Taliban 58–9, 90, 191
Taoism 8, 10
tele-evangelism 27
Thailand 112
theology 3, 46, 108, 168
Tonkinson, Robert 116–17
Tooker, Deborah 112–14

Touched by an Angel 27
transnationalism 188–91, 196, 201
transsexuality 78
Turner, Victor 127, 141–4
Tutu, Desmond 49
Tylor, Edward 39, 102–3

Unification Church 166, 200, 201
USA 1, 2, 5–6, 10, 12, 34, 35, 41, 44, 45,
    54, 55, 56–7.59, 69, 79, 87, 93, 104,
    153, 155, 171, 178, 180, 181, 185, 189,
    191, 201

van Gennep, Arnold 141–4
Vedas 9, 109, 149, 151
Vicar of Dibley 6

Weber, Max 50, 62–3, 70, 102
Williams, Raymond 21–5, 36–7, 42, 150
Wilson, Bryan 196, 197, 201, 206
Winnie the Pooh 173
Woolf, Virginia 33–4
world religions paradigm 8–13, 150

Xenophanes 105
Xhosa 110

yoga 107
Yoruba 11, 32
Yugoslavia 1, 181

Zulu 11